BUSINESS CLASS

David Cotton   Sue Robbins

COURSE BOOK

Longman

Contents

Using Business Class

Who is Business Class for?

Business Class is a Business English course for upper-intermediate to advanced students. It is designed both for students of business who wish to improve their communication skills in English and extend their knowledge of the business world, and for practising business people who need to use English more effectively in their work.

The course comprises 15 self-contained units which follow a clear structure, making it suitable for use with any size of class. The coursebook includes the complete tapescript and answer key, which means that it can also be used by students working independently.

Key features of the course

Business Class:

- offers a unique insight into a wide range of topical business issues and invites you to explore current thinking on important business topics and trends.
- is accompanied by two audio cassettes providing authentic recorded interviews with top business people.
- includes authentic texts from prominent business publications and the media, carefully selected for interest and relevance.
- gives you scope to practise the language and communication skills which are vital for people who need to use English in their business lives.
- develops your interpersonal skills, as the majority of the activities in the course encourage interaction and communication.
- helps you to achieve your aim of expressing yourself both in speech and in writing as effectively in English as in your own language.

Content and approach

Business Class is suitable for students from a wide range of business fields and functions. It consists of twelve topic/skills-based and three business skills-based units, all of which offer activities which integrate the various elements of the unit. This integrated approach makes it possible for you to study key aspects of grammar and essential vocabulary in context. All four language skills are practised and in each unit you will encounter the language that is most relevant to the business world. The business skills units provide an in-depth focus on presentations, negotiations and meetings. These units are designed to improve your performance and increase your confidence in these areas, and to provide practice in the key language they require. Each unit provides case study material which can be exploited in one or two teaching periods.

A typical unit contains the following sections:

Introduction

The aim of this section is to encourage you to think about the topic and to pool your knowledge with others in the group. The format varies and includes cartoons, photographs, questionnaires, short reading extracts or discussion topics.

Texts

Each unit contains two reading passages, and in some cases other, shorter materials such as advertisements. The majority of texts are authentic and are preceded by a pre-reading task, designed to make the task more readily accessible. You may be asked to perform a variety of tasks such as predicting content using headings/illustrations, skimming and scanning the text and studying key vocabulary. You will carry out tasks during and after reading which will help you to understand the text more fully. You may be asked, for example, to take notes, answer true/false questions, complete a chart or correct/complete a summary.

Vocabulary

Vocabulary has to be understood in the context in which it appears. Most of the tasks, therefore, appear after the texts and relate to them. Tasks include matching words from the text to their definitions or synonyms, deducing the meaning of words from their context, finding word partnerships, and word-building. In some units further extension work is also provided.

Language practice

As with vocabulary, the majority of the language tasks relate to the preceding text. The tasks provide contextualised practice in the structural areas that continue to cause difficulties even at an advanced level.

Listening

The listening material consists of recorded interviews with business people in well-known companies or with specialists in a particular field, in which they describe their work and discuss current business issues and practices. The material is treated in a similar way to the texts, with pre- and post-listening tasks designed to help you listen more effectively. Often you are asked to apply what you hear to a different but related task. For example, you may need to use the notes you took during a listening exercise in order to write a short report.

N.B. *For reasons of quality it has been necessary in some cases to re-record the original interviews. However, the original transcripts have not been changed in any way.*

Case studies

All the case studies generate a task based on simulation or role-play and involve you in such activities as discussion, problem-solving, decision-making and/or recommending courses of action. You will have the opportunity to put into practice the knowledge acquired while working through the unit, as well as using your existing linguistic resources and a wide variety of business skills in a challenging and realistic business task which will serve to recreate the atmosphere of the business world within a classroom environment.

Writing

Each unit contains a variety of realistic writing tasks which are often linked to the case studies, but which may appear at other points in the unit. All the writing tasks simulate those required by the London Chamber of Commerce and Industry in their English for Business examinations (levels two and three), e.g. writing letters, memos, sales leaflets, advertisements, articles, slogans, reports and press releases. Any student preparing for this examination will find the practice tasks in *Business Class* invaluable.

Complementary and Resource Materials

At the end of the book you will find the Complementary Materials section, which contains material such as role cards and checklists that you will need to carry out some of the writing and speaking activities. The Resource Materials Section which follows gives help with various related general business activities, such as writing letters and memos. You are referred to these sections at appropriate points in the book.

The authors

David Cotton is a senior lecturer in English as a Foreign Language at London Guildhall University. He has extensive experience of teaching English for Business and has written a number of text books for business English learners such as Agenda, International Business Topics, World of Business and Keys to Management. He has also been involved in developing training courses for teachers of business English in collaboration with the London Chamber of Commerce and Industry.

Sue Robbins has many years' experience in the field of ELT. She recently joined South Bank University, London, as a lecturer in English as a Foreign Language, teaching English for business. She has considerable expertise in the field of teacher training and development, having designed and taught a number of pre- and in-service courses for teachers of English to Speakers of Other Languages, including courses and seminars on English for Specific Purposes.

1

Brand Management

INTRODUCTION

1   **Can you match these famous brands with their makers?**

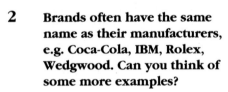

Cinzano	Nestlé
Marlboro	Rowntree
Smarties	McDonalds
Walkman	Levi Strauss
No. 5	Sony
Nescafé	Grand
501	Metropolitan
Big Mac	Chanel
	Philip Morris

Some famous brands . . .

2   **Brands often have the same name as their manufacturers, e.g. Coca-Cola, IBM, Rolex, Wedgwood. Can you think of some more examples?**

3   **Discuss the following questions.**
1   What is a company's main technique for building brand awareness?
2   What is 'brand image'?
3   Why do people wear Rolex watches? Or Cartier bracelets?
4   Which brands are you loyal to? Why?

TEXT 1

1   **Before you read, look at the title and subtitle.**
1   What are described as 'the purest treasure' and 'valuable assets'?
2   Do you expect the article to praise or criticise trends in brand management?

2   **Read the text and answer the following questions.**
1   What are the advantages to a company of building up a brand?
2   What mistake have brand managers been making in their marketing?
3   What do the terms 'brand-stretching' and 'taking a brand downmarket' mean?
4   Why is it dangerous to take a brand downmarket?
5   What is the thinking behind the appointment of 'brand-equity managers'?
6   How effective are price promotions in the short-term? And in the long-term?
7   What negative effect can price promotions have on brands?
8   What benefits can brand-stretching bring?

The purest treasure

Brands are among a company's most valuable assets. This month our management page looks at why they are so rarely treated that way

BRANDS are insubstantial things, mere symbols, names, associations. Sometimes they signal real differences between products. Sometimes they are pure illusion. Either way, brands are akin to a product's or company's reputation, and they influence consumers' perceptions. The wearer of a Rolex watch is concerned with more than keeping time; the BMW driver with more than getting from place to place. Brands add value by making customers loyal and, often, willing to pay more for the things branded. Roses by another name might smell as sweet, but they would no longer fetch $30 a dozen.

Despite the evidence of the value of brands, creating and sustaining that capital are often neglected by consumer-goods companies. Under pressure to make big short-run gains in sales, many brand managers are cavalier about the long-term commercial health of their products. Increasingly they are abandoning brand-building activities, such as advertising, in favour of tactics, especially price promotions, which aim to increase market share quickly. In 1980 promotions accounted for about a third of all spending on marketing, with advertising taking up the rest. Now, remarkably, the proportions have reversed.

A forthcoming book* by David Aaker, a marketing professor at the University of California at Berkeley, tries to cure brand managers of this myopia. Often, Mr Aaker argues, managers are not sufficiently aware of the damage that short-term thinking can do to good brands. A marketing plan centred on discounts and promotions, along with corner-cutting on quality, caused Schlitz, an American lager, to lose its position as a premium beer. In just five years, Schlitz went from $48m in net profits to $50m in losses.

Rarely can rivals inflict such severe damage. To launch a new consumer product in America can cost $75m-100m; even then, most fail. At the same time, old favourites become virtually invulnerable. In 19 of 22 standard product categories, today's leading brand was also on top in 1925. In the category of food blenders, consumers were still ranking General Electric second – 20 years after the company had stopped making them.

The failure of challengers to overcome the resilience of familiar names has led to

MANAGEMENT FOCUS

another tactic also prone to short-termism: brand-stretching. In their eagerness to extend a popular brand's recognition and reputation to a new type of product, says Mr Aaker, managers often overlook basic problems with the "fit" between the old name and the new item. Levi Strauss's attempt to stretch itself to cover a line of smart suits failed dismally. Worse, it hurt the core brand: it took a snappy advertising campaign to get Levi's jeans business back on track.

More perilous still are attempts to milk additional sales from premium brands by

taking them downmarket. Cadillac's reputation has still not recovered from its effort to attract lower-income car buyers with its cheaper Cimarron model in the early 1980s. Diluting Cadillac's snob appeal put off image-conscious buyers who might normally have been keen on the car. Undisciplined use of the Gucci name almost brought the company to ruin; at one point there were some 14,000 different Gucci products.

Part of the problem is that the organisation of most consumer-goods companies favours short time horizons. Brand managers at firms such as Unilever and Philip Morris usually stay in their jobs for just a year or two. Brand oversight by top management is generally *ad hoc*.

One solution suggested by Mr Aaker is for companies to hire or appoint people solely to monitor the status of brands. These "brand-equity managers" would be charged with taking a long view on guarding products' images, name associations and perceived quality. They would have the final say over marketing plans and the decisions of ordinary brand managers. Such a system is being tried at Colgate-Palmolive and Canada Dry.

But unless the incentive structure within the consumer-goods companies is changed, "brand-equity" managers will provide little more than another layer of bureaucracy. As Mr Aaker points out, the main reason for brand-related short-termism is shareholders' expectations of sparkling quarterly earnings. Because brand equity is hard to put a price on, punters must use returns as a guide to future performance. This is the source of pressure on brand managers to turn to promotions to boost sales.

Price promotions can have a dramatic short-term effect on a brand's sales, especially for some sorts of good. For fruit drinks, increases of more than 400% during the first week of a promotion are common. But a new study† by the London Business School shows that such promotions have no lasting effect on sales or brand loyalty. Some consumers switch temporarily to the promoted brand, but once the promotion ends, almost all of them go back to the one they normally prefer.

Promotions that merely offer a discount or a rebate can cheapen a brand's image. Since price is often a signal to consumers of a product's quality (witness luxury drinks like Chivas Regal), a brand that is always on special offer loses its appeal. Better, says Mr Aaker, to try promotions that reinforce the brand's image, such as American Express's leather luggage tags, or increase brand awareness, such as Pillsbury's baking contests.

Similarly, thoughtful brand-stretching can not only help a new product break into a crowded market but can also enhance the core brand's value. Frozen-juice bars and vitamin-C tablets have reinforced Sunkist's orange-tinted image of good health. But even a good "fit" has limits. Despite the association of a fruit-processor like Dole with all things tropical, Mr Aaker says the company would be stretching things too far if it opened a tropical-travel service. His advice to brand managers echoes the words of David Ogilvy, a legendary adman: "The consumer is no moron; she is your wife."

* Managing Brand Equity. By David A. Aaker, Free Press, $24.95. † The After-Effects of Consumer Promotions. By A.S.C. Ehrenberg, with Kathy Hammond and G.J. Goodhardt. London Business School preliminary report, August 1991.

VOCABULARY 1

1 **Match each word in the left box with a word in the right box to form ten common marketing expressions. Then use these expressions to complete the sentences that follow. Text 1 will help you.**

brand	premium	plan	product
consumer	market	brand	brands
marketing	price	offer	campaigns
advertising	special	loyalty	awareness
core	brand	share	promotions

1 .... are important brand-building activities.
2 Marketing tactics such as .... aim to boost sales quickly.
3 Because of their association with quality and status, ... often cost a bit more.
4 During a sale in a department store, many goods are on ....
5 The danger with brand-stretching is the damage that can result to the .... if it is not successful.
6 A good .... will guard the long-term interests of the brand it is promoting.
7 Launching a new .... onto the market is a costly and risky business.
8 Customers who always buy the same brand of goods are showing ....
9 .... is a measure of how well-known a product is in the marketplace.
10 In some sectors, the competition between companies for .... is fierce.

2 **Complete each sentence with the correct form of the underlined word. In some cases, you will need to use the negative form.**

1 advertise
- In our new campaign, our main .... medium will be television.
- Benetton produced a series of eye-catching .... for their products.

2 associate
- Engineering firms often work in .... with other companies on a major contract.
- When there is a financial scandal, business people often try to .... themselves from those involved.

3 consume
- Food, clothing and household products are all examples of .... goods.
- Wine .... is high in France, and on the increase in other European countries.

4 market
- To make money, you don't just need a good product – you also need excellent ....
- Some products are very innovative, but they simply aren't ....

5 produce
- Although the meeting went on for hours, it was rather ....
- Since we introduced the new pay structure, ... has improved enormously.

6 profit
- This line of raincoat is highly .... – we must discontinue it as soon as possible.
- If we are serious about improving the .... of these outlets, we should take a good look at staffing costs.

7 <u>promote</u>
- We expect all our .... activities to cost around £2 million.
- .... is a very important marketing function.

8 <u>rival</u>
- The .... between soft drinks companies, Coca-Cola and Pepsi Cola, is very fierce.
- Otis is known all over the world as a manufacturer of lifts. Its reputation in the industry is ....

9 <u>sell</u>
- Which is your best-.......................... product?
- Our .... force doubled when we took over our chief competitor.

10 <u>value</u>
- Our stock is so .... that it cannot be left unguarded.
- We were most impressed by the consultants we hired – their advice was ....

LANGUAGE PRACTICE 1

Relationships between facts

Study these examples from Text 1. Then choose words from the box to complete the sentences that follow. Use your dictionary and grammar book to help you decide which words are both appropriate and grammatically correct in each case.

Despite *the evidence of the value of brands, creating and sustaining that capital are often neglected by . . . companies.* (line 23)

Because *brand equity is hard to put a price on, punters must use returns as a guide to future performance.* (line 106)

Some consumers switch temporarily to the promoted brand, **but** *once the promotion ends, almost all of them go back to the one they normally prefer.* (line 120)

Since *price is often a signal to consumers of a product's quality . . . , a brand that is always on special offer loses its appeal.* (line 125)

Reason	because	as	so	since	therefore	consequently		
Contrast	although	despite	in spite of	but	however	nevertheless	yet	

1 Brand-stretching can be very risky. ...., it can also be very lucrative.
2 The value of price promotions is questionable, ... most consumers switch back to their usual brand when the promotion ends.
3 Companies have to keep their shareholders happy. ...., brand managers are under pressure to find ways of boosting sales.
4 .... a brand may sell well in one country, it may not sell at all in another.
5 Price is a signal of quality, ... consumers will often pay more for premium brands.
6 In 1991, advertising accounted for around a third of all marketing outlay, ..., in 1980, the picture was very different.
7 .... their disappearance from the market, General Electric's food blenders continued to rank second with consumers 20 years later!

1 **Before you read, discuss the following questions.**

1 How many of you are familiar with the brand name Levi?

2 How many of you own or have owned a pair of Levis?

3 What do you know about the company?

2 **Read the text and summarise the main points under the following headings.**

- the Levi achievement
- the company's development

- past marketing mistakes
- recovery and beyond

The Levi Story

Mistakes that failed to kill a classic product

[1] There are not many genuinely classic brands, but Levis have earned themselves a place among the Coca-Colas, Zippos, [5] Bics and 2CVs. Classic brands used continuously and in an unchanged format for 100 years are exceptionally rare in the clothing market, dictated as it [10] is by the fickle demands of fashion. Levi Strauss's achievement is formidable: from a small family firm to a massive international concern.

[15] The years in between have seen not only the evolution of a classic brand but also some massive, equally classic, marketing errors. The 501 initiative [20] is the nearest Levi Strauss has ever come to co-ordinated international marketing, and represents a serious attempt to re-focus the entire company [25] after several disastrous years in the international market.

In the early 1960s, Levi Strauss was sky-rocketing. American films and music had [30] spread to Europe and jeans had come to symbolise a new, youth culture. Kids decided that denim would become their uniform, a visible statement of a [35] new, exciting lifestyle. Levi Strauss was still a purely American company, with no overseas operation. Now that a brand new market had present-[40]ed itself, international expansion had to be looked at.

Initially, the company used local agents to sell the products which were shipped in from the [45] States. Teenagers trekked all over European cities, looking for a retailer who stocked the all-American jeans. There was still no international marketing, [50] let alone international advertising. The whole international success story happened almost by chance, and certainly without any co-ordinated effort from [55] San Francisco.

At the same time, in America, Levi Strauss diversified at a frenetic pace into all sorts of unrelated areas, includ-[60]ing Staprest trousers and Resistol hats. The Levi label was put on all these non-jeans products, and the company grew.

[65] By 1974, now a public company, Levi started manufacturing locally throughout Europe. It moved its European advertising account from Young and [70] Rubicam to McCann-Erickson, which took over all the non-American advertising. But Levi Strauss was coming unstuck: nobody knew what the Levi [75] name stood for any more. All the advertising for the different products was saying totally different things about the company and the unrelated pro-[80]ducts had begun to damage Levi's volume base – its jeans. What kid, seeing his dad buy Levi polyester trousers, was going to rush out and buy Levi [85] jeans? Levis were old-fashioned, said the consumers.

Something had to be done – and fast. The diversification programme was put into reverse [90] gear, and the Levi name was taken off unrelated products. The company retained the other brands, but distanced them from the jeans products, [95] or made them more jeans-related. Levi Strauss realised that it had to stop trying to drag value out of its most valuable property – its name – and go [100] back to its roots, becoming once again the premier jeans company in the world.

VOCABULARY 2

**Suggest an appropriate synonym (word or phrase with the same meaning)
for each of the following words from the text.**

1 genuinely (line 1)
2 fickle (line 10)
3 re-focus (line 24)
4 sky-rocketing (line 28)

5 expansion (line 40)
6 stood for (line 75)
7 volume base (line 81)
8 property (line 99)

LANGUAGE PRACTICE 2

Tenses

1 **Study the example from Text 2 and answer the questions that follow.**

*In the early 1960s, Levi Strauss **was sky-rocketing**. American films and music
had spread to Europe, and jeans **had come** to symbolise a new, youth culture.
. . . Now that a brand new market **had presented** itself, international expansion
had to be looked at.*

1 Why is the past continuous used in the first sentence?
2 Why is the past perfect used in the second sentence?
3 Which tenses are used in the third sentence? Why?

2 **The following text is about three seaside resorts in the south-west of England
which had a problem with their 'brand image'. Put the verbs in brackets in
the correct tense – simple past, past perfect or past continuous.**

*A new image for Torbay –
The English Riviera*

In the 1980s, the tourist trade in the Devon towns of Torquay,
Paignton and Brixham hit a slump. For some reason, visitors
[1]..................................... (stay away): even at the peak of the
summer, a third of the available hotel beds [2]....................................
(be) empty. Hoteliers [3].................................... (lose) money and
shopkeepers, too, [4].................................... (find) it hard to make a
living. Everyone [5].................................... (struggle). Something
[6].................................... (have) to be done.

The local tourist board [7].................................... (bring in) an
advertising agency and the explanation for the slump soon became
clear: in the 1970s, after a local government amalgamation, the
towns of Torquay, Paignton and Brixham [8]....................................
(start) using a collective identity in their marketing rather than their
individual names. However, the identity they [9]....................................
(choose) – Torbay – [10].................................... (confuse) people. Ten
years later, few holiday-makers actually [11]....................................
(associate) the name with the area; all the marketing up until then
[12].................................... (be) ineffective.

To overcome this problem, the agency [13]....................................
(drop) the name Torbay and [14].................................... (give) the
area a fresh image as The English Riviera instead. This was the
name people [15].................................... (use) in Victorian times to
describe the area, and reviving it in this way
[16].................................... (turn out) to be a wise decision: it
[17].................................... (give) the towns an appealing continental
flavour – and a much clearer image.

LISTENING

1 **Before you listen, discuss this opinion from one executive in the advertising industry.**

The purpose of most mass advertising is either to persuade consumers that your product is superior to those of your competitors, or to encourage retailers to give the product shelf space. Major food companies, car firms, banks, detergent manufacturers, and so on, have to spend a lot of money on advertising because there is actually not much difference between their products and those of rival companies. It's because the products are so similar that these companies spend a fortune persuading us that they're different!

2 **In this extract from the Channel 4 television programme, *Design and Technology*, Kate Farara, Account Executive at JWT Advertising Agency, and Roger Partington, Marketing Director at Rowntree Mackintosh, discuss advertising in general, and confectionery advertising in particular. Listen and take notes on the key points. Then complete the following programme review.**

Nestlé Rowntree's 'Gruesome Greenies' Smarties promotion

Review

The Technology Programme

This was another first-rate programme in an excellent series. Kate Farara of the JWT Advertising Agency and Roger Partington, Marketing Director at Rowntree, gave viewers a clear, informative account of the purposes of advertising.

Kate Farara pointed out that advertising can have different aims and work in different ways. Some advertising invites the consumer to make an immediate response, for example by filling in a coupon.

Another type, however, aims to [1].............................., especially about high-priced goods. Here, you're obviously not expected to respond immediately. You won't, for example, rush to a showroom to buy that new Renault you've just seen advertised in a TV commercial.

A third type of advertising addresses your needs, wants or desires. Such advertising is either designed to [2]....................................... or [3]............................... . Because there is no 'new news' about established brands, the aim of the advertiser in this case is to [4].................................... . This is vital with products such as cereal, chocolate and washing powder.

Roger Partington explained that his company spent a lot on advertising to ensure that Rowntree's brands [5].................................... . In the case of Smarties, Rowntree was trying to create [6]...................................., as he called it – children would feel proud to be seen with a tube of Smarties in their hand.

Although advertising is important, Roger Partington reminded viewers that it was just one part of the [7]......................................., which also includes elements such as [8]..................................... .

He explained the importance of market research, which provided Rowntree with a [9].................................... of consumer reactions to the products. Rowntree was, he said, above all a [10]....................................... company: the design of products and brands was largely determined by consumer opinions.

After talking about the advertising of new products, Kate Farara mentioned target audiences. Advertisers had to keep a careful watch on their [11]...................................... . While it was true that the target audience for Smarties had stayed the same since the 1950s, [12]............................... and advertisers had to take account of such changes.

One can only hope that other programmes in this series will be as good as this one. Verdict: Well worth watching!

CASE STUDY

Of Italian origin, Silvana emigrated to England from Lugano, Switzerland, with her family when she was ten years old. Later, she married Pierre, who was also Swiss, and worked in his designer clothing business in London. In 1980, they moved to Oxford and opened a French-style restaurant.

The restaurant was very successful, but Silvana found it difficult to get high quality after-dinner chocolates in England. She was so disappointed about this that she decided to return to Lugano and learn how to make them herself. A friend of hers owned a large chocolate factory there, and happily showed her how chocolates were manufactured. Back in England, she started producing hand-made chocolates for her restaurant clientele and friends. She used top-quality ingredients, and the chocolates were greatly praised by all who tasted them.

The idea of establishing a hand-made confectionery business came almost by chance. One day, on an impulse, they contacted a famous chain of quality food stores based in London. The firm's chief buyer expressed interest in their products, and the following week they went to London with their samples. To their astonishment, they left the buyer's office with an order for 30 kilos!

Seeing the potential in Silvana's 'hobby', the couple sold their restaurant and used the proceeds to set up Silvana Chocolates. Within a year, they were unable to cope with the demand and had to take on additional labour. Five years later, Silvana Chocolates was a flourishing business, producing a wide range of truffles, pralines and liqueur chocolates.

Today, the chocolates are selling well in the UK, but Silvana and Pierre are ambitious: they want the business to be much bigger. They would also like to expand into Europe as soon as possible. To do so successfully, they know they must create a stronger brand image – the chocolates don't really have a 'personality' at the moment – and devise a marketing plan to increase brand awareness – their products are still not widely known by the general public.

To discuss suitable ways of improving brand image and increasing consumer awareness, Pierre and Silvana have set up a meeting with a small advertising agency in London.

A brand with plans . . .

Role-play: Meeting

Work in groups of four as two pairs, one pair playing Pierre and Silvana, the other pair playing the account executives from the advertising agency. Read your role-cards and prepare for the meeting. When you have held your meeting, meet back as one group and compare your ideas.

Pierre and Silvana

Prepare for the meeting by thinking about your objectives (stronger brand image, increased consumer awareness, quicker growth in the UK, expansion into Europe). Try to come up with ideas for new packaging (people say it's dull), an attractive logo, and some catchy slogans for any advertising you decide to do – you will then be able to get the agency's reactions to them. Find out if the agency has other suggestions for marketing your products too.

Account executives

You know that Pierre and Silvana want Silvana Chocolates to grow faster and expand into Europe as soon as possible; they know they need a more clearly defined brand image and a proper campaign to increase consumer awareness. They will expect you to have ideas on new packaging (the present packaging is very dull). They will also need a new logo, and some suggestions for slogans, since you feel advertising will be an important part of their marketing plan. Other proposals for marketing their chocolates, such as special promotions, would also be well received.

WRITING

1 **Companies spend a lot of money developing slogans to promote their products. Many slogans use double meanings as a clever stylistic device.**

1 Can you explain the two meanings in the following slogans?
- 'We'll give you sound advice.' (hi-fi store)
- 'We offer you a good deal.' (bank)
- 'Make a snap decision.' (camera shop)
- 'Sea for yourself.' (Royal Navy recruitment advertisement)

2 Choose two or three of the following slogans and discuss what makes them successful.

The world's favourite airline

PURE GENIUS

ZANUSSI
THE APPLIANCE OF SCIENCE

PUT A TIGER IN YOUR TANK

Air Canada
A BREATH OF FRESH AIR

2 Read the following advertisement and write a letter of application for the post. You may invent any information about yourself that you wish.

BRANDS GROUP MANAGER

**To manage and inspire an able group
in growing some of the best known brands**

c.£36,000 + car   Central London

Although innovative brand management is often the basis of a marketing career, success in leading and managing a group of brand managers depends on a much broader range of talents. This new job, in an organisation whose name is a byword in its field and whose products are highly regarded, provides the chance to display genuine management ability, in controlling an able, committed and product-focussed team. A new marketing structure has been set up to anticipate and take advantage of changes and new opportunities in the market place. The ability to generate new ideas and perspectives which add to the success of established methods will therefore be crucial. For our ideal candidates, personality will be at least as important as background; certainly they'll be energetic (achievers always are), undoubtedly they'll be bright (a sharp intellect as well as formal qualifications) and inevitably they'll be highly proficient marketeers (inspired but not limited by their experience). Their background in substantial fmcg brand management, either in-house or in-agency – though both would be wonderful – should demonstrate commitment, success and, above all, the potential for further growth. Please send full details quoting reference WE 1091, to Dave Denny, Ward Executive Limited, Academy House, 26-28 Sackville Street, London W1X 2QL. Tel: 071-439 4581.

WARD EXECUTIVE
LIMITED

Marketing Sportswear

INTRODUCTION

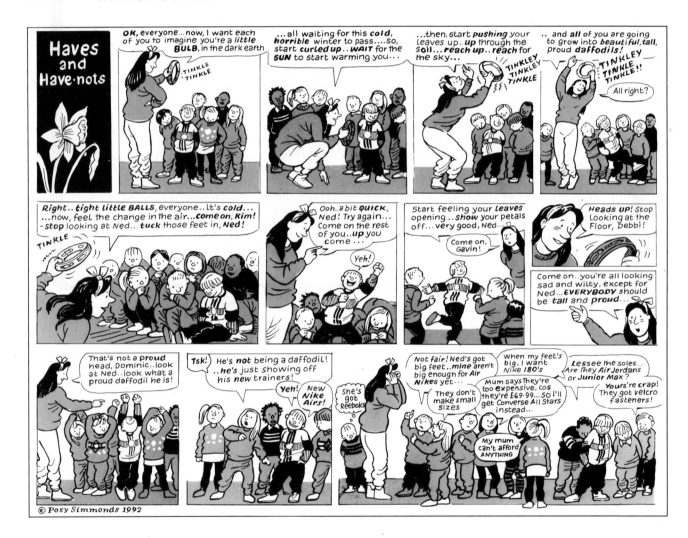

1 **Look at the first four pictures in the cartoon. What is the situation? Choose the correct answer.**

1 The children are in:
   a) a drama lesson
   b) an English lesson
   c) a sports lesson

2 The teacher wants the children to pretend to be:
   a) a tree
   b) an animal
   c) a flower

3 The children are:
   a) less than five years old
   b) between five and ten years old
   c) more than ten years old

2 **Read the whole cartoon and answer the following questions.**

1 Why are the children looking at Ned all the time?
2 How do the children feel about Ned?
3 How does the teacher feel in the last picture?
4 Which sports shoes do the children refer to?

3 **What do you think?**

1 How do children become this aware of sports shoe brands?
2 What pressures would/does this level of brand awareness put on parents?
3 How aware of brands were you at this age?
4 Do you own a pair of sports shoes? What influenced your choice?
5 Are sports shoes a status symbol?

TEXT 1

1 **Before you read, look at the title and subtitle.**

1 Which community is *'soul'* music associated with?
2 What does *'sole'* mean in this context?
3 Complete the following sentence.
   The article Soul to Sole is about how .... are challenging marketing traditions in the .... industry.

¹ There is a scene in Spike Lee's film *Do The Right Thing* of a white cyclist steaming along a Brooklyn street on a hot, hot ⁵ summer day. He bumps into Buggin' Out, one of the black kids hanging out on the street.

Buggin' Out is outraged. 'Not only did you knock me down, you stepped on my ¹⁰ brand new Air Jordans . . . and that's all you can say, "excuse me",' he shrieks, and lunges towards the cyclist.

For a Brooklyn boy like Buggin' Out his Nike Air Jordans are not just a pair of ¹⁵ sports shoes but a badge of pride. The real Buggin' Out will own as many as a hundred pairs of sports shoes costing anything from $50 to $150 each. All in all more than 44m pairs of sports shoes will ²⁰ be sold in the US this year.

For a handful of multinational manufacturers that dominate the $20 billion worldwide market, it all adds up to an extraordinarily buoyant business. But ²⁵ the market is changing, the axis of power is shifting away from the manufacturers towards the consumer.

It is not the technicians in Nike's research department or Reebok's ³⁰ marketing managers that dictate which styles will sell, but Brooklyn boys like Buggin' Out. The sports-shoe market is turning into a multinational's nightmare.

The sports shoe of today is the ³⁵ creation of three US companies, Nike, Reebok and Converse, which emerged in the 1980s. They used a combination of technical innovation and low-cost manufacturing to steal market share away ⁴⁰ from Adidas and Puma, the West German manufacturers that had dominated the market for decades.

These companies identified a need for smarter, more stylish shoes to suit the ⁴⁵ emerging sports of the 1980s. Nike went for running, Reebok for aerobics. They also developed a new system of subcontracting their manufacturing to companies in the low labour-cost ⁵⁰ economies of South Korea and Taiwan.

Soon sports shoes were worn by everyone from the Buggin' Outs in Brooklyn to the brokers and bankers on Wall Street and the clubbers in the night ⁵⁵ districts of Tokyo. Reebok, Nike and Converse were locked in a cycle of developing more and more styles and technical features to dangle in front of the consumer.

⁶⁰ The sports shoe began the 1980s as an unremarkable product, the humble trainer, which came in a choice of canvas or leather in black and white. It ended the decade as one of the most sophisticated ⁶⁵ and sought-after consumer products.

Some sports shoes come in leather. Others are covered with fur. The choice of colours, styles and trimmings is endless. Some have air pumps in the soles. Others ⁷⁰ have inflatable tops. There are Alphas. There are Air Jordans. There is even a sports shoe called the Beast.

Soul To Sole

The conventional wisdom is that the multinationals call the tune and the consumers dance to it. Well not with the sports shoe. **Alice Rawsthorn** tells the story

For Brooklyn Boys like Buggin' Out, Nike Air Jordans are not just a pair of sports shoes but a badge of pride

Ostensibly the multinationals have got it made. They have one of the hottest products on the market. ⁷⁵ They even have low manufacturing costs. But the tables are turning. The multinationals are so locked into the cycle of innovation that they have lost control of ⁸⁰ the market.

As soon as a new style or feature comes on to the market – the Pump by Reebok, a baseball boot with an inflatable sole, is the latest – the old sports ⁸⁵ shoes are dropped and the new style is taken up.

The culture of the sports shoe is textbook semiotics. In the States, the kids in one city go for one brand, and in a ⁹⁰ neighbouring town for another. Nike is hot in Chicago. In Philadelphia it is Adidas. Sometimes the styles and brands change from suburb to suburb or even from street to street. The choice of shoe, ⁹⁵ whether the laces are tied or not, even if it is a matching pair, speaks volumes about where someone lives and who they hang out with.

¹⁰⁰ The trends are set by the kids in the inner cities. The shoe worn today by the Puerto Rican kids along Bedford Avenue in Williamsburgh will soon spread to the suburbs and then out of New York over to the West Coast. It will ¹⁰⁵ then become big in Europe and even in the Far East.

The problem for the multinationals is that it is impossible to predict which type of shoe the kids will choose. A few years ¹¹⁰ ago British Knights became popular in Los Angeles but sales suddenly slumped when the local kids started calling them Brother Killers. In the London and Manchester clubs this spring ¹¹⁵ there was a craze for plain Puma trainers, an anti-fashion protest against the hi-tech styles from the States. It is the consumers, not the multinationals, that decide whether a new shoe will be a hit ¹²⁰ or not.

The multinationals are faced with potentially a phenomenally profitable market. They *must* keep coming up with new styles to keep ahead of their ¹²⁵ competitors. Yet they are now in a situation where they can sink million of dollars into developing a new product only to see it sink, inexplicably, without trace.

¹³⁰ Even if a new product succeeds, a sudden slump in sales may mean that the company is lumbered with high stocks of unsaleable shoes. The fact that most companies import their shoes from cheap ¹³⁵ production sources in the Far East complicates the problems, because they place their orders so far in advance that it is difficult to respond to sudden changes in the marketplace.

¹⁴⁰ The multinationals are developing defensive strategies. Converse gathers together groups of kids from the inner cities in the US to talk about the sort of trends and colours that they want to see. ¹⁴⁵ This forms the basis of its market research before it launches a new shoe.

Avia, one of the Reebok brands, sells small samples of new styles in a handful of inner-city stores on an experimental ¹⁵⁰ basis. It sees how sales go and monitors customers' comments. It then adapts the new shoe before going into full-scale production.

Nike has gone one step further. Given ¹⁵⁵ that it has little or no control over whether its shoes will sell, it has introduced an inbuilt-obsolescence to its products by deleting most of its range every six months. This means that most of its styles ¹⁶⁰ are automatically withdrawn and replaced by new styles after only a few months on the market.

But the multinationals are still struggling. Puma once developed a new shoe ¹⁶⁵ specifically, or so it thought, for inner-city kids in the US. It went as far as it could to be wacky. It covered the shoe in fur. It even called it the Beast. But the Buggin' Outs of Brooklyn just didn't want to buy it. ¹⁷⁰ Maybe the cyclist did.●

2   **The text is divided into two parts. Read the first part (lines 1-72) and complete the following summary (sometimes you will need to use more than one word).**

The writer describes a scene from Spike Lee's film *Do The Right Thing* to illustrate how [1].............................. young black Americans are of their [2]................................ . In reality, some may own up to a hundred pairs, costing between [3]................................ each.

With the market [4].............................. valued at [5]................................, the writer predicts that sports shoe sales for the year will reach [6].............................. in the United States alone. For the small number of major [7]................................ controlling the [8]..............................., sports shoes are clearly big business. But it seems it is the [9].............................. – no longer the [10]................................ – who are the new decision-makers.

The three American companies responsible for the modern sports shoe are [11]................................. . They [12]................................ in the 1980s, and succeeded in taking [13].............................. from long-standing market leaders, [14]..............................., by combining [15]............................... .

Nike, Reebok and Converse realised that there was a market for [16]............................... shoes, which were more suitable for 1980s sports like [17]................................ . The shoes took off. Everyone started wearing them, and the pressure was on to develop ever more [18]................................ to satisfy consumers.

Manufacturers certainly rose to the challenge: the 1980s saw the simple [19]............................... become a highly [20]................................ best seller.

3   **Read the second part of the text (lines 73-170). Then number the notes in the box from 1-10 to indicate their order of appearance in the finished article.**

NOTES

.... *Manufacturers' problem – no way of knowing which styles will be a hit.*

.... *The Beast – developed specially for inner city kids – unsuccessful.*

.... *Long lead times – multinationals can't react quickly to sudden changes in demand.*

.... *Inner-city kids start fashions – trends spread to suburbs, coasts, overseas.*

.... *Small-scale test marketing of new product – one way to reduce launch risks.*

.... *One answer to rapidly changing tastes – discontinue products after just a few months.*

.... *Multinationals driven by innovation cycle – new style/feature hits market, old shoes dropped.*

.... *Market potentially lucrative – but highly competitive and very risky.*

.... *Favoured brands differ from city to city, suburb to suburb, even street to street.*

.... *Market research with inner-city kids – one manufacturer's defence strategy.*

VOCABULARY

1   **Complete the following sentences with an appropriate word from the list. Make sure you use the correct form.**

develop	1 Three US companies .... a need for more stylish sports shoes.
dictate	2 Sports shoe manufacturers do a lot of market research before they .... a new product.
dominate	3 The multinationals have lost control of the market – it is the consumer who .... which styles will sell.
identify	4 By .... a system of sub-contracting in the Far East, the multinationals have been able to reduce their manufacturing costs.
launch	
	5 It is in the inner cities that new trends are ....
place	6 Because sports shoe manufacturers .... their orders so far in advance, they cannot always .... quickly to changes in demand.
set	
respond	7 Slow-selling shoes will probably be .... from the market and replaced by new styles.
withdraw	8 The market for sports shoes is .... by a handful of multinationals.

2   **Match each word in the left box with a word in the right box, using each word once only. Then use four of the expressions to write about the sports shoe industry.**

low-cost	production	basis	production
multinational	defensive	source	manufacturing
technical	experimental	manufacturer	department
research	full-scale	feature	strategy

LANGUAGE PRACTICE

Adverbs qualifying adjectives

Study these examples from Text 1. Then choose words from the box to complete the sentences that follow. Make sure you use the correct adverbial form.

It all adds up to an **extraordinarily** *buoyant business.* (line 24)
The multinationals are faced with potentially a **phenomenally** *profitable market.* (line 122)

exceptional	high	potential	special
technical	thorough	total	unbelievable

1 She is so rich – she bought an .... expensive pair of sports shoes today.
2 I can assure you, we only make .... superior products.
3 I disagree. It's a .... disastrous development.
4 Claude Longaud is a .... reliable manager.
5 We have come up with this .... designed package to meet your needs more closely.
6 What we need is a .... committed team.
7 We are very lucky – we have an .... motivated sales force.
8 These .... successful results mean we can go into production without delay.

WRITING 1

You work in the marketing department of a small US-based sportswear company. At present, the firm only manufactures sports clothing and accessories, but a proposal to diversify into sports shoes is under consideration. Your marketing director asks you to set down on paper the advantages and disadvantages of entering the sports shoe market to help her prepare for a meeting next week to discuss the proposed diversification.

LISTENING 1

1 In this interview, you will hear Neil Beeson, Puma's Senior Product Manager in the UK, talking about his company and its products. Listen and take notes under the following headings.
- product range
- endorsements
- target consumers
- product life
- football innovations
- Puma Disc System
- Puma's competitors
- advertising

The Puma Disc System

2 Now use your notes to write a brief article about Puma.

TEXT 2

1 Before you read, look at the title and picture caption. What do you expect the article to be about?

2 Read the article and find out what the following numbers refer to.

1 1989	3 £128m	5 1%	7 one in five
2 £1.6bn	4 68 million	6 £100	8 £1.5bn

Reebok pumps up the sales pressure

by Roger Tredre
Fashion Correspondent

[1] WAR was declared yesterday in the sports shoe industry. Reebok, the biggest selling brand of sports shoe in the [5] United Kingdom, launched its no-lace Insta-Pump running spike, the company's latest contribution to footwear technology.

The Insta-Pump, a successor [10] to the Pump, launched in 1989, represents the opening salvo in a pre-Olympics battle that will see sports shoe makers blinding the public with a barrage of high-tech [15] products and high-tech jargon.

The company has also developed the "revolutionary" Pump Custom Cushioning that inflates the mid-sole. Reebok's new Dual [20] Chamber running shoe has an additional gizmo, a lightweight electronic gauge on the side of the shoe to measure air pressure.

[25] For athletes, the Olympics represent the peak of sporting achievement. For the sports shoe industry, the games are a publicity opportunity. Reebok [30] alone, with sales of £1.6bn internationally, is spending £128m on advertising this year.

The US company brought along an American boffin to [35] demonstrate the new products yesterday at the Savoy hotel in London. Mark Fenton, manager of research and engineering trends at Reebok, is the [40] sports shoe industry's answer to Professor Stephen Hawking; he talked expertly about polyurethane airbags, electronic gauges and compression curves [45] By the end of his exposition, Mr Fenton's audience was much impressed, although some were none the wiser.

The Insta-Pump slips on like [50] a slipper. Instead of fiddling with laces, the athlete pumps up the shoe with a hand-held carbon dioxide canister to create a snug, customised fit. John Duerden, [55] president of Reebok's international division, said the effect was "like strapping yourself into a high-performance racing car".

Like many in the industry, [60] Mr Duerden is a master of understatement. The Insta-Pump, he said, represents "a quantum leap in athletic shoe technology".

The British bought 68 mil- [65] lion pairs of sports shoes last year, 1 per cent down on 1990. The new Reebok products, which will not reach the high street until spring 1993, are ex- [70] pected to cost well over £100.

Only one in five sports shoes is bought for sports use, but consumers are still impressed by new technology, even if it only [75] shaves hundredths of a second off the morning rush for the number nine bus.

Meanwhile, Reebok's rivals in the £1.5bn UK sports shoes [80] market are devising their own quantum leaps. This autumn, Converse launches its new "react" technology, containing a "unique" fluid in the mid-sole [85] heel component that responds to an athlete's movements. For the sports world, life is getting very complicated.

3 Read the text again and discuss the following questions. In each case, support your choice of answer with examples from the text.

1 What is the writer's main purpose?
   a) to inform
   b) to entertain
   c) to persuade
2 What style has the writer used?
   a) factual
   b) promotional
   c) ironic
3 What is the tone of the article?
   a) light-hearted and humorous
   b) heavy and serious
4 What is the writer's attitude towards his subject matter?
   a) enthusiastic
   b) unimpressed

LISTENING 2

You are going to hear an interview with John Williams, Account Executive for Reebok at Welbeck Public Relations. Listen and complete the following fact file.

FACT FILE: **Reebok**

Product range[1] ....

Target consumer[2] ....

Marketing philosophy[3] ....

Marketing techniques[4] ....
....
....

Sponsorship

Personal[5] ....

Competition: Junior[6] ....

             Adult[7] ....
....

Reebok Insta-Pump

Basic concept[8] ....
....
....

How it works[9] ....
....
....

Selling points[10] ....
....
....

Presentations

Work in pairs and take it in turns to give a mini-presentation to each other, one on Reebok's Insta-Pump shoe and one on Puma's Disc System shoe. Each time, the student who is listening to the presentation should take the role of an interested buyer, asking questions as appropriate. Prepare for your presentation carefully, using information from the unit. Design any support materials you feel may be helpful.

CASE STUDY

Discussion

Read the information in the box and discuss the questions that follow.

Michael Jordan – grace, charisma and a Nike success

Endorsements

Manufacturers of sports goods often use sports personalities to help sell their products. Sportsmen and women who agree to endorse a company's range of products usually sign a contract outlining the exact terms of their agreement.

Contracts vary depending on how well-known the personality is and the nature of the endorsement. Typically, a company might expect a personality to:

- make promotional appearances in person e.g. in-store, at trade fairs or other events;
- wear a company's product or logo when 'in action' in their sport;
- appear in advertising and/or mail-order catalogues;
- personalise products with their signature or photograph.

In return, a company might offer:

- fees in the form of e.g. lump sums, retainers, stage payments;
- free products;
- bonuses e.g. for winning, setting a new record etc.;
- royalties on product sales.

Endorsements can be very profitable, both for the sporting personalities and for the companies which sign them. Take the case of the famous American basketball player, Michael Jordan, one of the most graceful and charismatic players ever to appear on a basketball court. In one year alone, his endorsement of Nike helped sell one and a half million pairs of shoes – and earned him an estimated $20 million.

1 Which sports personalities do you associate with different sports manufacturers?
2 What are the possible drawbacks of endorsement to a company? Can you give some examples?

Role-play: Negotiation

The marketing director of a sports goods company manufacturing equipment, clothing and shoes, has set up a meeting with a major sports personality (and agent) to discuss a possible endorsement contract.

Work in groups of four as two pairs, one pair playing the company's marketing director and senior product manager, the other pair playing the sports personality and agent. Read your role-card and prepare for the meeting. Then role-play the negotiation, trying to agree, in principle, the terms of a contract.

Marketing director and senior product manager

It will be good for the company if you can sign this personality, but you know you are not the only offer on the table. Before the meeting, decide what you can offer and what you want in return.

Sports personality and agent

With fame on your side, you know you can sign endorsement agreements with any number of sports companies, but you like this particular firm. Before the meeting, decide what you can offer and what you want in return.

WRITING 2

1   Write a follow-up letter, summarising the points you agreed in the negotiation and noting any unresolved matters.

2   As public relations officer at a famous department store, you think it would be a good idea to invite a well-known sports personality to promote your own brand of sports products. Choose a suitable sports personality and write a letter, indicating how he or she might be able to help you e.g. by personal appearances in the store, training sessions for young people, photo opportunities and/or radio/TV advertising.

3

Marketing Ethics

INTRODUCTION

1   Discussion

Ethics are moral principles which govern attitudes and behaviour. Organisations which make ethical marketing decisions will probably be trusted by consumers and respected by the business community. Unethical marketing activities, on the other hand, can damage sales and destroy a company's reputation.

1   What unethical marketing activities can you think of?

2   What examples of unethical marketing can you give from your own knowledge or experience?

3   What kind of unethical marketing activities might go on in the pharmaceutical industry? And in the travel trade?

2   What do you think?

The Italian clothes manufacturer, Benetton, caused a lot of controversy when it ran a series of advertisements that were designed to highlight 'global concerns'. The company chose a picture of an AIDS victim – who died soon after the photograph was taken – for one advertisement and used the following picture in another:

Part of Benetton's controversial advertising campaign

1   Why did some people object to this advertisement?

2   Is it ethical to use the image of a dying man to advertise clothes?

3   The company's slogan is 'United Colours of Benetton'. What sense of unity are the images of two children of different races and a dying man meant to convey?

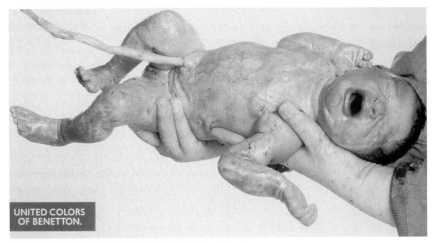

UNITED COLORS
OF BENETTON.

Benetton's new-born baby advertisement raised many objections

LISTENING 1

In this interview, you will hear marketing specialist, Francine Jason, talking about marketing ethics. Listen and decide which of the following short summaries most accurately reflects her comments. Give reasons for your choice.

1 Decisions have to be taken in business about whether a course of action is morally right or wrong. Benetton's new-born baby advertisement was unethical marketing and therefore gave rise to a lot of controversy. Marketing ethics relate to specific problems which managers have to deal with.

2 In business, decisions which involve ethical considerations can be very controversial. Benetton's decision to use a picture of a new-born baby in an advertisement was hotly debated, but whether it was right or wrong is a matter of opinion. Companies should operate within an established code of ethics.

3 Organisations have to take decisions of an ethical nature. The Benetton advertisement used a new-born baby to promote the company's goods. Some people believed this was ethical while others did not. Because marketing ethics are so subjective, it is not possible for companies to have policies about them.

TEXT 1

1   Before you read, look at the title and subtitle overleaf.

    1 Who is being interviewed?

    2 What about?

    3 What kind of comments do you expect him to make?

2   Read paragraph 1 and summarise the five charges against the pharmaceutical industry in your own words.

3   Read paragraph 2 and decide which of the following statements accurately reflect the content.

    1 Some people are beginning to have doubts about Glaxo's marketing methods.

    2 Glaxo's letter to the *Lancet* was an example of 'knocking copy'.

    3 One of Glaxo's products is called Omeprazole.

    4 Doctors are happy with Glaxo's promotional material.

The ethics of marketing drugs

The world according to Ernest

The methods used to promote and sell drugs are under attack, putting Glaxo, the world's second-biggest pharmaceuticals company, right in the line of fire. We asked the firm's chief executive, Ernest Mario, for his view

CRITICISM may be nothing new for the drug industry, but the ferocity of recent attacks is starting to worry even the most hardened executive. The industry stands accused of conducting promotional drives disguised as educational and fact-finding campaigns; of offering doctors, not pens and notepads but hard cash; of distorting data to suit its promotional needs; of blurring side-effects; and, perhaps worst as far as insiders are concerned, of bad-mouthing rival products and unnecessarily alarming doctors and patients.

Even Glaxo, long admired for its marketing, shocked the industry when in February 1990 it had a letter published in the *Lancet* saying that it had conducted tests on Omeprazole, a rival product made by Sweden's Astra, which had shown that the drug caused cancer. Such "knocking copy" had previously been taboo. More recently some doctors have raised worries about how hard Glaxo is pushing its products and whether some of its promotional material might even be confusing.

A question *The Economist* therefore asked Ernest Mario, an outspoken American, was:

● **Is Glaxo pushing too hard?** The *Lancet* letter, claims Mr Mario, was not a marketing ploy but a genuine attempt to bring to light important medical information. Naturally, he says he disapproves of public mud-slinging. But he admits that in the past few years pharmaceutical marketing has changed – often under Glaxo's leadership.

In the early 1980s Glaxo broke the mould by launching Ranitidine, its anti-ulcer cure, expensively around the world, rather than more conventionally in national markets. Glaxo was also one of the first to advertise directly to patients on American television, in a campaign about ulcers that was seen by 12m people and generated 581,000 visits to doctors. Ranitidine (branded as Zantac) is now the world's top-selling drug, accounting for half of Glaxo's £2.9 billion ($5.1 billion) sales.

According to Mr Mario the laws of the marketplace now apply as much to pharmaceuticals as to consumer electronics: once armed with a new product, a company must establish its market share as quickly as possible, before rival firms produce competitive brands. There are already four drugs similar to Ranitidine. In the past, drugs brought in good profits for a decade or more.

● **But does Glaxo "create" its markets?** Glaxo has built up one of the world's biggest sales-forces for drugs, 9,500-strong and growing; the firm is still recruiting in Europe in the expectation that several new products will be approved there. These days its marketing machinery goes into action far earlier in a product's life. While a new drug is being developed, Glaxo holds costly symposiums to which it invites experts – many of them doctors – who know about the disease the drug is designed to treat. Critics say the aim is to build a market while the drug is more an idea than a reality. Mr Mario says the drug companies use such symposiums to gauge market potential.

Once a drug is presented to regulators for approval, the marketing men get to work. After Imigran, an anti-migraine drug, was submitted to regulators for approval in mid-1990, Glaxo used public-relations firms to work out how to create demand. Doctors are to be blitzed with medical literature as well as being given guidelines on how to diagnose the disease. Medical authorities are to be persuaded of the economic savings derived from treating migraine. Fair enough, so long as such claims are true: developing brands and educating consumers matter as much to drugs firms as to others.

● **Might such heavy investment in development and marketing distort expectations inside and outside the firm?** Some doctors believe that these practices raise the stakes in a new product to such an extent that a company's scientific judgement might become clouded: that too little could be made of a drug's side-effects, and too much of its benefits. Mr Mario says that this is not possible. Any adverse information must be reported to regulators, he says, who are the industry's final arbiters. The claims made by drug firms about their products are also regulated.

Recently there have been complaints that Glaxo is confusing doctors in its promotion of Salmeterol, an anti-asthma drug that was launched in Britain last November, through claims about it potency. Although Glaxo has changed its promotional material for Salmeterol, Mr Mario believes that discussions about products should take place only with regulators. After all, drug firms do not have to publish data to get products approved, so even medical journals provide an incomplete view. Mr Mario believes that Glaxo should not be responsible for telling doctors about unfavourable reports on its drugs. It is the regulators who must decide.

● **But what about post-marketing studies? Don't they put an unreasonable burden on doctors?** Dr Bill Inman of the Drug Safety Research Unit, a charitable organisation based in Britain's Southampton, is opposed to another common pharmaceutical practice. Almost immediately after a drug has been launched, Glaxo and others establish small studies ostensibly to monitor the performance of their drugs in a normal population, rather than the one carefully selected for clinical trials. The idea is to spot any new adverse effects. But because doctors are paid for the exercise, Dr Inman regards it as a covert form of promotion, particularly as recruited patients often stick

Ernest Mario, Glaxo's Chief Executive

to the drugs after the study is complete.

Mr Mario does not think post-marketing studies are unethical: regulators have not yet managed to arrange a consistent system to handle later adverse reports, so the studies do the job.

He may be placing too much faith in regulators. America's Food and Drug Administration is in turmoil, overburdened and charged with corruption. In Britain critics believe that the relationship between drug firms and the Medicines Agency is too cosy. All information that passes between them about the approval of a drug is confidential. The agency is soon to be spun off from the Department of Health, financed solely by drug companies' licence fees. Moreover, recent surveys have shown that doctors are highly dependent on the industry's marketing men for information, which means that an appropriate debate on potential side-effects can never really take place. This may be why the World Health Organisation has gone so far as to suggest that sales-forces for drugs should be financed by the state.

4 The rest of the article is divided into four sections, each with a separate heading addressing a different question. Read each section in turn, noting the main points in the relevant column of the following chart. Check you understand all the key words, but don't worry about unfamiliar brand names or diseases. When you have finished, compare your notes in small groups.

Is Glaxo pushing too hard?	*But does Glaxo 'create' its markets?*	*Might such heavy investment in development and marketing distort expectations inside and outside the firm?*	*But what about post-marketing studies? Don't they put an unreasonable burden on doctors?*
KEY WORDS	**KEY WORDS**	**KEY WORDS**	**KEY WORDS**

KEY WORDS		KEY WORDS		KEY WORDS		KEY WORDS	
marketing ploy	generate	recruit	market potential	raise the stakes	regulator	ostensibly	corruption
break the	account for	marketing	regulator	clouded	arbiter	clinical trials	cosy
mould	market share	machinery	create demand	judgement	complaint	adverse effects	relationship
conventional	rival	symposium	guidelines	side-effects	confuse	covert	confidential
campaign		build a market	treat	adverse information		stick to	

VOCABULARY 1

Complete the following sentences with verbs from the list, making sure you use the correct form.

approve	build up	claim	conduct
gauge	launch	monitor	submit

1 New drugs always undergo a number of clinical trials before they are .... on to the market.
2 Some pharmaceutical companies organise symposiums as a way of .... the market potential of new products.
3 Before any drug can appear on the market, it must be .... to a regulatory body for approval.
4 In the fight for market share, drugs companies .... vigorous marketing campaigns.
5 Manufacturers often set up small studies to .... the performance of newly-launched drugs.
6 Some pharmaceutical companies have .... massive sales forces.
7 Marketing activities tend to start long before a new drug has been .... by the regulator.
8 It is sometimes hard to know whether the product benefits being .... by drugs manufacturers are actually true.

The article

Study these examples from Text 1. Then use 'a', 'an', 'the' or nothing at all to complete the text that follows.

*Criticism may be nothing new for **the drug industry**, but **the ferocity** of **recent attacks** is starting to worry even **the most hardened executive**. (line 1)*

*The industry stands accused of . . . offering **doctors**, not **pens** and **notepads** but **hard cash**. (line 4)*

*The Lancet letter . . . was not **a marketing ploy** but **a genuine attempt** to bring to light **important medical information**. (line 28)*

A major pharmaceutical group has started selling ¹............ cut-price drugs to ²............ hospitals in ³............ bid to increase its share of this multimillion pound market. Swedish multinational, SCP, hopes ⁴............ move will persuade ⁵............ hospital consultants to prescribe its anti-ulcer cure, Easit, instead of ⁶............ rival products.

'We have decided to offer ⁷............ hospitals ⁸............ 30% reduction on our products', said ⁹............ Reg Hastings, SCP's marketing director in ¹⁰............ UK. 'There is ¹¹............ intense competition for ¹²............ hospital market, and we must adjust our prices accordingly.'

On ¹³............ surface, this seems like ¹⁴............ saving for ¹⁵............ health service, but there are ¹⁶............ fears that ¹⁷............ move may simply be ¹⁸............ marketing ploy. 'You have to be very careful,' says Paul Humphries, ¹⁹............ Director of ²⁰............ Drugs Watchdog Unit in London. 'Price reductions are fine, but if ²¹............ price returns to its original level or even higher once ²²............ drugs have achieved ²³............ wider circulation, any savings will be wiped out.'

Easit's main competitors are Primec and Tanalas. Last year, Easit had only ²⁴............ 8% of ²⁵............ world market, while ²⁶............ Primec had ²⁷............ 15% share and ²⁸............ Tanalas, ²⁹............ market leader, accounted for ³⁰............ 39%.

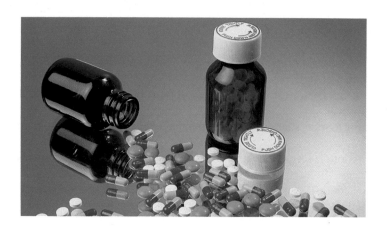

'If' sentences

1 **Study these sentences. Then answer the questions that follow.**

If I were offered an exotic holiday as a bribe, I'd probably accept it.

If I were president of Glaxo, I'd be very worried about the ferocity of recent attacks on the company.

Tobacco companies would quickly see their profits fall, if cigarette advertising was banned.

1 Are the situations referred to real or hypothetical?
2 Are the situations referred to in the present/future or in the past?
3 What structure is used to describe hypothetical situations in the present/future?

2 **Practise using 'if' sentences. Ask your partner: 'What would you do in the following situation?'**

1 As chief executive of a loss-making airline, you receive an anonymous telephone call warning you that a terrorist group is planning to place a bomb on one of your planes in the next seven days . . .

2 As a new recruit to the sales force of a prominent office equipment firm, you discover that you are expected to persuade customers to sign a service contract for every item purchased – without letting them know that the cost of spare parts and service calls increases sharply after the first year . . .

3 As purchasing officer for a major hotel group, you are considering refurbishment proposals from three different companies when a representative from one of the companies telephones and offers to buy you an exotic family holiday . . .

4 As copy-writer for a troubled package tour operator, you are asked to be more 'creative' in your descriptions and make the hotels and resorts on offer in your new holiday brochure sound more appealing than they really are . . .

LISTENING 2

Before you hear the second part of the interview with Francine Jason, discuss the following questions. Then listen and compare your answers with the comments Francine Jason makes on these points.

1 What is 'corporate hospitality'? Give some examples.
2 What is the difference between corporate hospitality and bribery?
3 Is it ethical to accept gifts in business?

TEXT 2

1 **Before you read, discuss the following questions.**

1 Holiday companies and travel agencies sometimes give misleading descriptions in their holiday brochures. Can you give some examples of such descriptions?

2 In your country, who is responsible for monitoring the activities of travel agents and/or tour operators? Is there a code of practice on holiday advertising?

2 The article summarises the results of a survey carried out by the consumer magazine, *Holiday Which?* Give yourself one minute to scan the text quickly and identify the survey's main findings. Then close your book and note down as many key points as you can remember. When you have finished, check your notes against the original article.

Holiday brochures under attack

[1]BRITAIN'S biggest holiday companies are producing misleading brochures two years after [5]the Association of British Travel Agents introduced a code of practice on the subject, according to a study by Holiday Which? [10]magazine, Michael Skapinker writes.

T_____, the UK's biggest tour operator, described Faliraki on [15]Rhodes as a former fishing village which had retained its atmosphere. Holiday Which? said it was "a sprawling, Costa-style [20]resort".

E_____, part of T_____, A_____,

the second biggest holiday company, told potential vis-[25]itors to some apartments that shops, tavernas and nightspots were within easy reach. In fact it was half a mile's walk to the nearest, [30]solitary bar.

A_____, the third biggest operator, published a brochure with a picture of a beach on the same page [35]as a description of a hotel. Holiday Which? found the beach was 12 miles from the hotel.

The magazine found bro-[40]chures from other operators with photographs taken in such a way as to hide unsightly features.

© The Financial Times

Marketing holidays – a competitive business

VOCABULARY 2

What do the underlined words in the following sentences mean? Choose the best definition.

1 The *Holiday Which?* survey found many examples of <u>misleading</u> holiday brochures. (line 3)
   a) undirected   b) disorganised   c) deceptive

2 Faliraki, a <u>former</u> fishing village, is situated on Rhodes. (line 15)
   a) well-known   b) one-time   c) built-up

3 Not all resorts <u>retain</u> their charm with the development of tourism. (line 16)
   a) keep   b) spoil   c) change

4 *Holiday Which?* described one place as a 'sprawling Costa-style resort'. (line 19)
   a) small and friendly   b) old and untidy   c) large and rambling

5 Brochure photographers try to keep <u>unsightly</u> features out of their pictures. (line 43)
   a) insignificant   b) unattractive   c) unseen

CASE STUDY

Porchester Tour Company (PTC), a medium-sized tour operator based on the south coast of England, has been receiving a growing number of complaints. Customers are dissatisfied with the standard of PTC's package holidays; many claim the company makes misleading statements in its brochures.

Annabel Kingstone chose a two-week holiday in Greece. PTC's brochure promised:

peace and relaxation off the beaten track on a little-known island of great beauty, charm and tranquility

traditional Greek hospitality in a comfortable family-run hotel full of local atmosphere

frequent ferry services to the mainland

lovely sunset walks through olive groves

miles of empty golden sands

When Ms Kingstone arrived, however, she found a sprawling resort overflowing with tourists. The nearest beach to the hotel was a kilometre away and rocky, there was one olive grove on the other side of the island, no traditional Greek dishes were served at the hotel which was staffed entirely by non-Greeks, the whole island was full of fast-food outlets and noisy bars and had a holiday-camp atmosphere. Escaping to the mainland didn't prove quite so easy either – the 'frequent ferry services' ran only three times a week and were very crowded.

On her return to the UK, Ms Kingstone wrote a letter of complaint to PTC but was refused a refund on her holiday. She was so dissatisfied, she wrote to the local paper, the *Porchester Gazette*, suggesting it might like to 'expose PTC's disgraceful business practices'. The paper followed up her story.

Having interviewed Ms Kingstone, the *Porchester Gazette* requested an interview with PTC to get the company's side of the story. The request was granted and the interview was set up at PTC's offices.

Role-play: Interview

Work in groups of four as two pairs, one pair playing two senior managers from PTC, the other pair playing two reporters from the *Porchester Gazette*. Read your role-card and prepare for your interview carefully, using the language in the box to help you.

Standing your ground

Well, as I said before . . .
As I've already said . . .
I see what you mean, but the point is . . .
What I'm saying is . . .
I think you've misinterpreted what I said.
You're missing the point.
No, that's not what I said.
It's (not) company policy to . . .
You must realise that . . .

Pushing your point

Let me come back to the point about . . .
I'm not sure you've really answered my question.
Are you saying that . . .?
To return to Ms Kingstone . . .
I'd just like to get this clear in my mind . . .
Let me put this another way . . .
Surely, that means . . .
Perhaps you can explain how . . .
Would you say that . . .?

Senior managers – Porchester Tour Company

Defend your company's reputation strongly: you must convince the reporters that you run a reputable business providing an excellent service to your customers. You organise hundreds of holidays a year and it is difficult to check all the details in your brochures. You have to rely on information given to you by local businesses and by your local representatives. You amend incorrect information in brochures as soon as possible. It is your policy to refund money to customers only in exceptional circumstances. Try to have a pleasant meeting with the reporters, but don't let them 'push you around'.

Reporters – *Porchester Gazette*

You must expect PTC's senior management to present the company's activities in a good light. However, you feel that the firm is unethical in its marketing techniques. You have information about other holiday-makers who have had bad experiences with these package holidays (give examples). Ask penetrating questions – you need to get plenty of good material so you can write a lively and provocative article – but expect to hear a lot of excuses from PTC. Don't forget to note down any comments that might make suitable quotes in your story.

WRITING

1. As Annabel Kingstone, write a letter of complaint to PTC.
2. As PTC's customer liaison officer, write a reply to Annabel Kingstone's letter of complaint.
3. As one of the reporters on the PTC/Annabel Kingstone story, write the article for the *Porchester Gazette*.

4

Presentations

INTRODUCTION

Discuss the following questions.

1 What is a 'presentation'?
2 For what purposes are presentations made in business?
3 What makes a presentation effective?
4 What is the worst presentation you have ever experienced?
5 Even experienced presenters can make mistakes during a presentation. Can you give any examples from first-hand knowledge?

VOCABULARY 1

Look at the following picture and use the words in the box to label each item correctly.

pointer	screen	podium
graph	felt-pen	notes
overhead projector (OHP)	slide projector	microphone
bar chart	pie chart	handout
whiteboard	flipchart	
overhead transparency (OHT)	table (figures)	

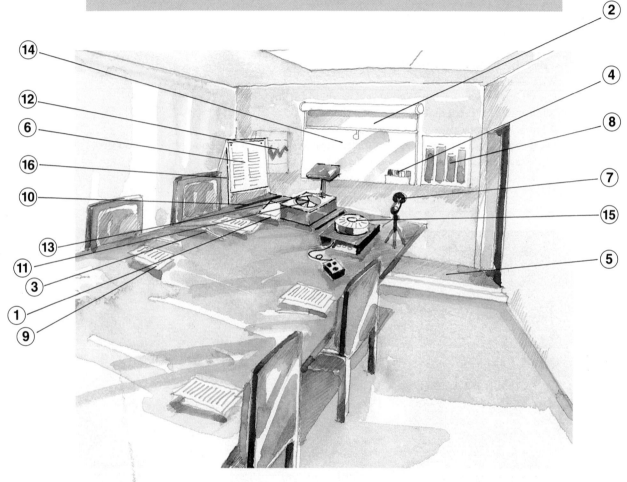

LISTENING 1

You are going to hear Alan Wroxley, Sales Manager of Brother, an electronics firm, talking about sales presentations. Listen and make notes under the following headings.

- presentation categories and techniques
- nerves: causes and cures
- ways of presenting information
- handouts
- how to be successful

TEXT 1

Read the text and answer the following questions.

1 Why did David Arnold start making critical comments about Marks & Spencer in his talk?
2 How did the audience react?
3 How did he interpret the audience's reaction – and respond?
4 What 'awful error of judgement' did the senior director bring to his attention in the coffee break?
5 How did David Arnold respond to this piece of news?
6 With hindsight, what was the true significance of the audience's body language?
7 What was David Arnold's 'biggest mistake'?
8 What did David Arnold learn from the experience?

MY BIGGEST MISTAKE

David Arnold

David Arnold, 36, is a director of studies at Ashridge Management College and a marketing consultant for such multinationals as Merck, Alfa-Laval and Boots. After a degree in English literature at University College London and in modern drama at London University, he began a career in publishing in 1979 as an editor for Mitchell Beazley. He moved to Ashridge in 1984 as marketing manager and later, after taking an MBA at City University, became a tutor on Ashridge's MBA course. His book, The Handbook of Brand Management, is published by Century Business.

MY BIGGEST mistake was failing to find out who was going to be in the audience before I gave a speech. It was two years ago, when I had been invited to be guest speaker at the annual management conference of a major clothing supplier, a company that relied on Marks & Spencer for more than 75 per cent of its sales.

My brief as guest speaker was to get the audience to think strategically about the changing market.

The conference was held at Gleneagles. I had to speak for an hour and a half to 70 managers, and when I began they were very subdued.

I decided to raise the level of challenge in order to get some reaction. When my first attempts proved unsuccessful, I turned to my last resort: I suggested that Marks & Spencer, their lifeline, was not the paragon of business success they thought it was.

Now this did spark some reaction, but the audience was still more subdued than most groups – so I actually started being rude about their beloved Marks & Spencer.

I justified these insults by saying I needed to make them take a different perspective, and even commented that I suspected the reason they were being quiet was because they were very loyal to their major customer.

I could see they were all thinking hard – they weren't asleep or anything – and I assumed they were thinking about company issues.

But at the end of the session, when we took a break for coffee, a senior director sidled up and said he had something to tell me.

He took me aside and informed me that the reason they had been so quiet was because sitting next to him in the front row was their chief customer in person: one of the head buyers of M & S. At that point, my heart hit my boots and I realised I had made the most awful error of judgement.

When I spotted the buyer, I remember going to enormous efforts to avoid him.

I managed to escape, but only at the expense of leaving my coat behind in the conference room, where everyone had assembled after coffee. I couldn't face going back in.

The other thing I couldn't face was sending the company an invoice for the agreed speaker's fee or for my expenses in travelling to Scotland.

Looking back, I remember there was a lot of fidgeting going on during my speech. I thought it was because I was talking about their most valued customer.

It was the squirming of the senior director in the front row that I remember most. Clearly, he was trying to make a judgement about whether he should speak up and halt me in mid-flow.

I think it would have been better if he had.

The night before, I had joined them for dinner and had become quite chummy with a lot of them, which is probably why I thought I was safe in taking the risk of winding them up.

But it was a mistake to assume I understood why people were reacting the way they were. It was a fatal assumption, because it was wrong. As a result, I was more critical about Marks & Spencer than I normally would have been, and certainly more than was necessary.

I still can't believe that, doing the job I do, I didn't find out who was there beforehand. I've had no communication with the company since, but the lesson to be learned is quite simple. In meetings, conferences or presentations of any sort, always make sure you find out exactly who you are speaking to.

Some hints for a successful presentation

PREPARATION

■ **Planning**   Plan your presentation carefully. Thorough preparation will make you more confident and help you to overcome your nervousness.

■ **Objectives**   Think about what you want to achieve. Are you aiming to inform, persuade, train or entertain your audience?

■ **Audience**   Whom exactly will you be addressing? How many people will be attending? What do they need to know? What do they already know? What will they expect in terms of content and approach?

■ **Content**   Brainstorm your ideas first. Then decide which are most relevant and appropriate to your audience and to your objectives and carry out any research that is necessary. Be selective! Don't try to cram too much into your presentation.

■ **Approach**   A good rule of thumb is to 'tell your audience what you're going to say, say it, then tell the audience what you've said'. Try to develop your key points in an interesting and varied way, drawing on relevant examples, figures etc. for support as appropriate. You might also like to include one or two anecdotes for additional variety and humour.

Plan your presentation carefully

■ **Organisation**   Think about how you will organise your content. Your presentation should have a clear, coherent structure and cover the points you wish to make in a logical order. Most presentations start with a brief introduction and end with a brief conclusion. Use the introduction to welcome your audience, introduce your topic/subject, outline the structure of your talk, and provide guidelines on questions. Use the conclusion to summarise the main points of your presentation, thank the audience for their attention, and invite questions.

■ **Visual aids**   If you have a lot of complex information to explain, think about using some charts, diagrams, graphs etc., on an overhead projector or flipchart. Visual aids can make a presentation more interesting and easier to understand, but make sure they are appropriate and clear – don't try to put too much information on each one.

■ **Rehearsal**   Allow time to practise your presentation – this will give you a chance to identify any weak points or gaps. You will also be able to check the timing, and make sure you can pronounce any figures and proper names correctly and confidently.

Rehearsing will help your confidence

DELIVERY

■ **Nerves!** You will probably be nervous at the beginning of your presentation. Don't worry – most people *are* nervous in this situation. Try not to speak too fast during the first couple of minutes – this is the time you establish your rapport with the audience and first impressions are very important. You may find it helpful to memorise your introduction.

■ **Audience rapport** Try to be enthusiastic – your interest in the subject matter will carry your audience along. Look around your audience as you speak – eye contact is essential for maintaining a good rapport. You will also be able to pick up signals of boredom or disinterest, in which case you can cut your presentation short.

■ **Body language** Stand rather than sit when you are delivering your presentation and try to be aware of any repetitive hand gestures or awkward mannerisms that might irritate your audience.

■ **Voice quality** You must be clearly audible at all times – don't let your voice drop at the end of sentences. If you vary your intonation, your voice will be more interesting to listen to and you will be able to make your points more effectively.

■ **Visual aids** Use your visual aids confidently, making sure you allow your audience time to absorb information from flipcharts and transparencies.

■ **Audience reaction** Be ready to deal with any hostile questions. Polite, diplomatic answers are a good disarming tactic, but if you should find yourself 'under fire', suggest that the audience keeps any further questions until the end of the presentation and continue with your next point.

LANGUAGE

■ **Simplicity** Use short words and sentences that you are comfortable with. There is no benefit in using difficult language.

Keep your language simple and clear

■ **Clarity** Active verbs and concrete words are much clearer and easier to understand than passive verbs and abstract concepts. Avoid jargon unless you are sure all your audience will understand it.

■ **Signalling** Indicate when you've completed one point or section in your presentation and are moving on to the next. Give your audience clear signals as to the direction your presentation is taking.

LISTENING 2

1   You are going to hear Alan Wroxley of Brother give a presentation on a
new range of fax machines. As you listen, make notes on the content and
structure of his talk. Then number the items in the box from 1-12 to reflect
their order of coverage.

FAX PRESENTATION

....   tell a personal anecdote

....   outline the major benefits of the new fax models

....   invite questions

....   introduce the subject of the presentation

....   sum up the main benefits of the new fax machines

....   welcome everyone

....   present some statistics (OHT)

....   thank and conclude

....   comment on market trends (OHT)

....   outline the purpose and structure of the presentation

....   sum up the statistics and their significance

....   mention handouts/graphics

2   Listen to the presentation again and note how Alan Wroxley deals with
each item. What does he actually say?

VOCABULARY 2

Complete the following presentation excerpts with suitable words from the boxes.

1-14
after that   finally
to start with   specifically
outline   bring you up to date
illustrate   purpose
then   thank
sum up   describe
tell you   concluding

15-28
indicated   talked
you will notice
draw your attention
interrupt   expand   move on
options   priority   referring
in conclusion   on balance
recommend   pointed out

'Good afternoon, everybody. I'd like to [1]................................ you all for being here.'

'My [2]............................... today is to [3]............................... about our corporate strategy for the next decade, and, more [4]..............................., to [5]............................... with our plans for Europe.'

'[6]............................... I'd like to [7]............................... briefly our current marketing policy in the UK. [8]............................... I'll [9]............................... some of the problems we're having over market share. [10]............................... I'll [11]............................... the opportunities we see for further progress in the 21st century. [12]............................... I'll quickly [13]............................... before [14]............................... with some recommendations.'

'Please feel free to [15]............................... me if you have any questions at any time.'

'Now I'd like to [16]............................... to Chart B showing our sales revenue and pre-tax profits over the last ten years. [17]............................... that although turnover has risen, our profits have not increased at the same rate.'

'I've [18]............................... about our current position in the UK and I've [19]............................... some of the problems we are facing. Well, what [20]............................... are open to us now? Where do we go from here?'

'As I have already [21]..............................., I think our first [22]............................... must be to build on the excellent results we have achieved in certain European markets. I'm [23]..............................., of course, to Italy and Spain. Let me quickly [24]............................... on those successes before we [25]............................... .'

'We should not forget the French market. Admittedly our results there have been poor so far, but there are signs the market is changing and we can learn a lot from our mistakes. [26]..............................., though, I think we stand to gain most from concentrating on southern Europe and I strongly [27]............................... we put all our efforts into further expansion in Italy, Spain and possibly Greece.'

'[28]..............................., may I thank you all for being such an attentive and responsive audience. Thank you also for your pertinent questions. Are there any final questions?'

LANGUAGE PRACTICE

Signalling

1 Study these examples of 'signalling devices' from Listening 2. Then write suitable headings for the groups of phrases that follow to summarise what each is signalling. As a guide to completing the exercise, a heading for group 1 has been given.

__Before doing so__, I would like you to look at some interesting statistics.
__What do these world statistics mean to us?__
__Let me give you an example__ that I think really brings out graphically what I mean.
__Now for__ some trends in the market.
__I'll start with__ memory models.

1
__Introducing the topic__
Let me start by . . .
I'll start by . . .
First of all, I'll . . .
Starting with . . .
I'd like to begin by . . .

2
....
Right, I've told you about . . .
We've looked at . . .
That's all I have to say about . . .
So much for . . .

3
....
Let me turn now to . . .
Let's move on to . . .
Turning to . . .
I'd like now to . . .
Next . . .
Let's look now at . . .

4
....
Where does that take us?
Let's look at this in more detail.
Translated into real terms, . . .
What does that mean for us?

5
....
For example, . . .
A good example of this is . . .
To illustrate this point, . . .

6
....
I'll deal with this later, if I may, but for now . . .
I'll come back to this question later in my talk.
I won't comment on this now, . . .
We'll be examining this question in more detail later on.

7
....
Let's recap, shall we?
I'd like to sum up now . . .
Let me summarise briefly what I've said.
Let me remind you, finally, of some of the points I've made.
If I can just sum up the main points . . .

8
....
Firstly . . . secondly . . . thirdly . . . lastly . . .
First of all . . . then . . . next . . .
* after that . . . finally . . .*
To start with . . . later . . . to finish up . . .

2 Working in pairs, make mini-presentations to each other to practise signalling different items. Choose one of the following topics.
- The advantages and disadvantages of flexitime.
- The advantages and disadvantages of open-plan offices.
- The advantages of working for a large company.
- How to motivate the workforce in large companies.

Role-play: Presentations

Choose one of the following situations and prepare a presentation to give to the rest of the group.

1 As sales director of an electronics company, you must make a presentation to launch your new range of telephone answer machines to the trade. Your presentation should cover the main features of each product and emphasise their selling points. The following extract from a sales brochure will give you some product ideas, but you may invent any information you wish about the company and its products.

Response 400

Complete sophistication made simple

Giving a good first impression is vital in business. So in creating the Response 400 combined telephone and answering machine for you, we've given you the means to record your welcome message digitally so it maintains consistent quality no matter how many times it's played. Easy to use yet with a wide range of advanced facilities, the Response 400 is hands-free, meaning you can hold a conversation and work without having to juggle with the handset. On the other hand, if you want to keep things *totally* confidential, you can listen to the messages left for you using the handset, so that no-one else can overhear. The useful LCD panel shows you the number as you dial it. You can also use it to time calls if you need to bill call costs to customers.

Answering machine features include:
■ Call screening ■ Call intercept ■ Volume control ■ Message counter ■ Message save ■ Message erase ■ Memo message with indicator ■ Conversation recording ■ Ring time selector ■ Answer only capability ■ Tape full alert ■ Single micro-cassette ■ Play, pause, fast forward and rewind ■ Digitally recorded announcement ■ Private record/playback via handset ■ Mains supply needed ■ Colour: Ice Grey.

Telephone features include:
■ 20-number memory ■ Last number redial ■ Ringer volume control ■ Inductive coupler ■ Secrecy button ■ *TouchTone** dialling ■ Wall-mountable ■ Hands-free operation ■ Call counter in answer-only mode ■ Programmable security code ■ Clock/call timer.

Remote access features:
■ Customer programmable security code ■ Remote switch-on and off ■ Play, pause, fast forward and rewind ■ Remote announcement change ■ Remote record ■ Remote message save and reset.

BUY	
excl. VAT	**£102.09**

ALSO AVAILABLE TO RENT
See page 126

ORDER DIRECT   0800 700 999

Remote Controller

Gives you access to your answering machine messages from anywhere in the world

Business and travel may take you anywhere in the world, but you can easily reach messages left on your answering machine and control it using this Controller from any phone.

Light, compact and simple to use, the Remote Controller can go with you everywhere so you're never out of touch with what's happening. It can be used with the BT Wren, Kingfisher II, Response 200 and 400, and the Falcon II answering machines and other manufacturers' answering machines which use tone signalling, and is also suitable for use as a tone dialling keypad to give you access to other services via the phone.

BUY	
excl. VAT	**£8.47**

ORDER DIRECT   0800 700 999

2 Choose or invent a company in one of the following product categories: food, sports goods, fashion, electrical products, health and beauty. As sales manager of that company, make a presentation to your sales force on the latest additions to your product range. Your presentation should cover the main features of each new product and emphasise their selling points. You may invent any information you wish.

3 As a member of the human resources department of a large multinational, you visit universities/colleges making presentations to students on your company and the job opportunities it offers graduates. Choose or invent a company to represent. You may invent any information you wish. If you have time, you might like to contact the company's PR department and ask for a copy of their annual report. This will give you a lot of information about the company's main areas of business, financial performance, product range, future prospects etc., and provide you with some useful visual aids.

Listen to each other's presentations, imagining you are a buyer/agent/distributor (1), sales rep (2) or student (3), as appropriate. Make notes as you listen, and use the following chart to provide constructive feedback on each presentation.

Aspects	Points to consider	Grade (1-5)*
Planning	evidence of careful preparation	
Objectives	clarity; appropriacy to audience/subject	
Content	extent; relevance; appropriacy; subject knowledge; research	
Approach	message support and reinforcement; variety; humour	
Organisation	coherence; clarity; appropriacy	
Visual aids	appropriacy; clarity; handling	
Delivery	pace; enthusiasm; rapport/eye contact; audibility; intonation; confidence; body language	
Language	clarity; accuracy; fluency; appropriacy; pronunciation; signalling	
Overall	clarity of message; achievement of objectives; interesting? enjoyable? informative? motivating?	
Other		

*Grade scale: 1 = unacceptable   2 = poor   3 = average   4 = good   5 = excellent
(i.e. could not do better in the time available)

Designer Appeal

INTRODUCTION

1   Look at the pictures and discuss the following questions.

1   How can you explain the difference in price between such similar looking products?

2   Would you pay £45 for a Lacoste polo shirt if you could buy one in Marks & Spencer for £15.99? Give your reasons.

FAVOURITE shirts get a new rough and tumble look for spring in washed down colours. In 100 stores at the beginning of March, this polo shirt will be available in navy, blue-green, purple and raspberry and costs £15.99.

The original Lacoste polo shirt, R.R.P. £45, available in 30 colours and containing 12 miles of pure cotton.

2   Read these advertising slogans and discuss the questions that follow.

The price may cripple you. The boots won't.

– Timberland (outdoor clothing and footwear)

We sell products to people who dream.

– Hermès (clothes, toiletries, accessories)

1   What image are Timberland and Hermès trying to create for their products?
2   What sort of person is their advertising probably aimed at?
3   What makes people buy their products?
4   Hermès and Timberland are upmarket companies. What other successful upmarket companies do you know of?
5   What difficulties do companies operating in upmarket 'niches' sometimes face?

Timberland
Walking tall

HAMPTON, NEW HAMPSHIRE

TRY this for size: if more American craftsmen were like the Swartz family, the country's protectionist lobbyists would have nothing to do. Founded by grandfather Nathan Swartz and now run by his son Sidney and grandson Jeffrey, the Timberland Company of Hampton, New Hampshire, is taking on the world in the market for rugged boots and shoes. And winning.

Low-cost foreign competitors have squeezed other American shoemakers out of business. While a few survivors are begging Congress for more protection against Asian imports, Timberland is rapidly increasing its exports — not only to Western Europe, but also to Hong Kong, Taiwan and Japan. It cannot compete on price with Asian producers. So it sells quality. In Europe it plugs the message: "The price may cripple you. The boots won't." Other American companies famed for high quality craftsmanship, like L.L. Bean, could follow Timberland's lead but don't. So could Stetson Boot and Shoe. There is a huge but hardly exploited market overseas for the sort of handsome, sturdy furniture made by the Shaker Workshops in Concord, Massachusetts. Several of the classic boatbuilders of New England could sail into world markets if they put their minds to it.

How does Timberland do it? **Lesson one**, say the Swartzes, is to make a better mousetrap. They started as Abington Shoe, making shoes for other makers. But in the early 1970s the Swartzes designed a rugged waterproof, insulated boot and set up a subsidiary to produce it, under the brand name Timberland. By 1978 more than 80% of their output was Timberland. They stopped manufacturing for others, and have not looked back. Sales rose from $68m in 1985 to $156m in 1989, sales abroad from next-to-nothing in 1978 to 30% of turnover.

Lesson two is to think long-term and remain relaxed about fluctuations in quarterly earnings. It helps that the company is run by a father and son. Mr Sidney Swartz, the president, describes Mr Jeffrey Swartz, the executive vice-president, as "my closest confidant and adviser". Both fervently hope that Jeffrey's two toddlers will grow up to be Timberland bosses. Family control, say the Swartzes, not only inoculates against rampant short-termism but also against take-over by a Wall Street whizzkid.

So does the company's share structure. When, in mid-1987, the

Where $500-a-pair boots really count

Swartzes made a public offering of Timberland stock, they took a leaf out of the German and Swedish corporate book. The B shares, with ten votes per share, were concentrated in family hands. The public was sold A shares with one vote per share. Business purists hate this. But it has worked. As Jeffrey Swartz admits, he and his father are better at making shoes than money. As Timberland's sales have soared, its net profit has sunk, from $9.4m in the year it went public to $6.4m in 1989. A conventional share structure would have left it vulnerable to predators.

Lesson three is not to panic about narrowing margins but hire a tough outsider to take the harsh corrective measures. Timberland's hard-man is Mr John Stevenson, a Lancastrian with more than 20 years in the shoe business. He persuaded the

Swartzes to do what they should have done earlier but had not the heart to: stop manufacturing in New England, where labour is scarce and dear, and concentrate more production in Tennessee, Puerto Rico and especially the Dominican Republic, where workers earn 70 cents an hour.

Lesson four is to know your customers. Timberland at one time tried to sell both to the adventurous sorts who like hiking, camping and boating and to fashion-conscious urbanites, more interested in the outdoor look than the outdoor life. This risked alienating both. So the company decided in America to stress the ruggedness, not the trendiness, of its products. It has made big donations to the Wilderness Society. It sponsors competitive yachtsmen and the annual Iditarod winter dog-sled race across the Alaskan tundra, where it equips competitors with snow boots that cost about $500 a pair to make.

In some foreign markets, though, Timberland has no choice but to aim at the rich. Japan is a prime example, with a 23% tariff on imported shoes, worked in a way that in effect adds a further 50%. So Timberland is forced to charge what Mr Jeffrey Swartz calls "silly prices", and the Japanese consumer gets stung for Japanese manufacturers' benefit. As usual.

TEXT 1

1 **Timberland thrives in a highly competitive market where many have failed. In its analysis, the article draws four 'lessons' from the company's approach. Before you read, try to predict some of the reasons for Timberland's success. Think in terms of the following areas.**
- the product
- administration
- production
- marketing

2 **Read paragraphs 1 and 2 and complete the following summary.**

Run by ¹........................., Timberland is based in ²......................... and sells
³......................... around the world. While growing pressure from ⁴.........................
has forced many of Timberland's American rivals out of business, Timberland has
continued to succeed, not least overseas, where the company has seen a rapid
increase in its ⁵......................... to ⁶......................... . Timberland does not
compete on price but on ⁷......................... .

3 **Read the rest of the article and note all the reasons it gives for Timberland's success. Then summarise the Timberland 'formula' as a list of guidelines for other upmarket companies.**

VOCABULARY 1

Complete the following sentences with words that are both appropriate and accurate in the context. Text 1 will help you.

1 In the early 1970s, the Swartzes set up a ...., manufacturing their rugged waterproof boot under the .... Timberland.
2 Between 1985 and 1989, Timberland's .... rose from $68m to $156m, with exports accounting for 30% of ....
3 The Swartz team tries to take a long-term view, not paying too much attention to .... in sales revenue from one .... to another.
4 Towards the end of the 1980's Timberland went ...., selling a proportion of its .... on the stock exchange.
5 Despite steady increases in sales, Timberland's .... fell by $3m between 1987 and 1989.
6 Timberland responded to the growing pressure on its .... by hiring a 'tough outsider' to take the harsh corrective .... that were needed.
7 Because of the shortage and cost of .... in New England, Timberland moved more of its .... to cheaper manufacturing centres.
8 Timberland has increased sales to Japan, despite the country's sizeable .... on imported shoes which sees the products selling at 'silly prices'.

LANGUAGE PRACTICE 1

Rise, raise, arise

Regular or irregular? Transitive or intransitive? These three verbs are often confused. Complete the chart, using the example from Text 1 and the definitions in the box to help you. Then choose the correct form of the correct verb to complete the sentences that follow. (Transitive verbs are verbs which take an object, intransitive verbs take no object.)

*Sales **rose** from $68m in 1985 to $156m in 1989.* (line 50)

infinitive	transitive or intransitive?	simple past	past participle	meanings (choose from the definitions in the box below)
rise				*
				*
raise				*
				*
				*
				*
arise				*

to occur/come into being/appear/become evident
to increase/go up/reach a higher level
to obtain/generate/acquire/collect (funds/support)
to bring up/put forward/mention
to reach a higher position/rank
to put up/cause to increase/make higher
to heighten/extend/intensify

1 The chairman .... the question at the next meeting.
2 Some unexpected difficulties have ....
3 The company's turnover has .... steadily in recent years.
4 In business, it is often necessary to .... finance for new projects.
5 I would like to .... an important point here, if I may.
6 She .... to a senior position in a very short time.
7 The government has .... interest rates again.
8 I hope this situation will not .... again.
9 The company could not afford to .... salaries in line with inflation.
10 Unemployment continues to .... steadily.
11 The problem .... through inadequate supervision.
12 The campaign certainly succeeded in .... awareness of the issue within the business community.

DISCUSSION

Working in small groups, try to come up with a suitable slogan to turn the picture on the left into an advertisement for Timberland footwear. The advertisement on the right for Timberland's clothing sale will help you. When you have finished, meet back as one group and compare your ideas.

THE BROGUE WEATHERBUCK PROTECTION £95 A PAIR.

TIMBERLAND PRESENTS A COLLECTION OF INEXPENSIVE CLOTHING THAT WON'T LAST LONG.
(WELL, IT IS THE START OF OUR SALE.)

The Timberland sale starts today. You'll find greatly reduced prices on many items of footwear, clothing and accessories, including sweaters, trousers and polo shirts. Unfortunately, the sale must end on January 25th. Proving that not everything from Timberland is guaranteed to last a lifetime.

TEXT 2

1 **Before you read, look at the title, the photograph and the caption.**

1   What image is the company projecting in the photograph?

2   Why is it important for Hermès to sell 'high-ticket' fashion items like the swimsuit?

2 **Read the article and summarise the main points under the following headings.**

- performance
- size of company
- product range
- acquisitions

- the Hermès brand
- target consumer
- administration
- company structure

High-ticket fashion

High-ticket fashion items drive demand for Hermès accessories and toiletries

[1] Hermès's sales rose steadily during the 1980s but fell 4 per cent last year to Fr2.5bn (£250m). The Gulf war kept jet-setters at home while the weak yen has [5] dulled Japanese demand for silk squares and crocodile-skin jeans. Hermès has trimmed its workforce and a nervous Christmas looms as the US threatens to slip back into recession and the British [10] market remains depressed. Sales in the US are 12-15 per cent down on last year.

"We should not be taken as a thermometer," Mr Dumas-Hermès [15] warns. The company's 250 outlets worldwide report that more expensive goods are selling slightly better than the lesser lines.

Sales of high-ticket fashion are more [20] important in that they drive demand for the accessories and toiletries which also bear the Hermès mark than as money-spinners in their own right.

The recent acquisitions of the English [25] shoemaker, Edward Green, and the 400-year-old Saint Louis crystal business demonstrate Hermès's conviction that the exploitation of its brand still has some way to go.

[30] But Mr Dumas-Hermès insists that he would not risk debasing the brand by attaching it to ever cheaper, lower quality goods. "We never risked being like a Pierre Cardin. We never licensed [35] our name. We never played with fire."

Hermès instead used the 1980s consumer boom to broaden its appeal from the *vieux riche* to the *nouveau riche,* spending heavily on advertising and [40] marketing in the process. "We sell products to people who dream. But is there only one way to think? One way to dream?"

Hermès has also tried to improve the [45] financial control its Paris hub exerts on the empire worldwide. Its head office administrative staff has been boosted at a time when the total staff figure has dropped. This has been done with one [50] eye on the prospect that Hermès's days as a family-dominated company may be numbered.

It was founded in 1837 by Thierry Hermès and is 90 per cent owned by [55] his descendants. A recent share restructuring created a limited partnership which can be dissolved only by a 75 per cent majority. A 9.7 per cent stake is administered by three French [60] banks, who have placed the shares with family-approved institutions and private investors. Sumitomo Corporation, the Japanese conglomerate, holds 1.2 per cent.

This structure permits the family to [65] opt for a stock quotation, although there are no immediate plans to go public. "But we must be prepared," says Mr Dumas-Hermès, giving the boy scout salute. "It may be necessary to be more [70] open. This is not the empire of one person."

■■■■ **VOCABULARY 2**

Complete the following sentences with appropriate words from the list. Text 2 will help you.

partnership	brand	quotation
control	outlets	stake
conglomerate	founded	workforce

1 Hermès responded to adverse market conditions by cutting back its ....

2 The company is very protective of the Hermès .... – there is no question of extending it to cover lower-priced goods of inferior quality.

3 A policy of tighter financial .... has seen an increase in administrative staff at head office while the number of employees at the company's 250 .... worldwide has been reduced.

4 .... in 1837 by Thierry Hermès, the company is 90% family-owned and run as a limited ....

5 A number of family-approved institutions and private investors have a small .... in the company, as does a Japanese ....

6 In the future, the company could decide to go public and obtain a stock .... but it has no immediate plans to do so.

■■■■ **LISTENING**

You will hear Victoria Ewin, Press Attaché at Hermès, talking about the company. Listen and complete the following fact file.

FACT FILE: HERMÈS

Key Products

- Silk scarf[1] ....
....
- Handbags[2] ....
- Ties[3] ....
....

Customer Profile

4 ....
....
....

Manufacturing

5 ....
....
....

Licensing

6 ....
....
....

The Future

7 ....
....
....

Company History

Market
wholesale
8 ....

Product
harnesses
saddles and harnesses
9 ....
10 ....
scarves
11 ....

Launch date
1837 ↓

12 ....

1950s

LANGUAGE PRACTICE 2

Prepositions

Complete the following text about Yves Saint Laurent (YSL) by replacing the missing prepositions.

YSL in upmarket mode

In a year when the diversified luxury goods conglomerate, LVMH, increased its net profits [1].......... 11 per cent, YSL's net profits are expected to have fallen [2].......... some Fr16 million [3].......... Fr235 million (£24.5 million) [4].......... turnover of Fr3.061 billion (Fr3 billion previous year), 82 per cent [5].......... which comes from its perfume, cosmetics and skin care division.

But things are not so gloomy off the profit-and-loss account. Mr Bergé has been praised [6].......... artificially lowering sales of YSL – which has a market valuation of Fr3.3 billion – to take the brand upmarket. The basic strategy is to distribute the products more selectively, especially in the important US market where couture and perfume retail sales under the YSL mark are currently [7].......... excess [8].......... $300 million. According [9].......... the US chief executive, Laurent Levasseur, the menswear line has caused the biggest problem.

"The clothes were being sold [10].......... half price in discount stores, and this did not help the public perception of the brand. Now our licensee, Bidermann, is concentrating [11].......... selling [12].......... the more upmarket department stores," he said.

This still means that menswear has a less prestigious distribution network than the luxurious Rive Gauche women's line where suits retail [13].......... $2,000 - $3,000.

"In New York the line can now only be found in two up-market speciality stores (Saks Fifth Avenue and Bergdorf Goodman) and our Madison Avenue boutique."

In accessories, which account [14].......... almost 25 per cent of the US couture division's retail sales, a different approach has been followed. YSL has started distributing items such as handbags, belts and jewellery, and this has enabled the company to have more power when dealing with the department stores.

"Our products are now sold to the collection buyer who will present the whole Yves Saint Laurent range together, rather than [15].......... the classification buyers who would place different products in different departments in their store."

If YSL has revamped its brand successfully, the improvement [16].......... couture sales could be dramatic.

CASE STUDY

Sheen PLC produces a range of upmarket leather goods, including clothing, giftware, travel goods and personal accessories. The company has done well in the past, but now seems to be out of touch with consumers. Sales are down and exciting new products are needed if the company is to regain its position and keep ahead of its competitors.

In an innovative move, Managing Director, Sandra Dickinson, has decided to involve the whole company in the decision-making process. She has set up a number of inter-departmental groups, each consisting of a representative cross-section of personnel, to act as informal product development teams.

In a memorandum to these 'task forces', she outlines their brief as follows: 'Give us a world-beating concept! Try to create something that has real potential to improve our profits . . . Your ideas could be the key to our future!'

Role-play: Presentations

Work in small groups, with each group member choosing a different role at the company, and brainstorm your ideas for a new leather product for Sheen PLC to develop. Choose your best idea and work out the details of its design, target market, marketing, production etc., inventing any information you wish. Prepare a presentation of your product to give to the other groups, using the guidelines in Unit 4 (page 38) to help you (see also page 145 for further guidance). Each group member should give part of the presentation.

Role-play: Meeting

When you have made your presentations, form larger groups with at least one member from each original group, and hold a meeting to be chaired by Sandra Dickinson. The purpose of the meeting is to choose *one* product (or range of products) for immediate development. Discuss the merits and demerits of each proposal, and try to reach a decision. If there are strong differences of opinion, put it to the vote (group members may not vote for their own product).

WRITING

1   Sheen PLC has just launched a luxurious new briefcase called *The Witness*. Featuring a built-in cassette recorder, microphone and speakers, the product is designed for professionals who attend meetings and need an exact record of what was said. *The Witness* comes in three different models and a range of colours, and retails at between £300-£750. You work in the publicity department at Sheen PLC, and it is your job to write a promotional leaflet for *The Witness*. The leaflet needs to be suitable for use by the sales force, in-store, and as an insert in the business press. Use the picture to help you, and invent any information you wish.

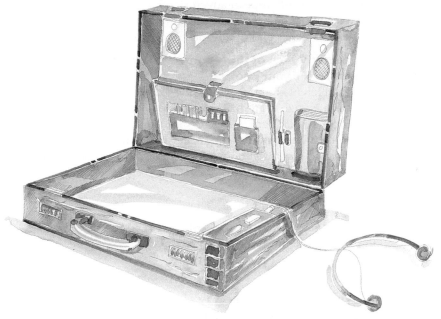

2   The new marketing director at Sheen PLC believes the company is missing out on opportunities in the sports goods market. As a starting point, he has asked you and all the other members of Sheen's marketing team to write a short informal report on any sport you are familiar with, indicating what opportunities you see for selling leather sports products.

6

Pan-European Advertising

INTRODUCTION

1 **Discuss the following questions.**

1 What is meant by 'pan-European advertising'?

2 What examples of pan-European advertisements can you give?

3 What are the advantages and disadvantages of pan-European advertising?

2 **What do you think? Which of these contrasting opinions do you agree with? Give reasons for your choice.**

a) Consumers in different countries vary widely in their needs and wants and ingrained consumer habits are hard to change. Marketing departments ignore these differences at their peril.

b) People desire the same products, no matter where they live. Sensible marketing targets the creation of 'world brands', standardised products that are marketed in the same way worldwide.

TEXT 1

1 **Before you read, look at the photograph and read the caption.**

1 What do you know about Benetton?

2 What are 'duty-free' television commercials?

3 How 'international' are the Benetton advertisements you have seen?

2 **Scan the text quickly and find the answers to the following questions.**

1 What point is illustrated by a balding British man and two French grandmothers?

2 What are NIH's – and how are they regarded?

3 Who are the following people and what views do they express?

- Alain Cayzac
- Jacques Arnaud
- Françoise Bonnal
- Joao Rapazote Fernades

4 What is significant about Procter & Gamble's Wash & Go commercial?

CONTINENT DIVIDES ON THE BOX

Le Monde

THE British swoon with delight over a television commercial showing a balding man who cannot get a photo-booth to work and instead loses himself in the pleasures of a good cigar. The French avidly follow the saga of two grandmothers holding forth on the shortcomings of a yoghurt. Neither ad is considered suitable for any other country.

That is the picture all over Europe. Films that aren't home-grown are referred to by advertising executives as NIHs – "not invented here" – and are frowned upon.

A study last autumn by the Alice advertising agency in conjunction with the Ipsos research institute asked 600 consumers from Germany, Britain, France, the Netherlands and Italy to watch 48 ads from all over Europe, all of which had won international awards. Even though the ads had been translated, the consumers liked the films from their own countries best.

The consumers only felt able to apply the label "pan-European" to a few of the advertisements. The films which held their attention were the ones with the simplest situations and the ones which appealed to their emotions or humour.

Five of the 10 best-liked films were British. Other popular commercials were a Spanish ad which shows a dog called Pippin packing her bags because she feels neglected by her television addict of a master; the Levi film in which a playboy uses his

United colours . . . the Benetton clothing company's 'duty-free' commercials are said to cross borders

jeans to tow a couple in a car and takes advantage of the situation to seduce the young woman; and the one about a blushing boy who has just bought some condoms from a woman pharmacist.

Alain Cayzac, chairman of RSCG-France said: "There are certain 'duty-free' campaigns, which are truly international, such as those by Marlboro, Benetton, Volkswagen and certain perfumes. They show real imagination, valued in all latitudes, and they put across for each of their products a feeling of serenity, fraternity, confidence or beauty."

But most commercials do not cross borders well. Françoise Bonnal, head of strategic planning at Young and Rubicam, said: "Each country has its own rhythms and sensibilities: the northern countries attach more importance to a rational element, while the south is more sensitive to form. The French and the British think humour and variety are more important, and the Spanish and Italians look for balance."

But how do you fuse the sparkling, light-hearted image sought by the French, the British sense of humour, the seriousness required by the Germans and the subtle effectiveness beloved of the Spanish and Italians?

One solution consists of producing a script which is identical in each country, with different actors and a translated soundtrack.

This was done with Wash & Go, the shampoo made by Procter & Gamble. The commercial used different actresses – blonde, brunette, sexy or the girl-next-door – supposedly in keeping with the sensibilities of the countries in which it was shown; France, Spain, Italy and the Netherlands.

However, if the production of ads on a pan-European scale is what many want, some members of the profession remain prudent. "We should not fall into schemes for the profit of technocrats thus emasculating creativity and production," said Jacques Arnaud, managing director of the Franco-American production company.

He is among a number of advertising professionals who are calling for the European Commission to prevent the harmonisation of national regulations which could extend to bans everywhere on commercials for alcohol, children's toys, insurance and medicines.

And if tastes and regulations are different, the structure of the publicity markets is hardly homogenous. In Portugal, where an ad rarely costs more than £20,000 (elsewhere the minimum is nearer £100,000), production houses frequently have to "handle the art of the limited budget", according to Joao Rapazote Fernades, director of the production company, Panoramica 35. He said: "European advertising should not be allowed to crush small countries which cannot participate in the creation of Europe-wide campaigns."

3   **Read the text again and complete the following summary.**

A survey of European advertising preferences undertaken by the Alice
[1]................................ and the [2]................................ research institute found that
[3]................................ tended to prefer advertisements [4]................................ . Only
[5]................................ of the advertisements – the ones with simple
[6]................................ which appealed to [7]................................ – were felt to be
truly [8]................................ . [9]................................ of the ten [10]................................
films were [11]................................ . The 'stars' of three other popular commercials
were [12]................................ , [13]................................ and [14]................................ .

The fact that most commercials do not [15]................................ means quite a
challenge for would-be pan-European advertisers: how to combine the
[16]................................ sought by the French, the sense of humour favoured by the
[17]................................, the [18]................................ preferred by the Germans and the
subtle effectiveness loved by the [19]................................ in a single advertisement
with universal appeal? One answer is to use the same [20]................................ for
every country but feature different [21]................................ and a translated
[22]................................ .

Pan-European production is one thing, pan-European regulation another. Some
[23]................................ are fighting calls for [24]................................ which could lead
to Europe-wide [25]................................ .

DISCUSSION

1   **How far do you agree with Text 1's assessment of British, French, German, Italian and Spanish national preferences?**

2   **How would you characterise the preferences of the following nationalities?**
- Brazilians
- Japanese
- Americans
- Russians
- Saudi Arabians

3   **How would these ideas influence any advertising you were planning for these markets?**

VOCABULARY 1

Match each word on the left with a word on the right. Then use four of the expressions to write about the advertising industry.

household	budget
price	company
TV	list
limited	commercial
media	rates
circular	campaign
strategic	names
production	letter
glossy	planning
competitive	brochure

LANGUAGE PRACTICE 1

Word stress

Some corresponding verbs and nouns have different stress patterns, e.g. àdvertise, advèrtisement. Mark where the stress falls in the following words. Then, working in pairs, read sentences 1-12 aloud to each other and check each other's pronunciation of the underlined words.

Verb	**Noun**
publicise	publicity
produce	product
create	creativity
analyse	analysis
conduct	conduct
contrast	contrast
prefer	preferences
participate	participation

1 One solution is to <u>produce</u> a script which can be translated for each market.
2 Centralised control of the European <u>advertising</u> industry could have a negative effect on <u>creativity</u> and lead to dull <u>advertisements</u>.
3 According to Alain Cayzac, Benetton succeeded in <u>creating</u> a truly international campaign. It also attracted a lot of <u>publicity</u>!
4 The Ipsos research institute <u>conducted</u> the survey in conjunction with the Alice <u>advertising</u> agency.
5 Consumers from five European countries <u>participated</u> in the survey. Their responses to 48 commercials from all over Europe were <u>analysed</u> in a report.
6 Developments in the <u>advertising</u> industry have been well <u>publicised</u>.
7 Their <u>analysis</u> yielded a number of interesting insights. The <u>contrast</u> in national <u>preferences</u> around Europe, for example, seems to be quite marked.
8 The Spanish dog Pippin leaves home because of her master's <u>conduct</u>.
9 Françoise Bonnal <u>contrasts</u> the rhythms and sensibilities of north Europeans with their southern European counterparts.
10 The British enjoy humour while the Germans <u>prefer</u> seriousness.
11 There are fears that <u>participation</u> in a truly European <u>advertising</u> industry might be limited to larger countries.
12 The article mentions a number of different <u>products</u> – cigars, yoghurt and jeans, for example.

LISTENING

1 **You are going to hear Stella Beaumont, Advertising Planning Manager at *The Guardian*, talking about pan-European advertising. Listen and take notes under the following headings.**
- criteria for success
- American Express
- dangers
- advantages

2 **Use your notes to draft some guidelines on pan-European advertising.**

'. . . an exceptionally good advertisement . . .' – Stella Beaumont

TEXT 2

1 **The article is about Benetton's approach to advertising. Before you read, from what you know of the company *(see Unit 3: Marketing Ethics)*, explain the choice of title.**

2 **Read the article and decide which of the following statements accurately reflect the content. Use the text to support your answer.**
1 Benetton's advertisements are hard-hitting.
2 The advertisement which featured a priest and a nun kissing was accepted in Catholic circles.
3 The purpose of Benetton's advertisements is to get people talking about the company.
4 Benetton's controversial advertisements have had an adverse effect on sales.
5 Benetton's audience is not always aware that the advertisements have an intended social message.
6 Black groups in America reacted badly to two of Benetton's advertisements.
7 Benetton tailors its advertisements to individual markets.
8 If a Benetton advertisement is successful in Europe, it will probably be successful elsewhere.

Tasteful

BENETTON'S colourful jumpers may be soft and woolly, but its advertisements are not. The Italian clothes maker's autumn 1991 campaign includes an ad picturing a not-so-platonic kiss between a priest and a nun clad in old-fashioned habits. "The affirmation of pure human sentiment," says Benetton. Offensive, say outraged Catholics.

Olivero Toscani, the photographer who dreams up and directs Benetton's advertising campaigns, says that the firm tries to distance its ads from boring old commercial considerations. They aim, says Mr Toscani, to capture people's attention, provoke reflection and "break through the barrier of indifference". As Benetton's sales grew by a healthy 24% in recessionary 1990, to 2.1 trillion lire ($1.7 billion), the ads clearly sell jumpers too.

But the firm is finding that convention-breaking is a ticklish business. Its spring 1991 campaign showed a group of tombstones, one sporting the Jewish star of David, just as the first Iraqi Scud missiles hit Tel Aviv. Accused of exploiting death for commercial purposes, Mr Toscani is this autumn countering with an off-putting (and full-colour) image of a gunk-covered newborn baby. The ad has already been rejected by *Child*, an American child-care magazine.

Benetton reckons its campaigns "address the major social issues of our time including AIDS, overpopulation, environmental problems and racial harmony." Its audience, however, often seems to miss the point. Two years ago a Benetton ad showing a black woman breastfeeding a white child created uproar among American blacks. The company looks set for a repeat performance. One ad in this year's autumn campaign depicts an angelic-looking white child embracing a black one whose hair has been shaped into devil's horns. Black groups are already starting to grumble.

In line with its "united colours" global philosophy, Benetton shows the same ads around the world. A campaign that backfires in one market often wins awards in others: the white-baby-black-breast ad that shocked America won awards in France and Italy. The missing link in Benetton's advertising policy may well be understanding where different countries' sensitivities lie.

Heavenly

▰▰▰ VOCABULARY 2

1 **Fill in the missing 11-letter word to make five common compound nouns.**

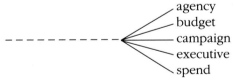

- agency
- budget
- campaign
- executive
- spend

2 **How many different compound nouns can you make with the following words?**
- sales
- market
- product
- marketing

3 **Quiz**
1 What do businessmen and women use to carry documents around? . . . . . .
2 In which room do company directors usually meet? . . . . . .
3 What gesture traditionally concludes a deal? . . . . . .
4 What do we call the total revenue of a company? . . . . . .

Now make up your own quiz items to test each other's knowledge of common business compound nouns.

LANGUAGE PRACTICE 2

Phrasal verbs

Complete the following passage by replacing the missing prepositions.

The 'Nova' goes better in Spain as 'Caribe' . . .

Marketing teams carry a lot of responsibility when it comes [1]........... choosing brand names that have to cross the language barrier. As many multinationals have found to their cost, names can take [2]........... unintended meanings when translated into another language.

We've all come [3]........... examples in the press, not least in the automotive industry – several car manufacturers, it seems, have run [4]........... problems on this front. One of General Motors' models, the 'Nova', translates into Spanish as 'it doesn't go' – 'no va'! The company changed the name to 'Caribe' for Spanish-speaking markets and sales shot [5]........... . One of Ford's new models turned [6]........... on the Mexican market as 'Caliente' – Spanish slang for 'street-walker'!

Such classic blunders soon show [7]........... and swift action usually saves the day. However, it does show how important it is for multinationals to carry [8]........... extensive research before they launch a new product!

CASE STUDY

UK-based patisserie chain, Gateau PLC, has its head office in Leicester, England. Over the last 25 years, the company has expanded rapidly and now has outlets throughout the European Community.

The success of the business is easily explained. Firstly, excellent quality products at reasonable prices: Gateau's wide variety of baguette sandwiches are always fresh, the pastries are delicious, the drinks – a good selection of teas, freshly-ground coffees and freshly-squeezed fruit juices – are good value for money, and there is always a fine choice of fruit/fruit salads. Products may either be consumed on the premises or taken away.

Another reason for Gateau's growth is the success of its development as a franchising operation. This has proven to be a very effective way of expanding the company quickly, and Gateau has built up quite an extensive network of franchises offering quality products, high standards of cleanliness and efficient service.

In the last five years, however, Gateau has met strong competition from other patisserie chains. These do not offer the same quality or range of products, nor is their service as good. Many people say their outlets have a less attractive decor too, yet they have had an impact on Gateau's profits.

Naturally, the Gateau management is worried about the situation. The company must continue to grow and, with ambitious plans to extend its franchise network further, must be seen to prosper. After much deliberation, Gateau has decided to respond by intensifying its promotion and has asked its advertising agency, Hudson-Bates-McGrath (HBM), to create a new pan-European advertising campaign along the following lines:

GATEAU PLC: ADVERTISING CAMPAIGN

Objectives:
- to inform consumers of the excellent food and drink and outstanding service on offer at Gateau
- to persuade consumers that Gateau patisseries are the *only* outlets worth visiting for a quick snack
- to reinforce Gateau's image as a *European* business

Target:
- actual and potential consumers living and working in major towns and cities throughout Europe

Media:
- TV (1 x 30-second TV commercial for transmission throughout October and November in all Gateau's European markets)
- print (1 x half-page advertisement to appear in selected national and regional newspapers throughout Europe)

Support:
- a special promotion to run simultaneously in all Gateau outlets

Approach:
- pan-European with limited tailoring to different consumer tastes and cultures in the target countries

Role-play: Presentations

Working in small groups, devise a suitable campaign for Gateau PLC. As HBM's creative team, decide on a concept for the TV commercial; draft the text and design some rough artwork for the newspaper advertisement; and devise an imaginative promotion to attract new customers and boost sales. When you have finalised your ideas, prepare a presentation to give to the other groups, illustrating your proposal with visuals on an overhead projector or flipchart. When you have made your presentations, try to decide which team came up with the best proposal.

WRITING

1 Eclair SA is a food manufacturing company based in Lyons, France. One of its main markets is the UK. Last year, the company introduced a new range of chocolate croissants which did not sell as well as had been expected. You work in the company's marketing department and you have been asked to design a promotional leaflet for circulation, via your usual distribution channels, to actual and potential customers in the UK, in an effort to boost sales. Invent any information you wish (See page 148 for further guidance).

2 As manager of one of London's biggest railway stations you receive the following letter from Eclair. Write a correctly laid-out reply, inventing any information you wish.

would like to carry out a special promotion for a new range of chocolate croissants which we expect to appeal greatly to British tastes.

Would it be possible to set up a stand promoting the products in your station during the week of January 14-18? We have in mind a stand sited in the middle of the concourse, with perhaps three or four people distributing free samples. Of course, we would not wish to interfere with the operation of your services in any way, or interrupt the movements of travellers.

If you agree to this proposal, could you let me know, please, what fee you would charge for the rental of the site per day? Would there be a discount if we rented for a period longer than a day – say three days?

I very much hope you will be able to give a favourable answer to my request.

Yours sincerely,

Monique Déon

Monique Déon
Marketing Manager

7

Negotiations

INTRODUCTION

1 **Discuss the following questions.**
1 What is a 'negotiation'?
2 How would you judge the success of a negotiation?
3 What makes a good negotiator?
4 Have you ever been involved in formal or informal business negotiations? Describe your experiences.

2 **What do you think?**
How appropriate is the following advice? Rank each suggestion on a scale from 1-10 (1 = essential, 10 = unhelpful) to indicate your opinion.

How to be a good negotiator

- try to get on well with your opposite number ☐
- use emphatic language ☐
- show respect for your opposite number ☐
- make suggestions to resolve disagreement ☐
- have clear objectives ☐
- be determined to win ☐
- say 'I don't understand', if that is the case ☐
- listen carefully ☐
- always compromise ☐
- discuss areas of conflict ☐

TEXT 1

Read the text and summarise the main points as a list of guidelines on negotiating.

The Art of Negotiation

There has been a great deal of research into the art of negotiation, and, in particular, into what makes a 'good' negotiator.

One point most researchers seem to agree on is that good negotiators try to create a harmonious atmosphere at the start of a negotiation. They make an effort to establish a good rapport with their opposite number, so that there will be a willingness – on both sides – to make concessions, if this should prove necessary.

Good negotiators generally wish to reach an agreement which meets the interests of **both** sides. They therefore tend to take a long-term view, ensuring that the agreement will improve, or at least not harm, their relationship with the other party. On the other hand, a poor negotiator tends to look for immediate gains, forgetting that the real benefits of a deal may come much later.

Skilful negotiators are flexible. They do not "lock themselves" into a position so that they will lose face if they have to compromise. They have a range of objectives, thus allowing themselves to make concessions, for example, "I **aim to** buy this machine for £2,000" and not "I **must** buy it for £2,000". Poor negotiators have limited objectives, and may not even work out a "fall-back" position.

Average negotiators look for immediate gains. Good negotiators have a range of objectives.

Successful negotiators do not want a negotiation to break down. If problems arise, they suggest ways of resolving them. The best negotiators are persuasive, articulate people, who select a few key arguments and repeat them. This suggests that tenacity is an important quality.

Finally, it is essential to be a good listener and to check frequently that everything has been understood by both parties.

TEXT 2

Read the advertisement and complete the following recruitment file.

JOB SPECIFICATION

Company[1] ....   Salary[5] ....

Location[2] ....   Benefits[6] ....

Position[3] ....   Contact[7] ....

Duties[4] ....

PERSON SPECIFICATION

Essential[8]	Desirable[9]
....	....
....	....
....	....
....	....
....	....
....	....

Dealing in the oil and fuels market is a high-powered activity, and Texaco Fuel and Marine Marketing is a major player within it. We deliver bunker fuels to ports worldwide, negotiating the sales of many millions of barrels of fuel each year.

So our small team is critical to profitability. Negotiating spot sales – both prices and volumes – with ship owners and shipping lines is exceptionally competitive. It calls for a clear head and keen commercial acumen. And, since you'll be working under pressure and in rapidly changing conditions, you'll need to be capable of rapid decision-making.

Sales Negotiator
What price sales success?

Most important is that you're a gifted communicator. Someone capable of both information gathering and communicating at all levels and with a wide variety of customers, both in the UK and abroad.

Obviously a strong sense of geography is valuable and both a European language and a background in the oil and marine industries would be useful though not essential. The key qualities are an eye for a deal, good telephone skills and the ability to work well within a team environment.

The price of achievement is high. For the right individual we offer a competitive salary and an attractive benefits package which includes a share option scheme as well as the prospect for career advancement within this world-leading oil company.

We are currently based in Knightsbridge but we are moving to brand new custom-designed offices in Westferry Circus, Canary Wharf. These offices will be part of one of the highest quality developments of its kind in Europe and will be linked to other centres in London by greatly improved road and rail transport.

To apply, please write with full CV to **Peter Sweetman, Human Resources Adviser, Texaco Limited, 1 Knightsbridge Green, London SW1X 7QJ.**

TEXACO ✪

 **LISTENING 1**

1   **In this interview, you will hear Siobhan Quinn, Sales Manager at Texaco, talking about negotiating. Listen and check whether the following statements accurately reflect what she says.**

1   Siobhan Quinn's full title is Manager, Bulk Sales, Texaco Fuel and Marine Marketing Department.
2   Negotiators are born not made.
3   It is important for both parties to achieve something in a negotiation.
4   Some 40% of Texaco's business is with non-native speakers of English.
5   Language affects negotiating strategy more than cultural considerations.
6   Personality influences negotiating strategy.
7   PLAS is a financial magazine.
8   Negotiating is a bit like dancing and boxing.

2   **Listen again, and make notes under the following headings and subheadings.**
- personality
  - buyer 1, and how to deal with him
  - buyer 2, and how to deal with him
- feedback
  - how negotiating works
  - negotiating without feedback
- advice
  - knowledge
  - skill

Canary Wharf, London

Some hints on negotiating

PREPARATION

■ **Planning**   Make sure you prepare properly. The less you prepare, the more you will be at a disadvantage and the less likely you will be to achieve a satisfactory outcome.

■ **Research**   Try to find out as much as you can about your opposite number and his or her business. Use the resources of a business library and/or talk to your business contacts.

■ **Objectives**   Try to take a long-term view and decide on a range of objectives so that you can be more flexible and offer more alternatives during the negotiation itself. Remember you are looking for a win-win situation of benefit to both parties, thus paving the way for further deals in the future.

■ **Limits**   Decide what your sticking point(s) must be and why. Knowing your negotiating limits and their reasons will help you negotiate more confidently and comfortably.

■ **Strategy**   Plan your negotiating strategy carefully, taking into consideration the personality and position of your opposite number, as well as your own strengths and weaknesses.

Prepare carefully, keeping your target in mind

TECHNIQUES

■ **Rapport**   Try to establish a good rapport with your opposite number from the moment you first meet, whether or not you already know each other. Some general 'social talk' is a good ice-breaker and bridge-builder in this respect.

■ **Parameters**   Confirm the subject/purpose of your negotiation early on and try to establish areas of common ground and areas of likely conflict before you move on to the bargaining/trading stage.

■ **Listen!**   Listening attentively at every stage of your negotiation will help to avoid misunderstanding and create a spirit of cooperation.

■ **Attitude**   Be constructive not destructive – treat your opposite number with respect, sensitivity and tact, and try to avoid an atmosphere of conflict. This will create a feeling of harmony and goodwill, which should encourage a willingness to compromise and ultimately lead to a productive negotiation.

■ **Approach**   Keep your objectives in mind – and try to keep a clear head. This will help you to concentrate on your key points. Try to resist the temptation to introduce new arguments all the time. Use the minimum number of reasons to persuade your opposite number, coming back to them as often as necessary.

Listen attentively at every stage

■ **Flexibility**   Be prepared to consider a range of alternatives and try to make creative suggestions for resolving any problems. Be prepared to make concessions and to compromise, if necessary, to avoid deadlock – but don't be pushed beyond your sticking point.

■ **Review**   Summarise and review your progress at regular intervals during the negotiation. This will give both parties a chance to check understanding – and, if necessary, clarify/rectify any misunderstandings.

■ **Agreement**   When you have reached agreement, close the deal firmly and clearly. Confirm exactly what you have agreed – and any aspects/matters that need further action.

■ **Confirmation**   Write a follow-up letter to confirm in writing the points agreed during your negotiation and clarify any outstanding matters.

LANGUAGE

■ **Simplicity**   Keep your language simple and clear. Take your time and use short words and sentences that you are comfortable with – there is no point complicating a difficult task with difficult language.

■ **Clarity**   Don't be afraid to ask questions if there is anything you don't understand. It is vital to avoid any misunderstandings that might jeopardise the success of your negotiation.

LISTENING 2

1 You are going to hear two short negotiations. In Dialogue 1, visiting American Jerry Mullins, on temporary attachment to Melford Furniture Group as part of an exchange programme with Melford's US parent, is talking to his UK boss, Charles Ramsay, about a training course. In Dialogue 2, Helen Dawson at Melford Furniture Group is talking to her old contact Hans Guertler about some second-hand cutting machines his German engineering firm has for sale. Listen to both dialogues and complete the following table.

Dialogue	Speakers	Purpose of negotiation	Outcome
1	Jerry Mullins + Charles Ramsay		
2	Helen Dawson + Hans Guertler		

2 Listen to Dialogue 1 again and decide which of the following statements about it are true.
1 Mullins and Ramsay established a good rapport with each other.
2 Mullins and Ramsay showed each other respect.
3 Mullins and Ramsay both used emphatic language.
4 Mullins had probably worked out his negotiating strategy before the meeting.
5 Mullins offered a creative suggestion to resolve an area of conflict.
6 Ramsay tried to avoid an atmosphere of conflict.
7 Ramsay showed a willingness to compromise.
8 The outcome of the meeting was unsatisfactory for both sides.

3 Listen to Dialogue 2 again and decide which of the following statements about it are true.
1 Dawson and Guertler established some common ground at the beginning of the negotiation.
2 Dawson indicated an area of conflict early in the negotiation.
3 Dawson and Guertler used polite language, showing tact and sensitivity.
4 Guertler made his sticking point clear regarding price.
5 Guertler did not make any concessions.
6 Dawson and Guertler were constructive and co-operative.
7 Dawson and Guertler summed up the main points they had agreed on.
8 The outcome of the negotiation was satisfactory for both sides.

Role-play: Negotiation

Working in pairs, role-play the negotiation between Jerry Mullins and Charles Ramsay from Listening 2/Dialogue 1, but this time try to ensure that the outcome is a win-win situation. Prepare for the negotiation carefully, using the hints on pages 66-67 to help you.

LISTENING 3

You are going to hear parts of a negotiation between Carson Martin, Vice-President of Toronto-based CM Kitchens Inc., and Pieter van Eck from Dutch kitchen equipment specialists, IPEA Holland. Listen and answer the following questions.

1 What are Carson and Pieter negotiating?
2 What agreement do they reach?

LANGUAGE PRACTICE

Study these phrases from Listening 3 and choose the most appropriate heading for each group from the list below. Then use each phrase once only to complete the negotiation transcript on page 70. You will need to think carefully about the meaning and the form of the missing language. When you have finished, listen again and check your answers.

- asking for clarification
- rejecting
- interrupting
- bargaining/trading

- making a suggestion
- stating your position
- agreeing
- asking for a reaction

1 ....
We just can't agree to . . .
. . . is out of the question.
No, I don't really think so.
I'd rather not . . .

2 ....
How's that then?
It depends what you mean when you say . . .
What do you have in mind?
Could you run through that again?

3 ....
We'll . . ., if you. . .
We might be able to make an exception, if you . . .
We're prepared to . . ., providing. . .
If you . . ., I could . . .
I was going to . . . but what if I were to say . . .?

4 ....
Why not?
Yes, of course.
I agree to . . .
That's a deal.

5 ....
I've got to stop you . . .

6 ....
What we're looking for . . .
We think . . .
We'd like to . . .
There's no way . . .
We wouldn't want to . . .
I guarantee . . .
I was hoping for . . .

7 ....
How does that sound . . .?
How do you feel about . . .?
What do you say . . .?

8 ....
Let's agree . . ., shall we?
How about . . .?
We could . . .
Do you want me to . . .?
. . ., say, . . .
I'd like to suggest . . .

Negotiation Transcript

Carson: ¹.................................. first on how to organise today's meeting, ⁽¹⁾...................................?

Pieter: Aha.

Carson: OK, well, ².................................. starting with the contract itself? Then ³.................................. move on to the product range, sales targets and discounts. ⁴.................................. for the morning session?

Pieter: That sounds fine. There's plenty to talk about there, for sure. ⁵.................................. start things off?

Carson: ⁶..................................? Go ahead.

Pieter: OK, well, as you know, we've signed up quite a few overseas agents recently. ⁷.................................. really is exclusivity – ⁸.................................. an exclusive agent can offer us more – more commitment, more motivation and better service. ⁹.................................. build up the relationship gradually, based on trust, and common interests . . .

Carson: ¹⁰.................................. right there, Pieter. Sorry, but ¹¹.................................. that. An exclusive agreement ¹².................................. . Absolutely impossible.

Pieter: Oh, ¹³..................................?

Carson: It's just that we're agents for a lot of big manufacturers, European, North American, a couple from the Far East, and we're locked into agreements with them. ¹⁴.................................. we can break them. In any case, ¹⁵.................................. – we've always handled competitors' products, it's the way we run our business.

Pieter: I see.

Carson: Look, exclusivity isn't everything, you know. ¹⁶.................................. look after your firm well ⁽¹⁶⁾.................................. give us the chance – there'll be no lack of commitment on our part. ¹⁷.................................. it.

Pieter: Hm, I suppose ¹⁸.................................., erm . . .

Carson: Yes?

Pieter: . . . if you offered us a realistic sales target for the first year.

Carson: I see. Well, I suppose ¹⁹.................................. 'realistic'. ²⁰.................................. exactly?

(Later that morning)

Carson: I want to be clear about this – ²¹.................................. for me?

Pieter: ²².................................. . What I'm saying is that ²³.................................. offer you a non-exclusive contract, ⁽²³⁾.................................. you stock our whole range of products and an agreed quantity of spare parts for each item.

Carson: Right.

Pieter: What I'd like to know now is are you prepared to commit yourself to a figure for sales growth, ²⁴.................................., over the next three years?

Carson: ²⁵.................................. .

Pieter: What, not even a rough figure?

Carson: ²⁶.................................. . It's going to depend on a lot of variables – any figure I give you won't be very accurate.

Pieter: OK, I won't try to pin you down on that. Let's move on to discounts. ²⁷.................................. 2% on orders up to $200,000, 5% on orders from $200,000-$500,000, and 10% for anything over that. It gives you a strong incentive to exceed your target. ²⁸.................................. that?

Carson: Well, I'm a bit disappointed, really. ²⁹.................................. at least 5% up to $200,000. It's the going rate over here – or weren't you aware of that?

Pieter: I'm sorry, I can't improve my offer on discounts. We've worked them out very carefully.

Carson: I see. Well, I don't know . . .

Pieter: How about this? ³⁰.................................. accept the discount rates, ⁽³⁰⁾.................................. help you with your mark-ups. ³¹.................................. set some limits, ⁽³¹⁾.................................. you can set your own mark-ups and we won't interfere.

Carson: Hm, yes, that'd be useful. It'd give us plenty of flexibility with our pricing.

Pieter: Exactly. ³²..................................?

Carson: Right, OK, ³³.................................. that.

Pieter: Great, ³⁴.................................. then. Let's summarise, shall we?

SKILLS PRACTICE

Role-play: Negotiation

**Work in pairs, one of you playing the Sales Director from Island Silks, the other
playing the Chief Buyer from Trendsetters Inc. (role card on page 145). Study
your role-card, and prepare for the negotiation carefully. When you have
finished negotiating, use the chart on page 72 to provide constructive feedback
on your opposite number's performance.**

Sales Director, Island Silks

Hong Kong

Island Silks, a medium-sized clothing company based in Hong Kong, operates in a highly competitive
environment and is in danger of losing market share to Thai silk manufacturers. As Sales Director, you are
delighted, therefore, to have the chance of a contract with Trendsetters Inc., a major American clothing retail
chain, based in New York. Trendsetters is interested in buying 50,000 silk scarves from your new 'Miriam
Designer Collection' at a unit price of $US50, including the cost of insurance and shipping to the US.

   You have some temporary cash flow problems at the moment. It is November 1, and you really need a deal
which will bring in some money quickly. You know that Trendsetters will require the scarves as soon as
possible as the company is approaching its peak selling period (the six weeks before Christmas). Despite your
cash flow problems, however, you would prefer not to deliver before early December, as you are behind
schedule with your orders and must give priority to existing customers. Also, you know Trendsetters will expect
a wide range of colours and patterns, and, although your factory can cope with this, it will cost more and mean
employing extra staff.

   Your objective is to negotiate a satisfactory deal for your company. Use the following points system as a
guide to your priorities. You should try to score as many points as possible, and will need to decide your
objectives, negotiating limits and strategy accordingly.

Decisions	Points	Decisions	Points
Delivery Date		*Terms of Payment**	
Nov. 15	1	By irrevocable letter of credit:	
Nov. 30	2	90 days presentation	1
Dec. 7	3	60 days presentation	2
		30 days presentation	3
Different Patterns		at sight	5
20	1		
15	2	*Discount*	
10	3	4%	0
		3%	1
Colours		2%	2
12	1	1%	3
10	3	0	5
6	4		

Aspects	Points to consider	Grade (1-5)*
Name of negotiator:		
Planning	was well-prepared	
Objectives	took a long term view; had a range of objectives; wanted to achieve a win-win outcome	
Rapport	established a good rapport	
Parameters	identified areas of conflict/ common ground early on	
Listening	listened well	
Attitude	was constructive not destructive; showed respect, tact and sensitivity; tried to avoid conflict	
Approach	stayed cool-headed; stuck to a minimum number of arguments	
Flexibility	considered alternatives; made creative suggestions; was willing to compromise	
Language	used language effectively; was fluent, articulate and persuasive	
Overall	competent? effective? skilful? successful?	
Other comments		

*Grade scale: 1 = unacceptable   2 = poor   3 = average   4 = good   5 = excellent (i.e. could not do better in the circumstances)

WRITING

1   As Sales Director at Island Silks, write a follow-up letter to the Chief Buyer at Trendsetters Inc. to confirm the points agreed in your negotiation. Take the opportunity to forward details of a new range of silk garment designs which you will be able to offer shortly and suggest Trendsetters might like to consider an order for these too.

2   As Chief Buyer at Trendsetters Inc., write a follow-up letter to the Sales Director at Island Silks to confirm the points agreed in your negotiation, and ask to be kept up to date on future additions to the company's range of silk garment designs.

3   As Chief Buyer at Trendsetters Inc., you are anxious to cash in on the latest fashion for silk designer shirts. Write a fax to Thai Silks in Bangkok requesting some samples as soon as possible and asking for a quote (CIF New York) for supplying 5,000 shirts. Ask whether you could expect delivery within four weeks of placing an order and request full details of the company's payment terms.

4   When Helen Dawson bought Hans Guertler's second-hand cutting machines (see Listening 2), he confidently predicted that the Melford Furniture Group would have no problems with them. In fact, difficulties have arisen, and Jim Ross, Melford's Head of Sales, has just received the following memorandum from the company's Production Director.

MEMORANDUM

MELFORD FURNITURE GROUP PLC
MELFORD HOUSE · DANIEL STREET ·
BATH · AVON BA2 7RS
TELEPHONE: (0225) 311670

To: Jim Ross, Head of Sales

From: Jack Hartley, Production Director

Date: 5/5

Subject: Cutting machines

At first the machines we bought from Guertler seemed to be running well, but now we're running into problems with them.

They are not producing goods of the same quality as our existing machines nor are they working as fast. As a result, we're having to carry out more frequent inspections, and reject a larger number of finished products.

In order to complete the contract with Country Furnishings satisfactorily, we need more time to work on the equipment. Bill tells me that a few minor adjustments to the machines here and there could improve their performance, so I'm letting him check them out.

I know this is an important contract for us and I know Derek Wright can be 'difficult' about delays, but we really have no alternative.

As Jim Ross, write to Derek Wright, Managing Director of Country Furnishings, and explain that you are unable to supply the wardrobe units and dressing tables he ordered in time. Be tactful and assure him that you are doing all you can to supply the goods with a minimum of delay. You will need the following details.

Mr Derek Wright
Managing Director
Country Furnishings
Beacon Row
Tamerton
Devon

8

Headhunters

INTRODUCTION

1   **Discuss the following questions.**

1   What is a 'headhunter'?
2   Do you react in the same way to the term 'executive search consultant'?
3   What other recruitment methods can you think of?
4   What are the advantages and disadvantages of each one?

2   **Read the cartoon and answer the questions that follow.**

1   In the first four pictures, who does the cartoonist lead us to believe Clive is talking to?
2   Who is he actually talking to?
3   Why is his wife annoyed?
4   Why do you think the headhunter is calling Clive?
5   Is Clive interested?

3   **What do you think?**

1   How would it feel to be 'headhunted'?
2   Is the poaching of senior personnel from a company simply part of executive life, or is it an unethical activity?
3   In western countries, executives tend to switch jobs several times in their careers, whereas in Japan, with its policy of lifetime employment, most executives stay with one company throughout their working lives. Which system is better for the employer? And for the employee?

LISTENING 1

1 In this interview, you will hear Francis Wilkin, an Executive Search Consultant at Russell Reynolds Associates, talking about his job. Listen and take notes under the following headings.
- the role and status of the headhunter
- areas of corporate and personal specialisation
- the distinction between executive search companies and recruitment agencies
- the type of people headhunters target
- methods used to identify candidates
- the 'craft' and 'art' of headhunting

2 Listen again and answer the following questions.
Francis Wilkin mentions the following figures. What do they relate to?
- 50%
- £60,000
- 15,000

Two sides of the recruitment business . . .

TEXT 1

1 Before you read the text on page 76, look at the title and subtitle. What do you think the article is about? Choose the best answer.
a) how to attract the attention of headhunters
b) what to do if you receive a phone call from a headhunter
c) how to become a headhunter

2 Read paragraphs 1 and 2 and summarise the trends and statistics quoted in your own words.

Bait for the headhunters

That unexpected phone call offering a plum job with another firm isn't always just a matter of chance. Given a little planning, the talent scouts can be directed to your door. Stephanie Jones explains how.

"NATURALLY, I was headhunted into my present job," a typical City whizz-kid boasts. "Headhunters ring all the time. During Big Bang they phoned us so often that we put their calls over the office loudhailer. Then we'd have a laugh when the headhunter said: 'Confidentially, I have a uniquely exciting opportunity that might just interest you . . .'"

Being headhunted is not only for young bloods and famous chief executives. Almost 90 per cent of the top 1,000 companies use executive search consultants to find senior people. In the last few years they have been joined by smaller companies, accounting and law firms, chartered surveyors, architects, private hospitals, the media, and even local authorities and Government departments.

So how do you attract those ego-trip phone calls which spell a new career opportunity?

John Harper, 33, has been headhunted three times. His first job was as a graduate trainee with Procter & Gamble where, after five years, he was a brand manager on Pampers, which he had launched in the UK market.

He was invited to Kenner Parker (the American toy and games manufacturer responsible for Trivial Pursuit, Monopoly and Care Bears) where in five more years he rose to be European marketing and operations director.

Then he was lured away into Avis, the car-hire giant, and two years later headhunted again into the job he started last week as international marketing director for Reebok, the sportswear company. He won't quote figures, but each time he moved his salary and benefits showed substantial improvement.

Not one of these positions was advertised. Indeed, before his latest move he was not considering a career change at all.

So his advice to those hoping to hit the headhunt trail is born of experience:

■ First, start out with a large international company. Procter & Gamble, Unilever, Shell, IBM and Mars, for example, offer not only excellent training but a ready-made network of contacts around the world, arguably more helpful to a

John Harper: It pays to cultivate people, to keep visible, and to drop hints when you're ready to move on

career than being a Harvard alumnus.

■ Secondly, ensure you are noticed by superiors. Headhunters frequently find people through referrals from a source, usually a more senior person who suggests suitable names. Successful and highly-respected mentors should be cultivated, so that they will think of you when approached.

Pass the word around if you have itchy feet

■ Thirdly, make an impression outside your company. The research departments of search firms take note of executives mentioned in the Press and trade journals.

You can't be sure exactly which particular self-publicising effort led to an approach (headhunters rarely reveal how they found you, and it is naive to ask) but developing a profile stands you in good stead.

Whenever Kenner Parker was launching another toy or game, John Harper's name repeatedly cropping up in Marketing, Marketing Week and the Financial Times played a useful part in his progress.

■ Fourthly, when you want to move –

and don't stay in the same job, with the same company, for more than five to seven years – make it known. According to Harper it's rare, and only when you're hitting the big time, that a headhunter will call out of the blue.

Most headhuntees have put out the word that they are looking, and have taken the initiative by sending their CV to selected research consultants. When moving from Kenner Parker to Avis, Harper passed his CV to fifty searchers, identified through friends, contacts and other headhunters.

The likelihood that one of the search firms will be looking for someone just like you is remote, so it's wise to cast your net widely. Harper was headhunted into Avis by Bruce Rowe of Rowe International in Paris - not only one of his targeted search consultants, but a fellow ex-Procter & Gamble man, which underlines the value of his first piece of advice.

■ Finally, keep in with headhunters. This includes a willingness to act as a source. Harper admits he would not recommend anyone he was currently working with – it would conflict with his allegiance to his employer. But he will mention outstanding people he has worked with in the past.

3   **Read paragraphs 3-7 and complete the following record card.**

H

Name: John Harper

Age: [1] ....

Qualifications: [2] ....

Career:

    First job

        Company [3] ....
        Position [4] ....
        Length of employment [5] ....

    Second job

        Company [6] ....
        Position [7] ....
        Length of employment [8] ....

    Third job

        Company [9] ....
        Length of employment [10] ....

    Current position

        Company [11] ....
        Position [12] ....

4   **Read the rest of the text, and summarise John Harper's advice to would-be headhuntees in the following chart. You will need to infer the reason for his fifth piece of advice. The first one has been summarised for you.**

	Advice	Reason
1	start with a large international company	excellent training and an immediate circle of contacts
2		
3		
4		
5		

VOCABULARY

What do the underlined words in the following sentences from Text 1 mean? Choose appropriate substitutes from the list.

marked	flattering	excellent
highlights	let it be known	represent
behind	becoming visible	persuaded
appearing	very successful	changed jobs

1 '. . . how do you attract those <u>ego trip</u> phone calls which <u>spell</u> a new career opportunity?' (lines 22 and 23)
2 '. . . the American toy and games manufacturer <u>responsible for</u> Trivial Pursuit, Monopoly and Care Bears . . .' (line 33)
3 'Then he was <u>lured away</u> into Avis . . .' (line 37)
4 '. . . each time he <u>moved</u> his salary and benefits showed <u>substantial</u> improvement.' (lines 43 and 44)
5 '. . . <u>developing a profile</u> stands you in good stead.' (line 74)
6 'John Harper's name repeatedly <u>cropping up</u> in *Marketing, Marketing Week* and the *Financial Times* . . .' (line 78)
7 '. . . [it's] only when you're <u>hitting the big time</u>, that a headhunter will call out of the blue.' (line 87)
8 'Most headhuntees have <u>put out the word</u> that they are looking . . .' (lines 89-90)
9 '. . . which <u>underlines</u> the value of his first piece of advice.' (line 105)
10 '. . . he will mention <u>outstanding</u> people he has worked with in the past.' (line 113)

LANGUAGE PRACTICE

Giving advice

Whether advice comes across as helpful and friendly or rude and abrupt depends on the situation, the choice of language, and, if the advice is delivered verbally, on the tone of voice used. Study these examples from Text 1 and the language in the box. Then practise giving advice in the role-play that follows.

*Successful and highly-respected mentors **should** be cultivated.* (line 62)
***Pass** the word around if you have itchy feet.*
***It's wise to** cast your net widely . . .* (line 99)

Giving advice	
You ought (not) to . . .	*Why don't you (try) . . . ?*
You could always (try) . . .	*Can I suggest you . . . ?*
Have you . . . ?	*My advice would be to . . .*
I (would) advise you to . . .	*If I were you, I'd . . .*
It might be an idea to . . .	*I would recommend you . . .*

Work in pairs, one of you playing Student A, the other Student B. Read your role-card and prepare for the meeting, drawing on Text 1 and your own ideas.

Student A

As a successful business person, you have been headhunted several times. Now, a contact of yours who is hoping to be headhunted for the first time has come to you for guidance. Give as much advice as you can during your meeting.

Student B

As you are hoping to be headhunted for the first time, you have sought the advice of a contact of yours who you know has been headhunted several times. Get as much guidance as you can during your meeting with this successful business person.

Tenses

Present or present perfect, simple or continuous, active or passive? Read the following passage about headhunting and put the verbs in brackets in the correct form.

The Ritz – favoured haunt of London's headhunters

Once a list of suitable candidates [1]..................................... (draw up), the lead consultant [2]..................................... (set up) appointments to meet them all. At these preliminary meetings, the consultant usually [3]..................................... (start) by presenting the job on offer in some detail, and then [4]..................................... (ask) about the candidate's background so he can assess how far it [5]..................................... (match) the needs of the client and, also, how interested the candidate is. At this stage, no commitment [6]..................................... (seek) by the headhunter - he [7]..................................... (simply try) to size the candidate up, just as the candidate [8]..................................... (seek) to learn more about what [9]..................................... (offer) by the company. After these initial discussions, the headhunter [10]..................................... (report back) to his client and the relative merits of different candidates [11]..................................... (discuss) in depth. At this point, a short-list [12]..................................... (draw up) and the real negotiating begins!

TEXT 2

1   **Read the advertisement and complete the following summary.**

This advertisement was placed by [1].................................., a [2]....................................
company with offices in [3].................................... and [4].................................... . As a result of
[5]...................................., the company is looking for two [6].................................... . Applicants
should [7].................................... or send a [8].................................... to [9]....................................
quoting [10].................................... .

2   **Which of the following must candidates be able to offer?**
  a) two European languages (including mother tongue)
  b) the ability to grow professionally
  c) evidence of excellent interpersonal skills
  d) managerial skills
  e) energy and creativity
  f) a postgraduate qualification
  g) work experience in a similar field

Hertfordshire   Amsterdam

European Executive
Search & Selection

Outstanding Packages

This is a unique opportunity to make a real impact on the future success of an international business.

We are one of the leading search and selection companies focussed on the European IT industry. As part of our strategy for growth we are opening a network of offices in key European countries, in order to provide our clients with both pan-European and local market solutions.

This expansion has created the need for two addition Consultants to be based either in our Hertfordshire or Amsterdam offices.

We will consider only the best, ambitious individuals with an exceptional background and obvious potential, who meet our key requirements:

* High calibre graduate.

* Aged 27 - 35.

* Proven ability to build and develop client relationships.

* A background in Search, Selection or HR within the IT industry.

* Possess a combination of drive and resourcefulness.

* Fluency in a second European language desirable.

For a completely confidential discussion, please phone Vanessa Lurie or a send a detailed Curriculum Vitae to her at the address below, quoting reference AR1.

GOODMAN GRAHAM
AND ASSOCIATES

8 Beaumont Gate, Shenley Hill, Radlett, Herts WD7 7AR.
Telephone: 0923 855515. Fax: 0923 854791

LISTENING 2

1 **Listen to the second part of the interview with Executive Search Consultant, Francis Wilkin, and check whether the following statements accurately reflect what he says.**

1 Headhunting fees are not based on an accepted 'industry standard'.
2 There are two opposing forces at work in a person considering a job change.
3 People who are dissatisfied with their current salary are perfect targets for headhunters.
4 Closing a deal is the hardest part of the search process.
5 Clients have no redress if a selected candidate should leave soon after joining the company.
6 Headhunters sometimes fail to finalise a deal for apparently rather trivial reasons.

2 **Listen again, taking notes on the key points. Then summarise what Francis Wilkin says on the following subjects:**

■ headhunters' fees/salaries
■ the search and selection process
■ an 'embarrassing moment'

CASE STUDY

Nick Burford, an Executive Search Consultant, received the following brief from a US company, Hi-Style Inc.

RECRUITMENT BRIEF – HI-STYLE INC.

Company Background

Head office:	New York, USA
European HQ:	Zurich, Switzerland
Turnover:	£350 million
Products:	clothing; perfume; beauty/health products
Main markets:	USA, Switzerland

Job Specification

Position:	Marketing Director, Europe
Location:	based at European headquarters
Duties:	oversee all aspects of the company's marketing in Europe; implement new strategies for expansion in Europe
Salary:	minimum £120,000 (negotiable) and substantial benefits package, including relocation expenses

---

Person Specification

	Essential	Desirable
Qualifications:	degree; marketing diploma or specialisation	MBA
Skills:	good communication skills; fluency in two European languages (one must be German); excellent negotiating skills	IT expertise
Background:	marketing upmarket fashion and health/beauty products in Europe	experience of developing new distribution outlets
Qualities:	hard-headed, innovative; able to work in a team; leadership qualities	even-tempered, outgoing, creative

Having identified and interviewed a number of possible candidates for the post, Nick Burford's recommendation to Hi-Style management was Peter Kahn, currently European Marketing Director at Cosmetics International. Hi-Style decided to offer Peter Kahn the job and asked Nick Burford to set up a meeting with him to discuss the terms and conditions of employment.

Discussion

Nick Burford made the following notes when he met Peter Kahn. Read them and discuss the questions that follow.

NOTES   Action

Meeting with Peter Kahn

- visited Kahn at home, met wife (Paula) and three children – big house in a smart area of London

- Paula charming/sociable – runs own business (specialist food store) 'doing really well'
NOT keen on going to Zurich – 'full of bankers isn't it?'
wonders how the Swiss will like Peter (Anglo-Indian) bossing them around

- two sons (Prakesh and Rhalib) about to go to private schools

- daughter (Jane) just started university

1 How might this information affect Peter Kahn's decision on Hi-Style's job offer?
2 How might it affect his negotiation position (objectives, limits, strategy) when it comes to discussing terms and conditions?

Role-play: Negotiation

Work in groups of three, one of you playing Peter Kahn (role card on page 146) and the other two playing Hi-Style's Managing Director and Director of Human Resources respectively. Read your role-cards and prepare for the negotiation carefully, using the hints on pages 66-67 to help you.

Managing Director and Director of Human Resources, Hi-Style Inc.

You want Peter Kahn for the job, but not on *any* terms. You have worked out the following negotiating position and, although you are prepared to compromise a little, you are not going to let him 'push you around'.

Salary	£120,000 (i.e. 20% more than his present salary)
Bonuses	A 'golden hello' i.e. bonus for making the move to Hi-Style of £24,000 plus a yearly bonus depending on the company's financial performance but guaranteed not to be less than one month's salary
Accommodation	A housing allowance: Hi-Style will pay 50% of the cost of rented accommodation (usually the firm only pays 20%)
Car	Negotiable – room to offer something a bit special if he has had to make too many concessions!
Hours of work	No fixed hours
Length of contract	Three years: probationary period of six months, at the end of which the contract can be terminated by either side – if Peter Kahn leaves before the end of his contract, he may not take up employment with one of Hi-Style's competitors within the next twelve months
Health	Free membership of a private health insurance scheme
Employment for Paula	A position as personal assistant to one of the middle managers could be offered (no higher position would be available to her)

WRITING

Depending on the outcome of your negotiation, choose one of the following tasks.

1 Write a summary of the main points agreed during your negotiation as a basis for drawing up a contract. When you have finished, exchange summaries with your opposite number(s) for checking.

2 As Peter Kahn, write a letter to Nick Burford complaining that he failed to give you enough relevant information about Hi-Style and its requirements and therefore wasted your time putting you in touch with the company.

3 As Hi-Style's Managing Director/Director of Personnel, write a letter to Nick Burford expressing your disappointment with Peter Kahn and complaining about the waste of your valuable time on such an unsuitable candidate.

Corporate Culture

INTRODUCTION

1   **Read this extract from *Corporate Cultures*, a book by Terrence Deal and Allen Kennedy, and discuss the questions that follow.**

Marvin Bower, for years managing director of McKinsey & Company and author of *The Will to Manage*, described the informal cultural elements of a business as 'the way we do things round here.' Every business – in fact every organization – has a culture. Sometimes it is fragmented and difficult to read from the outside – some people are loyal to their bosses, others are loyal to the union, still others care only about their colleagues who work in the sales territories of the Northeast. If you ask employees why they work, they will answer 'because we need the money.' On the other hand, sometimes the culture of an organization is very strong and cohesive; everyone knows the goals of the corporation, and they are working for them. Whether weak or strong, culture has a powerful influence throughout an organization. It affects practically everything – from who gets promoted and what decisions are made, to how employees dress and what sports they play. Because of this impact, we think that culture also has a major effect on the success of a business.

1   What is 'corporate culture'?
2   What is meant by 'strong' corporate culture?
3   What is the relationship between corporate culture and success?

2   **What do you think?**

At the heart of corporate culture – and critical to a company's success – are the 'shared values' which, says *Corporate Cultures*, 'provide a sense of common direction for all employees and guidelines for their day-to-day behavior'. A company like Caterpillar, for example, revolves around 'an extraordinary commitment to meeting customer needs' – symbolised in their slogan '24-hour service anywhere in the world'. According to Terrence Deal and Allen Kennedy, 'often companies succeed because their employees can identify, embrace, and act on the values of the organization.'

What, in your opinion, are the shared values behind the following businesses?
- McDonalds
- Rolls–Royce
- Christian Dior
- Sony
- The Walt Disney Company
- IBM

3   **Read the cartoon and discuss the following questions.**
1   Who does Rupert run into?
2   What kind of corporate culture does BBDX have?
3   Why is Rupert looking blank in pictures 1-4?
4   Why does Rupert smile in picture 6?
5   What is the cartoon's message?

The caring company

A strong 'corporate culture' is said to help firms succeed. Does it?

[1] The greeter at a Wal-Mart store might be surprised to know he is living proof of one of the oldest saws of management theory. Instilled by the late Sam Walton, [5] Wal-Mart's deeply ingrained corporate culture of frugality, hard work, service to customers and paternalism towards employees has contributed as much to its success as its slick distribution system and [10] 'everyday low prices'.

Management thinkers have long associated a strong corporate culture – the beliefs, goals and values that guide the behaviour of a firm's employees – [15] with superior long-term performance. The theory is that strong cultures can help workers march to the same drummer; create high levels of employee loyalty and motivation; and provide the [20] company with structure and controls, without the need for an innovation-stifling bureaucracy.

In a new book, John Kotter and James Heskett, both professors at Harvard [25] Business School, report on their four-year study to examine the link between corporate culture and economic performance*. To do this, the authors calculated (from survey responses) [30] 'culture-strength indices' for over 200 big American firms. Companies such as Wal-Mart, J.P. Morgan and Procter & Gamble scored highest; bankrupt, but still operating, American airlines scored [35] among the worst.

Messrs Kotter and Heskett then tried to correlate the strength of the firms' cultures with their economic performance over an 11-year period. [40] Their analysis did show a positive correlation between strong cultures and long-term economic success, but it was a weaker association than most management theorists would have [45] expected. Strong-cultured firms seemed almost as likely to perform poorly as their weak-cultured rivals. The popular view that a strong corporate culture invariably leads to success, they [50] concluded, was 'just plain wrong'.

Perhaps they should not have found this so startling. Strong cultures, even

*Corporate Culture and Performance.
Published by Free Press, $24.95.

MANAGEMENT FOCUS

those which once made a company successful, can also be an obstacle to [55] change – just ask the top managers at IBM. Too strong a culture can lead to corporate arrogance and insularity. America's General Motors and Britain's BP are two notorious examples. At its [60] worst, a strong but misdirected culture can lead all of a firm's employees to run, hand in hand, in the wrong direction. So what makes a corporate culture a competitive weapon, rather than a [65] liability?

To find out, the researchers dug deeper. Two smaller groups of strong-cultured companies were selected for closer study. The first comprised high-performing firms whose net profits had, [70] on average, increased by three times as much over an 11-year period as those in the second group. A group of 75 investment analysts, who between them had followed the 22 companies in the [75] two groups, were then asked whether corporate culture had had any impact on each firm's performance. Overwhelmingly – and surprisingly, since culture is the sort of 'soft' [80] information that analysts are thought to ignore – they said that a strong culture had helped the high performers. They were equally convinced, however, that the low performers had been hindered [85] by their cultures.

What is it about the cultures of the

---

high-performing companies that makes them successful? The authors' theory is that firms whose cultures seem [90] consistently to produce long-term economic success share one fundamental characteristic: their managers do not let the short-term interests of shareholders override all else, but care equally about [95] all of the company's 'stakeholders'.

Over the long-term, mind you, the authors believe that these interests converge. 'Only when managers care about the legitimate interests of [100] shareholders do they strive to perform well economically over time, and in a competitive industry that is only possible when they take care of their customers, and in a competitive labour market that [105] is only possible when they take care of those who serve customers – employees.' That sort of thinking seemed to go out of fashion in America in the takeover and debt-crazed 1980s, when [110] many firms paid so much attention to the short-term interests of their shareholders that customers or employees often seemed to have been forgotten.

[115] To test their idea, Messrs Kotter and Heskett asked the investment analysts to rate a larger number of firms by how much each valued customers, shareholders and employees. Managers [120] and employees at the companies were also interviewed; their views closely matched those of the analysts. Of these, 12 firms were identified whose cultures stressed all of the three big corporate [125] constituencies – customers, employees and shareholders. A further 20 were identified which did precisely the opposite (whose managers, according to the analysts, cared mostly about [130] 'themselves').

Over the 11-year period, Messrs Kotter and Keskett found that the 12 firms in the first group increased their revenues, on average, by four times as [135] much as the 20 companies in the second group; their workforces expanded by eight times as much; and their share prices increased by 12 times as much (by 901%, against 74% for the second [140] group). Perhaps most impressively, however, the net profits of firms in the first group soared by an average of 756% during the period, compared with an average increase of just 1% for [145] companies in the second group.

TEXT 1

1 Before you read, look at the title and subtitle. What theory is the article questioning?

2 The article focuses on a four-year research study undertaken by two Harvard Business School professors, John Kotter and James Heskett. Read it carefully and complete the following research synopsis.

RESEARCH SYNOPSIS: *CORPORATE CULTURE AND PERFORMANCE*			
Aims of the study	**Methods/ procedures**	**Findings**	**Conclusions**
1	survey over 200 big US firms and calculate their culture-strength indices	2	
to correlate the strength of the firms' cultures with their economic performance over an 11-year period		3	4
5	two smaller groups selected for closer study		strong cultures had helped the high performers but had equally hindered the low performers
6	7	8	

3 What do the following companies have in common, according to the article?
- IBM
- General Motors
- BP

WRITING 1

The editor of a prominent business magazine has asked you to submit a short review (maximum 120 words) of *Corporate Culture and Performance* for a book feature she is planning for the next issue. Base your article on the information in Text 1.

VOCABULARY

Complete the following sentences with the correct form of the underlined word.

1 analyse
   - By .... their results in some detail, the professors were able to reach some interesting conclusions.
   - Investment .... evaluate the investment merits of different stocks and shares.
   - If you work in financial management, you probably need to have an .... mind.

2 bankrupt
   - During a recession, it is not uncommon for people to face ....
   - We are almost .... because two of our major customers can't pay us.

3 bureaucracy
   - Government departments, hospitals, and other large organisations can be very ....
   - .... seem to enjoy giving you masses of paperwork to deal with.
   - 'Red tape' is a derogatory term for excessive ....

4 character
   - Fast-growing firms are often .... by a strong corporate culture.
   - The .... of an organisation is formed, to some extent, by its leader.
   - What are the .... of a weak corporate culture?

5 economy
   - What sort of .... system do you have in your country?
   - Strict financial controls ensure that an organisation's resources are used ....
   - Some countries have a mixed .... while others have a high degree of state control.

6 innovate
   - Sony has always been seen as an .... in the field of hi-fi equipment.
   - In certain areas of business – for example, high fashion – it is important to be .... and keep coming up with new styles and original designs.
   - .... – or stagnate!

7 research
   - Cambridge University has a worldwide reputation in the field of scientific ....
   - Pierre works in our R & D department. He's one of ten ....
   - The effects of the factory environment on shop floor workers have been extensively .... by a well-known industrial psychologist.

8 theory
   - Higuchi is an impressive and entertaining .... – we enjoy listening to his ideas.
   - The study was largely ...., and therefore of limited value to us.
   - In ...., there's no reason why we couldn't produce such a revolutionary product, but the costs would probably be prohibitive.

LANGUAGE PRACTICE

Phrasal verbs: 'stand'

Match the verbs with their correct definitions (1-6). Then complete the sentences that follow (7-12), using each verb once only. Make sure you use the correct form.

1 to stand down   a) to take someone's place (e.g. while they are out of the office or on holiday)

2 to stand for   b) to be better than somebody/something or distinctive in some way

3 to stand out   c) to represent
4 to stand by   d) to defend
5 to stand up for   e) to be ready to act
6 to stand in   f) to resign or withdraw

7 We all know that the name 'Sony' .... technical excellence.
8 If the company chairman is on a business trip, his deputy will usually .... for him.
9 Our sales manager will be giving the presentation, but a technical salesman will be .... to help him.
10 In this company you don't get anywhere by being modest. You have to .... yourself.
11 The managing director was asked to .... and a new appointment was made.
12 As an example of strong corporate culture in the fast-food sector, McDonalds certainly ....

Phrasal verbs: 'keep'

Now do the same with these verbs.

1 to keep up   a) to follow/inform yourself about
2 to keep up with   b) to avoid (e.g. a topic)
3 to keep on   c) to maintain good relations with
4 to keep to   d) to maintain/continue
5 to keep in with   e) to prevent from rising/hold at a low level
6 to keep down   f) to continue employing
7 to keep off   g) to stick to/adhere to (e.g. a rule, a promise, etc.)
8 to keep from   h) to prevent/stop

9 We hope to .... the deadline and finish the project on time.
10 The chairperson .... the forthcoming redundancy programme because she didn't want to upset anyone.
11 Product prices had to be .... for the firm to remain competitive.
12 If you work in the computer industry, you need to .... the latest technology in software and hardware.
13 Some of the company's longest-serving workers would have been .... if the economic conditions hadn't been so unfavourable.
14 I have been .... doing important jobs because of this report. It's been incredibly time-consuming.
15 Our firm is known for craftmanship and we intend to .... the high standards we have set.
16 It's usually worth .... your superiors, even if you don't like them.

LISTENING

You are going to hear Angela Baron, Manager of Organisation and Human Resource Planning at the Institute of Personnel Management in London, talking about corporate culture. Listen and take notes under the following headings.

- 'bureaucratic' culture
- 'facilitating' culture
- achieving a personal-corporate culture match
- personal-corporate culture mismatches
- achieving a positive corporate culture

Angela Baron at The Institute of Personnel Management in London

TEXT 2

People at all stages of their careers need to understand culture and how it works because it will likely have a powerful effect on their lives. People just starting their careers may think a job is just a job. But when they choose a company, they often choose a way of life. The culture shapes their responses in a strong but subtle way. Culture can make them fast or slow workers, tough or friendly managers, team players or individuals. By the time they've worked for several years, they may be so well conditioned by the culture they may not even recognize it. But when they change jobs, they may be in for a big surprise.

Take an up-and-coming executive at General Electric who is being wooed by Xerox – more money, a bigger office, greater responsibility. If his first reaction is to grab it, he's probably going to be disappointed. Xerox has a totally different culture than GE. Success (even survival) at Xerox is closely tied to an ability to maintain a near frenetic pace, the ability to work and play hard, Xerox-style.

By contrast, GE has a more thoughtful and slow-moving culture. Success at GE is a function of being able to take work seriously, a strong sense of peer group respect, considerable deference for authority, and a sense of deliberateness. A person of proven success at GE will bring these values to Xerox because past experience of GE's culture has reinforced them. But these same values may not be held in high esteem elsewhere.

Bright young comers at GE could, for example, quickly fizzle out at Xerox – and not even understand why. They'll be doing exactly what they did to succeed at GE – maybe even working harder at it – but their deliberate approach to issues large and small will be seen by insiders at Xerox as a sign that they 'lack smarts'. Their loss of confidence, self-esteem, and ability will be confusing to them and could significantly derail their careers. For Xerox, the loss of productivity could be appreciable.

This is no imaginary scenario. It happens again and again at Xerox, General Electric, and many other companies when managers ignore the influence of culture on individual approaches to work. Culture shock may be one of the main reasons why people supposedly 'fail' when they leave one organisation for another. Where they fail, however, is not necessarily in doing the job, but in not reading the culture correctly.

© Addison Wesley Publishing Company Inc.

Read the extract from *Corporate Cultures* on the opposite page and summarise what it says on the following subjects:

- the importance of understanding culture
- the Xerox culture
- the General Electric culture
- the relationship between culture and success

WRITING 2

You have agreed to write a short article (200-300 words) on corporate culture for your company's in-house magazine. Use the following brief from the editor and the information in the unit to help you.

> Thanks for agreeing to write about corporate culture for us. Could I suggest that you start by saying what corporate culture is and giving a few examples? Then perhaps you could follow on with a brief description of the various types of culture found in large organisations. Finally you could explain why it's important for people to be aware of corporate culture when they choose jobs. – Ed

DISCUSSION

Work in groups and discuss the following questions.

1 Where would you place yourself in terms of your preferred corporate culture? Mark your position with an X and discuss your choice with the other members of your group.

facilitating culture   *bureaucratic culture*

2 Do you think this preference might change in time?
3 Have you ever been in a situation where your personal culture didn't match the culture of an organisation/group you belonged to? Describe your experiences.

CASE STUDY

The EuroDisney theme park

Before the EuroDisney theme park opened, east of Paris, it received strong criticism from anti-American elements of the French media who accused the park's management of behaving in a heavy-handed, authoritarian manner. EuroDisney was criticised for its policy concerning the way employees should be dressed. The company had announced a dress code which specified the Disney look required of its 12,000 workers.

Female staff had to wear 'appropriate underwear'. Fishnet stockings and suspenders were not allowed. Neither were dark lipstick, leather trousers, miniskirts, false eye-lashes, highlighted hair and very high heels. Male staff had to observe certain rules too. Hair should not be too long; beards and moustaches were banned, as were visible tattoos and earrings. Finally, both sexes had to have an 'equilibrium between height and weight'.

The dress code caused quite a stir. A government inspector supported the media critics, saying the Disney dress code violated personal liberty. An American who applied for the job was told that he would have to shave off his moustache. He commented, 'I wasn't interested in the job offer after I learned of the dress code. These kinds of attitude have no place in France or anywhere else in the modern world.'

EuroDisney – a controversial outfit?

Role-play: Meeting

Dissatisfied with the dress code, a group of English-speaking employees at the theme park have asked for a meeting with the EuroDisney management. Work in small groups, with half of you playing the EuroDisney employees, and the other half playing the EuroDisney management. Read your role-cards and prepare for the meeting. Then try to reach a satisfactory resolution of your differences of opinion.

Employees

You want to persuade the park's managers to either change their dress code or get rid of it completely. Prepare your arguments carefully and work out your strategy for the meeting.

Management

You do not want to get rid of the dress code since you are very conscious of the need to maintain EuroDisney's image in the eyes of the public. Work out your arguments for keeping the dress policy and agree on a strategy for the meeting.

WRITING

An English language newspaper, the *Paris Tribune*, publishes a selection of letters from readers in its Business Section each week. The letters are generally controversial, giving rise to lively debates.

Write a letter to the editor of the newspaper commenting on the dress code of EuroDisney, and arguing strongly for or against retaining it. When you have written your letters, compare them, and decide which is the most suitable for publication.

Caution: People at work!

INTRODUCTION

1 **What do you think? How far do you agree with the following statements?**
1 People are the most important resource a business has.
2 Management should always use the negotiating machinery of the union to make organisational changes.
3 Changing the pay system of a company will usually be resisted by the unions.
4 Length of service not ability/responsibility should determine an employee's salary.
5 Most countries neglect the talents of women in the workplace.
6 Business should do more to encourage women employees.

2 **Answer the following questions. Then discuss your answers in small groups.**
1 What do you know about union-management relations in Britain?
2 What are industrial relations like in your country?
3 Do women have equal employment opportunities in your country?
4 How easy is it for women to reach senior positions in your country?

TEXT 1

1 **Before you read, look at the title, subtitle and picture.**
1 Which company is the article about?
2 What does the company produce?
3 What area of the company is the article about?

2 **Scan the text quickly for information about Ilford and complete the following summary.**

> Ilford Ltd. is located in [1]......................... and has a workforce of [2]......................... .
> The company, which has two sister [3]......................... in Europe, is part of
> [4]......................... which was bought in [5]......................... by [6]......................... . Ilford
> manufactures [7]......................... . The company's head of human resources is called
> [8]......................... and it is his job to oversee [9]........................., the company's new
> programme for [10]......................... work practices, pay and conditions.

3 **Look again at the title of the article. Why is it a clever way of introducing the text?**

Ilford puts people into sharp focus

Fiona Thompson explains how the photographic materials company developed its personnel blueprint

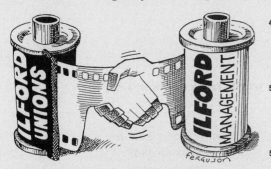

Management is determined that nobody should be kept in the dark about changes which are being introduced at Ilford's plant in Mobberley, Cheshire.

Impact, Ilford's programme for a comprehensive restructuring of work practices, pay and conditions, is now under way. And the company's aim – that none of Ilford Ltd's 1,400 employees should be left in the dark about the programme – has meant an exhaustive series of consultative meetings.

The process is being overseen by the company's head of human resources, Frank Sharp. The changes in Impact echo those in other companies which have adopted the human resources title alongside an attempt to achieve fundamental changes in employment culture. These companies often want to move away from traditions of industrial relations conflict, and integrate the management of people into their strategy.

According to Sharp, the impetus for setting up Impact was an acknowledgement by the board a few years ago that the company was in a mature industry; that a substantial effort had been put into engineering, science and marketing in the previous 10 to 15 years, 'and we could not see how the business would further prosper and become more profitable unless we tackled the people side'. It was a radical move for Ilford which, until then, 'had not regarded personnel as contributing in any way to the strategic direction of the business'.

Ilford, number one in sales in the world monochrome market, makes and sells photographic materials, chemicals and equipment. It is part of Ilford Group, which has two other manufacturing plants, in France and Switzerland, and was bought by the large US paper company, International Paper, in 1989. The UK company traditionally operated along inflexible lines, with strict demarcation between the different unions and rigidly enforced differentials based on 43 grading bands.

Impact is nothing less than a complete overhaul of how Ilford's employees work, their pay and conditions. Impact's three aims are:

- To implement organisational change involving a move away from detailed job descriptions and a lot of different jobs to a number of core jobs with many fewer grades;
- To devise specific training and development plans for each employee; and
- To develop an improved pay and reward policy.

The consultative process to devise a framework for a reward policy was launched last April in workshops attended by all the shop stewards and departmental managers. The managers then held a series of team meetings with never more than 15 employees at a time, to encourage maximum feedback.

'We started with a blank sheet of paper and said 'What would you like?' And we literally got everything from 'turkeys at Christmas' to 'deunionise',' says Sharp.

By the autumn, a nine-point framework was devised. Key elements of the reward policy, aimed at getting a simpler, fairer pay system, include substantially fewer grades, and the introduction of job evaluation, performance rewards and personal development discussions. The new grade structure will reduce the present 43 grades to between six and 12.

Each employee's job will be put into one of the new grades using a method of job evaluation – almost certainly the work profiling system of consultants Savile & Holdsworth – involving the employee. Each grade will have a negotiated base rate of pay to be determined by the market rate and Ilford's performance. The banding for each grade would be very wide to allow for performance payments agreed once a year between each employee and her/his boss. Getting to this stage has been a painstakingly slow business. Last April, it was intended that the new reward policy would be implemented on January 1, the normal date for pay increases.

But management had been 'too optimistic', Sharp acknowledges. 'Hindsight is a marvellous thing. In reality, to use a racing analogy, it was a 10-furlong race and the finishing point was to get everybody on board, understanding what the reward process was about. But while some departments started the race around the eighth furlong, others hadn't even saddled up the horse months later.'

But he does not see the delay as a failure. 'We had never gone through consultation before. The lesson we had learned is that if you are going to involve people, you must be prepared to accommodate their views and satisfy them before you move on, otherwise you risk failure.'

The organisational change at Ilford – involving the move away from a lot of different jobs to a number of core jobs – is a third complete, says Sharp.

The change was sorely needed, particularly as Ilford has had the same structure in place for many years despite having decreased from a multi-site organisation with 7,000 to 8,000 employees in the early to mid-1970s to a one-plant operation with 1,400 employees now.

In the scientific products department, for example, after detailed management-workforce discussions on what its new role should be and who should accept what responsibilities at what level, the consensus was that the department would actually function more effectively without supervisors.

Consequently the staff have taken on more responsibility and have been given the tools to carry out certain new tasks, like statistical process control.

The organisational changes, while providing much greater job satisfaction for some, inevitably leave some less happy as well. 'If a new role demanded more people-management skills, we didn't just take someone because they'd been there 20 years and done a good job. We tried to measure objectively through discussion and tests who had the 'best' skills.'

Some got bigger jobs, some moved sideways and others transferred to different roles elsewhere in the company.

In a small number of instances, this has meant salary decreases. Not surprisingly, there was union resistance. MSF, the technical and white-collar union representing the managers and scientists, accepted that some of its members' positions would change but wanted them to maintain their present grades, performance rates and income.

'We couldn't accept this as it wouldn't be seen as equitable by other people doing a bigger role,' says Sharp.

There was no question that the Impact proposals had to happen, according to Sharp. 'In the 1980s life for manufacturing companies became much more competitive. It will become even more so in this decade. We have got to ensure that the company can respond quickly and effectively.'

4 **Now read the text and summarise the main points under the following headings.**

- the thinking behind Impact
- why Impact was necessary
- how Impact was developed
- Impact's main features
- the timetable for change
- the impact of Impact

VOCABULARY 1

Complete the following sentences with appropriate words from the box. Text 1 will help you.

consultative process	core jobs	employment culture
human resources	industrial relations	job evaluation
market rate	performance payments	reward policy
union resistance	shop stewards	white collar

1 Frank Sharp is head of .... at Ilford.
2 The Impact programme is an attempt to change the company's ....
3 The new system of pay was only agreed after a long .... involving employees, union officials and managers.
4 After identifying a number of .... within the company, Ilford was able to work out a fairer system of pay.
5 Under the new pay system, some workers had lower salaries. Naturally, this led to .... at first.
6 Employees who are also union officials are known as .... – they are used to negotiating with management.
7 Before management can decide what a job is worth, they must have some system of ....
8 In the past, ... in Britain have been characterised by bitter fights between unions and management.
9 The unions which represent the interests of office workers are known as .... unions. What are the unions representing factory workers called?
10 Workers generally become unhappy if they know they're being paid below the .... for their job.
11 The .... at Ilford is based, to a large extent, on how well the employee performs in the job. Personal development discussions are a key element of the system.
12 The company's new grade structure allows for annual .... for every employee.

LANGUAGE PRACTICE 1

Spelling

Identify and correct the eight common spelling errors in the following sentences.

1 Ilford manafactures photographic equipment.
2 Shop stewards frequently have to negociate with management.
3 The level of responsability of each job will be taken into account.
4 Management tried hard to accomodate the views of their workers.
5 The personel department took each employee's perscnal development seriously.
6 In the past, the company put most effort into enginering and science.
7 The proccess of change is often slow.
8 Workers at Ilford are payed in line with market rates.

Phrasal verbs: 'take'

Match the verbs (1-8) with their correct definitions. Then answer the questions that follow (9-16).

1 to take aback	a) to make a written note of something
2 to take down	b) to start doing something which someone else began
3 to take in	c) to shock/surprise
4 to take (time) off	d) to hire/employ
5 to take on	e) to behave badly toward someone even though it is not that person's fault that you are upset
6 to take up	f) to stay away from work for a short period
7 to take over	g) to deceive
8 to take out on	h) to pursue

9 In what business situation might an employee be completely taken aback?
10 Why is it important not to be taken in when you are interviewing someone for a position?
11 What is a good reason for taking time off work? And a bad reason?
12 In what sort of economic conditions do companies take on additional workers? And when do they lay off employees?
13 If your boss gave you a hard time, who would you take it out on?
14 Who usually takes over if the chairman of a company falls ill?
15 What do firms usually take up before they employ you?
16 Who usually takes down the minutes of a meeting?

LISTENING 1

You are going to hear John Lawrence, Human Resources Manager at Ilford Ltd., talking about Impact. From what you know of the programme already, try to predict how he might answer the following questions. Then listen and note what he actually says.

1 What are you trying to change?
2 How are you going about this?
3 How far have you got?

LISTENING 2

Listen to the second part of the interview with John Lawrence and make notes under the following headings.

- the immediate and long-term future
- the current position
- the process of change
- the Ilford culture

Making an impact on people – Ilford UK

WRITING 1

Use your notes from Listening 1 and 2 to write a brief follow-up article to Text 1, updating readers on developments at Ilford.

TEXT 2

1   **Before you read the article, study the three charts below and answer the following questions. Then make up some questions of your own about the charts to ask each other.**

1   In which managerial functions can you find the highest percentage of women directors?
2   What are the two main factors which make women feel unequal to men at work?
3   Which sector has the highest number of women managers?
4   What percentage of senior managers in sales and marketing are women?
5   What percentage of women directors feel disadvantaged by domestic commitments?
6   Which three sectors have the smallest percentage of women managers?
7   What do these statistics say about career opportunities for women?
8   What do these statistics say about gender stereotypes?

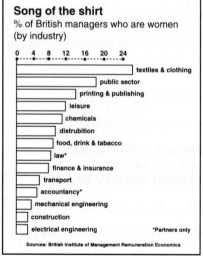

Song of the shirt
% of British managers who are women
(by industry)

0 4 8 12 16 20 24

- textiles & clothing
- public sector
- printing & publishing
- leisure
- chemicals
- distrubition
- food, drink & tabacco
- law*
- finance & insurance
- transport
- accountancy*
- mechanical engineering
- construction
- electrical engineering   *Partners only

Sources: British Institute of Management Remuneration Economics

© The Economist

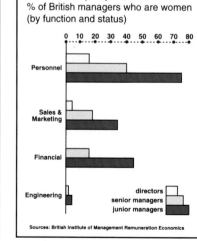

Good with people
% of British managers who are women
(by function and status)

0 10 20 30 40 50 60 70 80

Personnel

Sales & Marketing

Financial

Engineering   □ directors
                     ▨ senior managers
                     ■ junior managers

Sources: British Institute of Management Remuneration Economics

© The Economist

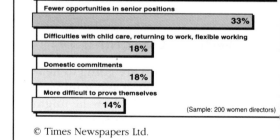

WHAT MAKES WOMEN FEEL UNEQUAL

Male attitudes   37%

Fewer opportunities in senior positions   33%

Difficulties with child care, returning to work, flexible working   18%

Domestic commitments   18%

More difficult to prove themselves   14%

(Sample: 200 women directors)

© Times Newspapers Ltd.

The spare sex

WOMEN IN MANAGEMENT

Few women get far in business. That is not just their loss, but their employers'. Hire women managers, promote them, create the right conditions to keep them, and companies will see the results on the bottom line. In black

1 Though women make up over 40% of the western workforce, the firms they work for promote very few of them far. In America and Britain alike, women hold about 2% of big-company board
5 seats. Where women do get to run big companies, it is not by climbing the ordinary corporate ladder. The lone female chief executive of a *Fortune* 500 company, Marion Sandler, of Golden West Financial, a Californian
10 savings bank, shares the post with her husband. They bought the bank together. Katharine Graham, chief executive of The Washington Post Company until taking the chairmanship last year, inherited the firm from her father.

15 Talented women are not the only losers when companies fail to hire them or later refuse them promotion. Assuming that most women are potentially as good at filling executive jobs as most men (quite a big if; we come to it later),
20 those companies are limiting their pool of available management talent by around half. Of recent graduates, 52% in America and 44% in Europe are women. The company that fails to recruit them now will find its pool of middle
25 managers inferior to that of a wiser employer in a few years' time; likewise, which matters more, its upper management ten years later, if (as is likely) it goes on displaying the same bias further up the ladder.

30 A 1990 survey of women quitting large companies, carried out by Wick, a Delaware consultancy, found that only 7% wanted to stop working altogether. The rest planned to join other firms, to work as freelance consultants, or
35 to start their own businesses. When BP carried out a similar exercise among graduate trainees recently, the leading reason women gave for going was not marriage or motherhood, but dissatisfaction with their career prospects. At
40 one Johnson & Johnson unit, departing female managers complained that they had felt isolated from their male colleagues.

Fellows like us

Could it be that this lack of esteem is justified?
45 Given the chance, would women really be as good at running large firms as men? Most research on the way gender differences affect women's careers lies within the murky disciplines of comparative psychology and
50 organisational behaviour. A lot of what it says is too contradictory or anecdotal (or sometimes obviously biased from the outset) to carry much weight. Yet some findings ring true.

First, people who work in large organisations
55 have an innate tendency to hire and promote those who resemble themselves. 'Our managers are all white, middle-aged men, and they promote in their own image,' says one woman.

If looking odd in positions of power is
60 women's first big barrier to top jobs, feeling odd in them is the second. 'People come up to you at a party, and say "Aren't you bright?" It isn't a compliment,' says a female director at a London investment bank. Men are expected to be
65 assertive. Women are not, and often do not feel happy being so.

Made to choose between being thought pushy and being actually self-effacing, women tend to choose the latter. Within mixed groups,
70 even highly qualified women put their views less forcefully than men, and listen much more than they talk. Strident counter-examples – Margaret Thatcher is an obvious one – leap to mind just because they are so rare.

75 In one study, researchers taped seven university faculty meetings. With one exception, the men taking part spoke more often and at greater length than their female colleagues.

Slow change

80 Senior managers' attitudes to women's employment are changing more slowly than corporate image-makers would have you believe. Women's employment 'is much like the environment – it's seen as essentially a window-
85 dressing question,' says one senior woman executive about her bosses. 'If [stockmarket] analysts or anyone who mattered cared about it, then they would care too.'

Tokenism abounds. Such female directors as
90 there are are disproportionately likely to be found running bits of the firm without profit-and-loss responsibility – personnel or public relations, for instance – that offer little prospect of promotion to the top posts. Alternatively, they
95 may be part-time advisers. Of the 30 female directors on the boards of Britain's biggest 100 companies, 26 are non-executives.

It can be done

If a firm does genuinely want to use the talents of
100 women more effectively, how should it go about it? The watershed dividing different employers' approaches is positive discrimination. Some use quota schemes. At Pitney Bowes, an American office-equipment manufacturer, 35% of all
105 promotions must go to women, 15% to non-whites. Some companies even tie managers' pay to their fulfilment of such schemes.

Positive discrimination can hurt the women it is designed to help. Bosses compelled to hire
110 women to fulfil some quota are unlikely to take them seriously. 'If you feel people are just there because you had to have them, then you work around them, not with them. Then they feel under-utilised, because they probably are,' says
115 Nancy Gheen, a personnel manager at Monsanto.

Organise accordingly

The real change in the way companies think about women managers will come when they
120 change the way they think about jobs.

Most women want to have children. Raising a family requires time off, and shorter working hours, for somebody, either husband or wife. To keep good women, firms need to find ways of
125 giving them those things, yet using them efficiently. That normally involves letting women with small children work flexible hours, not requiring them to relocate or travel at a moment's notice, or even letting them share
130 their jobs with someone else.

In exchange, women may have to accept lower pay, or slower promotion, until they return to full-time work. Such programmes have been dubbed 'mommy-tracks'.

135 Companies exist to make their shareholders money, not to engineer social change. Though mommy-tracks are to firms' ultimate advantage, since they help keep good staff, in the short term they will sometimes prove to be inconvenient
140 and expensive. In the irritation of having to change their ways, employers should not forget to take into account the costs of turnover among employees. Part of the money spent training those who leave has gone down the drain.
145 And back-of-the-envelope calculation of the costs of replacing a manager of ten years' standing, earning $70,000, suggests that the time it takes the new manager to get fully on top of the job is worth $25,000. If a replacement has
150 been sought from outside, headhunters' fees, advertising and interviewing could double that.

Sisters, chief executives, your interests coincide. One day your identities might too.

2   Read paragraphs 1-3 and complete the following statistics.

1   Women make up more than .... of the western workforce, but, in the US as in the UK, hold just .... of seats on the boards of large companies.

2   Women account for .... of recent graduates in the US and .... of recent graduates in Europe.

3   A survey carried out by Wick revealed that .... of women leaving large companies left not because they wanted to stop work but because ....

3   The rest of the text is divided into four sections, each with a separate heading. Read each section in turn, noting the main points in the following chart. When you have finished, compare your notes in small groups.

FELLOWS LIKE US
SLOW CHANGE
IT CAN BE DONE
ORGANISE ACCORDINGLY

Presentations

How does the position of women in the US/UK compare with the position of women in your country? How do you feel about opportunities for women? Working in pairs, make mini-presentations to each other on one of the following topics. Feel free to state your personal opinion and use your notes from Text 2 to help you.

- The role of women in management.
- Managerial prospects for women.
- The employment of women – past, present and future.

10

LANGUAGE PRACTICE 2

Conditional sentences

Study the following pairs of sentences, paying particular attention to the type of conditional used (first, second, third or 'mixed'). How does the second sentence in each pair differ in meaning from the first?

1 ■ 'Assuming that most women are potentially as good at filling executive jobs as men . . ., those companies are limiting their pool of available management talent by around half.' (lines 17-21)
  ■ If most women were potentially as good as men at filling executive posts, companies would be limiting their pool of available management talent by around half.

2 ■ 'Given the chance, would women really be as good at running large firms as men?' (lines 45-46)
  ■ If women have the chance, will they really be as good at running large firms as men?

3 ■ 'If looking odd in positions of power is women's first big barrier to top jobs, feeling odd in them is second.' (lines 59-61)
  ■ If looking odd in positions of power is women's first big barrier to top jobs, feeling odd in them would be second.

4 ■ 'Made to choose between being thought pushy and being actually self-effacing, women tend to choose the latter.' (lines 67-69)
  ■ If women are made to choose between being thought pushy and being actually self-effacing, women have tended to choose the latter.

5 ■ 'If stockmarket analysts . . . cared about it, then (senior managers) would care too.' (lines 86-88)
  ■ If stockmarket analysts had cared about it, then senior managers would have done too.

6 ■ 'If a firm does genuinely want to use the talents of women more effectively, how should it go about it?' (lines 99-101)
  ■ If a firm does genuinely want to use the talents of women more effectively, how will it go about it?

VOCABULARY 2

Working in pairs, discuss the meaning of the underlined words.

1 'Where women do get to run big companies, it is not by climbing the ordinary corporate ladder.' (lines 6-7)
2 'Men are expected to be assertive.' (line 65)
3 'Made to choose between being thought pushy and being actually self-effacing, women tend to choose the latter.' (line 68)
4 'Strident counter-examples . . . leap to mind just because they are so rare.' (line 72)
5 'Women's employment "is much like the environment – it's seen as essentially a window-dressing question."' (lines 84-85)
6 'Tokenism abounds.' (line 89)
7 'The watershed dividing different employers' approaches is positive discrimination.' (line 102)
8 'And back-of-the-envelope calculation of the costs of replacing a manager . . . suggests that the time it takes the new manager to get fully on top of the job is worth $25,000.' (lines 145 and 148-149)

CASE STUDY

For Manfred Englemann, Managing Director of a Swiss-based chemical company, the appointment of a Regional Marketing Manager for Asia was proving rather difficult. At first, it had all seemed fairly straightforward. Johann Straub appeared to be the logical and safe person for the job. He was hard-working, dependable and experienced. You wouldn't expect fireworks from him, but he wouldn't let you down.

However, not all the directors shared Manfred's opinion. When he suggested Johann Straub to them several raised objections. He 'wasn't up to the job'. He 'lacked drive'. 'I think Gail Partington would be a much better candidate,' said Jean-Claude Longaud, Personnel Director. To Manfred's surprise, several other directors nodded their agreement.

Gail Partington was an American national who had made a big impression at the company in a short time. Given the Scandinavian market to look after, she'd built up business there so quickly that the area now made a substantial contribution to group profits. There was no doubt she wanted the Asian position – she'd told most people that already, and hinted that, if she didn't get it, she might have to leave the company.

The mention of Gail Partington was not exactly music to Manfred's ears. He considered Gail an ambitious woman who could be rather disruptive if she didn't get her way.

'I should point out,' said Manfred, 'we've always had a policy of not sending women to Asia. In my opinion, it's a sensible policy. I'm not saying Gail isn't qualified for the job – clearly she is. But this is a very sensitive position. If we put the right person in charge, this area could become our most profitable market. I've nothing against Gail, but she is rather . . . how shall we say . . . direct. She likes to say what she thinks.'

'You mean she's honest and sincere, don't you?' cut in Jean-Claude Longaud.

'If you wish,' replied Manfred, a little irritated by the interruption. 'The point I was making was that if we send Johann Straub, we'll be sending a good man to do the job, and we wouldn't have to worry about the cultural problem – Straub would be accepted wherever he went. Right?'

Manfred needed support and he got it from Pieter Junker, Technical Director. 'There is the added problem with Gail that she's part of a dual-career family – her husband's a pretty successful photographer.'

'That's no problem,' said Jean-Claude. 'I know for a fact that he supports her completely, he won't hold her back if she wants to go. He'll go too, and so will the children – they're very young.'

Manfred shook his head, unconvinced. 'The husband and children may hate Japan once they get there. The point is, surely, that all the countries she'll be working in are male-dominated. People there aren't used to seeing women in important positions, they wouldn't know how to cope with someone like Gail as Regional Marketing Manager. She might be all right looking after existing business, but what about getting new business?'

'She did all right in Scandinavia,' pointed out Tony Simmons, Marketing Director. 'If she could repeat that performance in Asia . . .'

'Come on now,' said Pieter Junker, 'you can't compare the two markets. In Scandinavia, there're loads of women in top positions. Of course Gail's not out of place there, but in Asia it's a different matter. Let's face it, Manfred's right. Johann Straub is our only realistic choice.'

Manfred Englemann gave his friend a grateful glance. 'Thanks Pieter for seeing it my way. I know there's a risk we may lose Gail if she isn't chosen, but is Asia right for her?'

It was Jean-Claude who answered. 'We'll never know, will we, unless we send her there. So let's risk it.'

Manfred looked hard at Jean-Claude. There was a short silence. Then he smiled, a little ruefully. 'You've always been rather impulsive, Jean-Claude, but I suppose that's part of your charm. I prefer to make a reasoned choice, though – if you don't mind.'

Discussion

Working in pairs or small groups, discuss the following questions.

1 Is the company's policy of not appointing women to posts in Asia acceptable?
2 Would Asian businessmen feel uncomfortable if they had to deal with a female regional manager?
3 What are the main arguments for appointing Johann Straub? And Gail Partington?
4 Who should be appointed to the position?
   a) Johann
   b) Gail
   c) someone else

Role-play: Meeting

Manfred Englemann arranges a meeting with Gail Partington to explain – politely but firmly – why she is unsuitable for the position in Asia. Gail Partington, on the other hand, is determined to persuade Manfred that she is not only suitable, but the best person for the job! Working in pairs, role-play the meeting between Manfred Englemann and Gail Partington.

WRITING 2

A group of young journalists is planning to launch a new consumer magazine called 'Ambition'. Aimed at women aged 20-40 who wish to have a professional career as well as a family, the magazine will give readers vital business information and practical advice on how to reach the top of the corporate ladder. You have been asked to produce a promotional leaflet introducing the new magazine and inviting readers to send in a coupon entitling them to a substantial discount on the first three issues. Every coupon received will also be entered in a 'lucky draw' offering some fabulous prizes.

11

Team-Building

INTRODUCTION

1 John Nicolson is one of Britain's leading experts on the skills involved in running businesses and getting the best out of the people who work in them. To him, this depends totally on managers having the right relationship with the people they work with and those people in turn having a healthy attitude to their jobs and to themselves. So how do you see yourself? And how do other people see you?

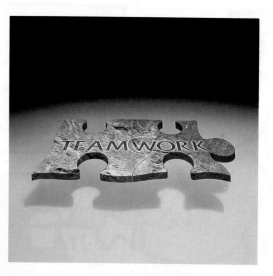

Write a brief profile of yourself (approximately five lines), outlining your personal qualities and highlighting any strengths and weaknesses you feel you have. Then write a brief profile of your partner, outlining his or her strengths and weaknesses as you see them. Use the list of personal qualities to help you. When you have finished, work with your partner and compare the profiles you have written. Discuss any differences between them and try to agree an 'accurate' profile of each other.

STRENGTHS		WEAKNESSES	
confident	thorough	arrogant	obsessive
enterprising	tolerant	opportunistic	uncaring
humorous	caring	frivolous	nosy
ambitious	prudent	ruthless	indecisive
helpful	focused	controlling	tunnel-visioned
forceful	supportive	bullying	interfering
competitive	generous	combative	irresponsible
open to change		wishy-washy	

2 Complete the following self-analysis questionnaire, designed by John Nicolson, and work out your score using the specified points system. Then compare results with your partner.

WHO DO YOU THINK YOU ARE?

		TRUE	FALSE
1	I reckon I can do things as well as most people	☑	☐
2	It's not easy being me	☐	☑
3	When I have to make a presentation, I'm terrified of making a fool of myself	☑	☐
4	It's not often that I think of myself as a failure	☑	☐
5	There are lots of things about myself I'd change if I could	☑	☐
6	I am rarely bothered by other people's criticism	☐	☑
7	Other people tend to be more well-liked than I am	☐	☑
8	If I have something to say, I usually go ahead and say it	☑	☐
9	I don't often feel ashamed of anything I have done	☐	☑
10	When people say complimentary things about me I find it hard to believe they really mean it.	☐	☑

Score two points for each 'True' answer to questions 1, 4, 6, 8 and 9; score zero for every 'False' answer. For questions 2, 3, 5, 7 and 10, score two points for each 'False' answer; score zero for each 'True' answer.

The higher your score, the better the opinion you have of yourself. A score of 14 or more suggests that you are quite confident; not necessarily conceited, but you certainly like yourself well enough, and there's no danger of other people being made to feel uncomfortable by any signs of self-loathing in you.

A score of 8 or less suggests that you have serious doubts about yourself and your value to the world. It may of course be a temporary state of affairs – perhaps the result of some recent misfortune. But if this is your normal condition, other people are bound to pick it up, and the risk is that they will accept your low estimate of yourself and hence find it difficult to respect you.

3   What do you think?

1   What personal qualities are essential in a good manager?
2   What professional skills/abilities are essential in a good manager?
3   What approach to people should a good manager have?

TEXT 1

1   In its analysis, the article on page 106 lists eight characteristics of 'great managers'. Before you read, try to predict what they might be. Scan the text quickly to see if your predictions were accurate.

2   Read the text and decide which of the following comments you would expect the writer to agree with. Use the text to support your answers.

Successful managers . . .

1   are happy when their staff make progress in the company.
2   try to be positive even when times are difficult.
3   tell head office if any of their staff make mistakes.
4   praise their staff as often as they can.
5   encourage employees to speak out if they are unhappy.
6   make sure they know what's going on outside their organisation.
7   keep in touch with their staff and customers.
8   never dislike any member of their staff.
9   concentrate on their employees' strong points and try to correct their weak ones.
10 ignore people's weak points, pretending they don't exist.
11 enjoy new challenges.
12 don't find it easy to delegate responsibility.

How to be a great manager

[1] AT THE MOST general level, successful managers tend to have four characteristics:

- they take enormous pleasure and pride in the growth of their people;
[5] - they are basically cheerful optimists – someone has to keep up morale when setbacks occur;
- they don't promise more than they can deliver;
[10] - when they move on from a job, they always leave the situation a little better than it was when they arrived.

The following is a list of some essential tasks at which a manager must excel to be truly [15] effective.

Great managers accept blame: When the big wheel from head office visits and expresses displeasure, the great manager immediately accepts full responsibility. In everyday working [20] life, the best managers are constantly aware that they selected and should have developed their people. Errors made by team members are in a very real sense their responsibility.

Great managers give praise: Praise is [25] probably the most under-used management tool. Great managers are forever trying to catch their people doing something right, and congratulating them on it. And when praise comes from outside, they are swift not merely to publicise the fact, [30] but to make clear who has earned it. Managers who regularly give praise are in a much stronger position to criticise or reprimand poor

performance. If you simply comment when you are dissatisfied with performance, it is all too [35] common for your words to be taken as a straightforward expression of personal dislike.

Great managers make blue sky: Very few people are comfortable with the idea that they will be doing exactly what they are doing today [40] in 10 years' time. Great managers anticipate people's dissatisfaction.

Great managers put themselves about: Most managers now accept the need to find out not merely what their team is thinking, but what the [45] rest of the world, including their customers, is saying. So MBWA (management by walking about) is an excellent thing, though it has to be distinguished from MBWAWP (management by walking about – without purpose), where senior [50] management wander aimlessly, annoying customers, worrying staff and generally making a nuisance of themselves.

Great managers judge on merit: A great deal more difficult than it sounds. It's virtually [55] impossible to divorce your feelings about someone – whether you like or dislike them – from how you view their actions. But suspicions of discrimination or favouritism are fatal to the smooth running of any team, so the great [60] manager accepts this as an aspect of the game that really needs to be worked on.

Great managers exploit strengths, not weaknesses, in themselves and in their people: Weak managers feel threatened by other people's

[65] strengths. They also revel in the discovery of weakness and regard it as something to be exploited rather than remedied. Great managers have no truck with this destructive thinking. They see strengths, in themselves as well as [70] in other people, as things to be built on, and weakness as something to be accommodated, worked around and, if possible, eliminated.

Great managers make things happen: The [75] old-fashioned approach to management was rather like the old-fashioned approach to child-rearing: 'Go and see what the children are doing and tell them to stop it!' Great managers have confidence that their people will be working in [80] their interests and do everything they can to create an environment in which people feel free to express themselves.

Great managers make themselves redundant: Not as drastic as it sounds! What great managers [85] do is learn new skills and acquire useful information from the outside world, and then immediately pass them on, to ensure that if they were to be run down by a bus, the team would still have the benefit of the new information. No [90] one in an organisation should be doing work that could be accomplished equally effectively by someone less well paid than themselves. So great managers are perpetually on the look-out for higher-level activities to occupy their own time, [95] while constantly passing on tasks that they have already mastered.

© The Independent

VOCABULARY

1   **Finish the list of adverbs. Then, using each adverb once only, complete the sentences that follow.**

adjective	adverb
basic	basically
common	....
constant	....
full	*fully*
true	*truly*
virtual	....

1 There are .... *virtually* no women in top positions at our company.
2 ....*basically*...., a good manager is someone who knows how to handle staff well.
3 It is ....*commonly*...... believed that leaders are born not made.
4 In business, you need to be ....*fully*.......... aware of what your competitors are doing.
5 We have quite a reputation for our innovative approach to product design – we are ...*constantly*.../ on the lookout for new ideas.
6 I am ....*truly*........ delighted to hear of your promotion – it is well deserved.

2 The following pair of words are frequently confused. Choose the correct word to complete each sentence. Then write sentences of your own to illustrate the meaning of the other five words.

> ensure; assure
> dissatisfied; unsatisfied
> effective; efficient
> morale; moral
> criticism; critic

(handwritten notes: make sure; make sb comfortable, feel sure; not satisfied; stronger, very unhappy; quickly, more than effective; feeling, way of behaviour, principles; disapproval, person who give negative opinion)

1 A good manager will .... that his staff have an opportunity to express their opinions.
2 In my opinion, the demand for this product is still largely ....
3 The new machine is very .... – it is quick, clean and very economical to run.
4 The .... of the story is that if you must dismiss someone, you had better do it quickly.
5 Our new advertisements have come in for a lot of .... – many people consider they are in poor taste.

LANGUAGE PRACTICE

'If only ... .'

Study these examples. Then, working in pairs, practise making excuses and giving advice. Use the phrase *'if only ...'* to discuss the complaints that follow. (For more help on giving advice, see page 78.)

A 'There just aren't enough hours in the day to do all the things I have to do. **If only** I had more time ...'
B 'Well, why don't you manage your time better? If I were you, I'd delegate more of my work.'

A 'I always have far too much to do, but I never get paid overtime. **If only** I wasn't so overworked and underpaid ...'
B 'It might be an idea to think about employing a secretary. And you should try saying 'no' when your boss gives you more work to do. Maybe you could ask for a rise, too.'

1 'My staff never seem to listen to me, so they always get things wrong. I spend hours each day telling them how to do things properly.'
2 'Head office is always cutting my budget. I never have enough money to do anything properly.'
3 'They never let me run things my way. Someone's always checking up on me. If it isn't head office, it's that regional manager who's always on my back.'
4 'I'm always being interrupted in my office when I have an important call, or when I want to get down to writing a report.'
5 'The paperwork is unbelievable. I'm up to my eyes in it. I have to read through a stack of papers in my in-tray every morning.'
6 'They're always moving the goalposts. They give me a sales target to meet, then they raise it three months later.'
7 'I wish someone would tell me what's going on in this place. I'm always the last to know about any new policy.'
8 'My area manager never praises me. I'd like more feedback from him. A pat on the back now and then. Frankly, I've no idea what he thinks of my work.'

■■■■■ **TEXT 2**

Read the text and study the chart. Then, working in pairs, try to decide which of Dr Belbin's personality type(s) you represent.

Successful teams

One of the most important functions of a manager is to build a team which will perform effectively and contribute to the success of a business.

The art of team-building has been studied by many people, but possibly the most interesting work on the subject has been done by Dr Meredith Belbin. His original insight has been to identify the individual roles which are crucial to a successful team. He argues that while individuals in a management group have their formal job titles – accountant, designer, marketing director, production manager, etc. – they also perform a variety of 'personality team roles': the ideas person, the organiser, the unorthodox genius, the stickler for detail, the diplomat, and so on.

Dr Belbin's team-role theory states that there are nine key personality types and a team will work most effectively if it has them all. However, a successful team need not be made up of nine members since some people may be more than one personality type. Thus a team of three could work together very successfully if, among them, the members combined the nine personality types.

USEFUL PEOPLE TO HAVE IN TEAMS

Type	Symbol	Typical Features	Positive Qualities	Allowable Weaknesses
Company Worker	CW	Conservative, dutiful, predictable.	Organising ability, practical common sense, hard-working, self-discipline.	Lack of flexibility, unresponsiveness to unproven ideas.
Chairman	CH	Calm, self-confident, controlled.	A capacity for treating and welcoming all potential contributors on their merits and without prejudice. A strong sense of objectives.	No more than ordinary in terms of intellect or creative ability.
Shaper	SH	Highly strung, outgoing, dynamic.	Drive and a readiness to challenge inertia, ineffectiveness, complacency or self-deception.	Proneness to provocation, irritation and impatience.
Plant	PL	Individualistic, serious-minded, unorthodox.	Genius, imagination, intellect, knowledge.	Up in the clouds, inclined to disregard practical details or protocol.
Resource Investigator	RI	Extroverted, enthusiastic, curious, communicative.	A capacity for contacting people and exploring anything new. An ability to respond to challenge.	Liable to lose interest once the initial fascination has passed.
Monitor-Evaluator	ME	Sober, unemotional, prudent.	Judgement, discretion, hard-headedness.	Lacks inspiration or the ability to motivate others.
Team Worker	TW	Socially-orientated, rather mild, sensitive.	An ability to respond to people and to situations, and to promote team spirit.	Indecisiveness at moments of crisis.
Completer-Finisher	CF	Painstaking, orderly, conscientious, anxious.	A capacity for follow-through. Perfectionism.	A tendency to worry about small things. A reluctance to let go.
Specialist	SP	Single-minded, self-starting.	Brings knowledge or skills in rare supply.	Contributes only on narrow front.

The perfect team . . .

Simulation: Team-building

Form management 'teams' of at least three but no more than nine people. Elect a leader and discuss the personality composition of your team, using Dr Belbin's classification. Summarise your collective strengths and weaknesses on paper. Then try to 'complete' your management team by headhunting the personality type(s) you lack from the other teams.

LISTENING

You are going to hear Peter Wallum, Director of Strategic People, talking about people management. Listen and take notes under the following headings.

- Strategic People
- team-building: obstacles and problems
- management training
- 'Dilemma'
- the ideal team
- culture
- mavericks

Dilemma

Pan-European Teamwork

Slowly they entered the room in ones and twos, anxiously looking for familiar faces. Some took refuge in intense conversation to avoid the searching eyes of strangers. Others were preoccupied rearranging papers.

The Scandinavians were the first to arrive, conspicuous in their plaid jackets and open-necked shirts. Exactly on the stroke of nine o'clock the Germans entered, debating with their Austrian colleagues. The US participants followed, introducing themselves to everyone they passed.

Then two hesitant figures in dark, pin-stripe suits filled the doorway, their formal handshakes unmistakably betraying them as the British representatives. The seats around the circle of tables were almost filled and the buzz of polite conversation began falling off when the Italian participants, dressed in fine tailored suits, were the last to arrive.

The group of managing and marketing directors from nine national subsidiaries of a large international company had gathered in a European capital city for a three-day meeting with a dual purpose.

Their primary task was to draw up a pan-European marketing strategy to exploit the EC's single market. The meeting was also seen as an opportunity for the executives to learn about working within a multicultural team, and to recognise how it differed from their team-working back home. I was one of two consultants assigned to facilitate the process and crystallise the learning.

As with many multicultural groups, the first difficulties emerged over language. The meeting was conducted in English, but not all the participants were equally fluent or confident about expressing themselves. Not surprisingly, native English speakers dominated the early discussions, until the facilitator asked others for their ideas.

This intervention, however, only exposed another cultural trait that impeded progress. Impatient with the time it took others to formulate their views, British and US participants frequently interrupted the long periods of silent contemplation with even more suggestions of their own. To construct coherent arguments in a non-native language takes time and requires concentration.

The use of only one language was the most obvious barrier to multicultural teamworking. As the first working session progressed, however, the comments made and ideas proposed revealed how unconscious cultural biases and corporate myths dominated the participants' thinking.

French executives argued for their proposal, since it was manifestly the most logical. No, said the Germans, their approach should be endorsed because it was technically superior and had a proven track record. No one gave serious consideration to the Danish proposal. The ideas produced by the Italians were seen as elegant and seductive, but impractical.

The members of this multicultural team, brought together for the first time, reacted like all human beings: In the absence of more reliable information, they made liberal use of preconceived stereotypes about the nations they did not know. Or where they had some experience, they generalised by using one past incident to predict the behaviour of that nationality.

Like 'groupthink', where all members of a team home in on one powerfully argued but possibly flawed idea, this multicultural team was taking refuge in simplistic stereotypes and over-generalisations.

To address this obstacle to effective teamworking, time was taken to learn about the characteristic behaviour of the nations present. Each national group had to act as informants on their own culture, and heard how their cultural behaviour influenced the perceptions and attitudes of others.

This cathartic activity produced much laughter. The linear, time-conscious Northern Europeans discovered the mysteries of their Latin colleagues' flexible

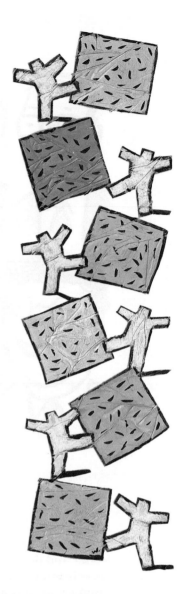

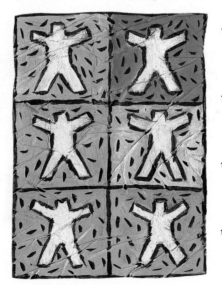

approach to time and capacity to deal with several projects simultaneously. The Anglo-Saxons learned about alternatives to adversarial relationships in industry from the consensus-orientated Scandinavian managers.

Each group explored the emphasis it placed upon personal relationships in getting things done, cultural preferences for long-term outcomes and the importance attached to being liked, a theme that proved sensitive for many of the executives.

Many significant messages and difficult observations were delivered in jest and mimicry throughout the remainder of the meeting. But all the participants acknowledged the pain of learning, and the importance of more accurate perceptions in putting together a draft marketing strategy.

Yes, they agreed, it might need more work, but their future efforts would be less likely to be side-tracked by superficial differences of culture.

TEXT 3

Read the article by Robert J Brown, director (Europe) of Moran, Stahl & Boyer, specialists in intercultural management and note the key points under the following headings.
- the problems of working in multicultural groups
- how cultural pre-conceptions affect people's views and attitudes
- overcoming obstacles to effective teamwork

WRITING 1

The international construction company you work for frequently sends small mixed-nationality project teams overseas. During these assignments, team members spend a lot of time together and have to co-operate closely with each other. As a senior member of the Personnel Department, you have been asked to draft some guidelines to help project members work more effectively as a team. Your guidelines should outline the kind of problems mixed-nationality project teams might face and offer some practical advice on how to overcome them. Use your notes on Text 3 to help you.

CASE STUDY

Universal Systems PLC specialises in computing and office automation systems for the financial services sector. Dennis Mitchell, the company's top salesman and an outstanding systems analyst, had always been a difficult person to manage, but his unconventional behaviour was starting to cause real problems at the firm.

1   Listen to Dialogue 1 between Managing Director, Jack Cooper, and Technical Director, Philip Seymour and note the main points.

Dennis Mitchell was an exceptionally brilliant student at university, graduating in computer science with first class honours. After leaving university, he worked briefly for a scientific research institute, then left and spent the next 18 months travelling around the world. He then joined Universal Systems PLC as a salesman. He was top salesman in his first year and within three years was earning more than everybody else in the firm thanks to the performance-related commission system.

2   Listen to Dialogue 2 between Jack Cooper and Dennis Mitchell and note the main points.

Unfortunately Jack Cooper's conversation with Dennis made very little difference: not only did Dennis continue to behave inconsiderately towards his colleagues, he became more and more erratic. Having demanded his own office space partitioned off from the rest of the sales team, he started playing his radio loudly because it helped him to be 'creative'. Then, one day without warning, he disappeared for almost a week and no one had any idea where he was. When he finally turned up it was to announce that he had clinched a major deal with a prominent Saudi Arabian bank which the company had been pursuing for some time. He was very pleased with himself, but no one else was.

3   Listen to Dialogue 3 between Jack Cooper, Robert Barrett, Personnel Director, and Heather Crompton, Head of Sales and note the main points.

It's time for Jack Cooper to have another talk with Dennis Mitchell.

Discussion

Divide into two groups according to whether you will role-play Dennis Mitchell or Jack Cooper in the negotiation that follows. Discuss the situation at Universal Systems PLC and analyse your position.

Group 1: Dennis Mitchell
Decide on three reasons for staying at the company, two reasons for being uncertain whether to stay or leave, and one reason for leaving the company.

Group 2: Jack Cooper
Decide on three reasons for keeping Dennis Mitchell, two reasons for being uncertain whether he should stay or leave, and one reason for getting rid of him.

Role-play: Negotiation

Work in pairs, one of you playing Dennis Mitchell, the other playing Jack Cooper. Read your role-card and prepare for the negotiation carefully. Try to agree a workable arrangement that will resolve the situation.

Dennis Mitchell
You want to stay at Universal Systems but not at any price. Think carefully about your objectives/strategy. Drawing on your group discussion, draft your negotiating position on paper, outlining the concessions you want from the company – and the concessions you are prepared to make. Try to reach an agreement with Jack Cooper.

Jack Cooper
Universal Systems is prepared to keep Dennis Mitchell, but not at any price. Think carefully about your objectives/strategy. Drawing on your group discussion, draft your negotiating position on paper, outlining the concessions you want from Dennis Mitchell – and the concessions you are prepared to make. Try to reach an agreement with Dennis Mitchell.

WRITING 2

Write a follow-up letter to either Dennis Mitchell or Jack Cooper, summarising the results of your negotiation. The tone of your letter should reflect whether your meeting was successful or not from your point of view.

Meetings

INTRODUCTION

1   **Discuss the following questions.**
1   What are the main reasons for holding a meeting?
2   What is the role of the chairperson?
3   Why are so many meetings unsuccessful?

2   **Describe a meeting that you have attended recently. How effective was it and why?**

VOCABULARY

Complete the following sentences with appropriate words from the list.

agenda	casting vote	consensus	minutes	circulate
apologies	chairperson	items	arising	conduct

1   In all formal meetings and most informal meetings, there is a .... whose job it is to .... the business of the meeting and to ensure that the meeting's objectives are achieved.
2   It is helpful in both formal and informal meetings to have an ...., listing the points that are to be discussed. It is usual to .... this in advance so that participants can prepare adequately for the meeting.
3   If there are too many .... on the agenda, it is inevitable that the meeting will be over-long and so less effective.
4   After formal meetings, the secretary writes up the ...., an official record of the discussion that has taken place.
5   If you cannot attend a meeting, it is customary to send your .... to the chairperson, who reads out the names of any absentees at the beginning of the meeting. After naming absentees, the chairperson may ask if there are any matters .... out of the minutes of the last meeting.
6   When decisions must be taken, the chairperson hopes there will be a .... on what should be done. Otherwise, a vote must be taken and sometimes the votes for and against are equal. If this happens, the only way to break the deadlock is for the chairperson to give his or her ....

Make meetings work for you

Preparation is the key to success

1 Do you dread meetings more than Monday mornings? Do you find them boring, unproductive and far too long? Meetings are central to most organisations; people need to 5 know what their colleagues are doing and then take decisions based on shared information and opinions. How well you present yourself and your ideas, and how well you work with other people, is crucial to 10 your career.

RUNNING A MEETING

Only call a meeting if you (and your colleagues) are quite clear about its purpose. Once you are certain of your objective, ask 15 yourself whether it could be better achieved through alternative means, such as a memo. Meetings called on a routine basis tend to lose their point. It's better to wait until a situation or problem requires a meeting. If in 20 doubt, don't waste time having one.

If you're sure a meeting is the solution, circulate a memo several days in advance specifying the time and place, objectives, issues to be discussed, other participants 25 and preparation expected. Meetings should be held in the morning, if possible, when people are usually more alert, and should last no more than an hour. Six is the optimum number of participants for a good 30 working meeting. Inviting the whole department (more than 10) increases emotional undercurrents such as, 'Will my suggestions be taken seriously?' Larger meetings can be productive as 35 brainstorming sessions for ideas, provided participants can speak freely without feeling they will be judged.

A successful meeting always leads to action. Decisions should take up the bulk of the 40 meeting minutes, including the name of the person delegated to each task, and a deadline for its completion. Circulate the minutes after the meeting and again just before the next one.

45 Draw out quieter members of the group. Encouragement helps create a relaxed and productive atmosphere. Do not single out any individual for personal criticism – they will either silently withdraw, upset and 50 humiliated, or try to come up with excuses rather than focusing on the problems in hand. Save critical comments for a private occasion.

If you're talking for more than 50 per cent of 55 the time, you're dominating the meeting.

ATTENDING A MEETING

However informal the meeting, it always pays to prepare a few key points in note form to put across or discuss. If you're 60 unprepared, you will not be able to concentrate on what your colleagues are saying and others are less likely to listen to you because you will either waffle or sound hesitant.

65 Don't memorise notes or read them out like a sermon. This inhibits your natural gestures: the eye contact and body language that is essential to effective communication. If you cannot answer a question, don't be afraid 70 to say, 'I don't know but I'll find out and get back to you by . . .' (give a definite date). Phrase your criticisms and proposals positively. Seek to offer solutions rather than to complain.

75 Arrive early and sit close to the chairperson to ensure that you aren't ignored. If you're late, apologise and find a seat quickly and quietly. Don't try to sneak in as if you're invisible.

© Cosmopolitan

TEXT 1

Read the text and complete the following chart.

	DOs	DON'Ts
chairperson	1 have a clear purpose 2 .... 3 .... 4 .... 5 .... 6	1 go on for more than an hour 2 .... 3 .... 4 ....
participants	1 .... 2 .... 3 .... 4	1 .... 2 .... 3 sneak in if you're late

LISTENING 1

You are going to hear Roger Myddleton, Legal Director and Company Secretary at Grand Metropolitan, talking about meetings. Listen and take notes under the following headings.

- formal and informal meetings
- objectives
- chairing meetings
- mixed-nationality meetings
- participating in meetings
- minutes

WRITING 1

Using information from Text 1 and Listening 1, draw up a set of guidelines entitled 'How to hold a successful meeting'. It may help you to think in terms of the following areas.

- objectives
- the role of the chairperson
- the role of participants
- administrative considerations

LISTENING 2

The informal discussion you are going to hear takes place in an advertising agency and concerns Charles Drake, a copywriter who is to be made redundant. Frank Harrison, Account Director, Derek Jordan, Creative Director, and Jennifer Walton, Personnel Director, are meeting to decide when, where and how he should be told the news. Listen and note what they decide and why.

WRITING 2

Use your notes from Listening 2 to write the minutes of the meeting between Frank Harrison, Derek Jordan and Jennifer Walton.

LANGUAGE PRACTICE

Match each item on the left with the correct description on the right. Then use each phrase once only to complete the excerpts from Listening 2. When you have finished, listen again and check your answers.

I'm afraid I don't agree with you.	making a suggestion
Could I just come in here. . .?	reformulating
In other words. . .	moving to a new point
I absolutely agree.	giving an opinion
I think. . .	setting objectives
Let's recap.	asking for an opinion
How about. . .?	interrupting
What do you think. . .?	disagreeing
What we've got to do. . .	summarising
We ought to move on. . .	agreeing

Frank: Let's get started then. [1]................................... is, er, discuss how Derek's interview with Charlie should go . . .

Jennifer: Well, I think it's usually useful to break this kind of news midweek, rather than doing it on a Friday afternoon.

Frank: Certainly, [2]................................... . . .

Jennifer: . . . There should be a package we offer him, and quite a few details to sort out.

Frank: Yes certainly. Erm, I think [3]................................... now, so the next question is, erm, you know, how are we going to do it, and where? [4]..................................., Jennifer? . . .

Derek: . . . I haven't really thought this through, but, erm, I mean, [5]................................... it might be better to do it outside the office in a sense.

Jennifer: [6]................................... . It needs to be you in your managerial role, not you in your role as a personal friend. . . . I certainly think it should be done, er, somewhere in the office, and preferably in his office rather than in yours . . .

Frank: Well, [7]................................... a lunch, Derek, in a quiet pub or restaurant?

Derek: So, the in-between thing, it's a working lunch. It's work, but it's not in the office. It could be a compromise, yes.

Jennifer: Well, [8]................................... please? I tend to think it might be better if you did do it in the office . . .

Frank: I mean, Jennifer, you've had a lot of experience of this. How do people react when they . . .

Jennifer: People tend to be rather shocked, they tend to be angry, but rather briefly, and they do tend to . . .

Derek: [9]..................................., they're not able to formulate an immediate and rational response . . .

Frank: Give him the background.

Derek: Yes, I mean but briefly, you're saying that I should get to the point and say 'you know, Charlie, it has been decided that, basically, you are being made redundant, and the normal terms and conditions of our contract will apply . . .

Frank: Ok, so [10]................................... I think we're agreed, Derek, that you will actually be telling Charles . . .

Derek: Yes.

Frank: And that you'll do it, er, inside the company, and you'll do it probably in your office. Right?

Some useful language for participating in meetings

Giving an opinion

(strong) *I'm convinced we should use an agent.*
I'm sure the Japanese market has big potential.
I have no doubt the new factory will make life a lot easier.

(neutral) *I think we need a bigger sales force.*
As I see it, we must build up our middle management.
In my opinion, we should offer a bonus.

(tentative) *It seems to me we should try to diversify.*
I tend to think our designs are old-fashioned.
I feel our competitors are more market-orientated.

Agreeing

(strong) *I totally agree.*
I agree entirely with Peter.
I quite agree.
I couldn't agree more.
Absolutely!/Precisely!/ Exactly!

(neutral) *I agree with you.*
I think you're right.
That's true.

(tentative) *Mmm, maybe you're right.*
Perhaps.
I tend to agree.
I suppose so.

Checking comprehension/re-formulating

To put that another way, …
If I follow you correctly, …
So what you're saying is…
Does that mean…?
Are you saying…?

Expressing reservations

You have a point, but…
I agree to some extent, but…
I suppose you're right, but…
Maybe that's true, but…

Disagreeing

(strong) *I don't agree with you at all.*
I totally disagree.
You're quite wrong about that.
It's out of the question.
Of course not.
Rubbish!/Nonsense!/No way!

(neutral) *I don't really think so.*
I can't see that, I'm afraid.
I'm afraid I can't agree with you there.

(tentative) *Mmm, I'm not sure.*
I tend to disagree.
Do you really think so?
Is that such a good idea?

Making a suggestion

(neutral) *I suggest (that) we buy from the French supplier.*
I would suggest strengthening our management team.
My suggestion would be to spend more on R & D.

(tentative) *We could sell the business.*
Perhaps we should make a takeover bid.
It might be worth setting up a joint venture.
What about appointing a new agent?
Why don't we borrow some more money?

PITFALLS OF INTERNATIONAL MEETINGS

[1] More than six years ago the US futurist John Naisbitt wrote: '...the more technology in this society, the more people want to get together.' But even he could [5] not have envisaged the dramatic growth in the number of international meetings over the past few years.

Unique with all these meetings, which range in size from a few to more [10] than a thousand, is that many of the participants leave their culture to meet in another. Unfortunately, what is not unique is that many of the meetings fail to accomplish their objec- [15] tives to a very high degree.

The purposes of these meetings are varied, ranging from exchanging information to rewarding performance and creating opportuni- [20] ties for professional development. Often, as in the case of IBM Europe and other companies, the meetings are staged to introduce new products and [25] make a sales pitch to top customers. IBM tries to get its top customers away from their normal business environment and gather them in a location [30] that creates an atmosphere that 'puts them in the right frame of mind and then allows us to do some high level selling'.

During the past year, I [35] have attended a number of international meetings and witnessed first-hand serious administrative and planning problems, all of which undermined the chances of success.

[40] A classic bungle was the arrival of participants' material three days after one meeting ended. In another case, the audio visual equipment required by a presenter was delivered as the meeting [45] was ending. At yet another meeting, the audio visual equipment was the wrong format, and the presenter was unable to show his video tapes.

International meeting organizers are [50] sometimes guilty of even the most fundamental blunders. For example, at one meeting, pork was the only meat served to the many Moslems attending. At a three-day seminar, staged by an [55] American company, the absence of any scheduled social activities drew complaints from the many European participants.

Company gatherings often show the [60] most serious shortcomings. One very 'process' orientated meeting reflected the corporate culture. It encouraged small group discussions and group reports. Many of the participants wanted, [65] and were expecting, more formal presentations by senior executives.

International meetings can be costly to stage, especially if they are poorly or-

ganized and fail to achieve the desired [70] results. To have any chance of success, the foremost issue to consider is the purpose of the meeting. Only when that has been clearly articulated can organizers begin to plan the meeting and deter- [75] mine whether it has been a success.

At international meetings with participants from many different cultures, unique issues are bound to arise. For example, the timing of meals and the se- [80] lection of the menu, the listing of names and titles, the use and language of business cards, the necessity of interpreters or translators and getting materials through customs are all factors that [85] must be taken into account by the organizers.

It's especially important to allow participants who travel long distances sufficient time to rest, physically and mental- [90] ly, before the meeting begins. One large US-based organization ignores this completely, expecting travellers from Europe after a nine-hour-plus flight to attend a four-hour meeting the day they [95] arrive. The following day, meetings are scheduled to begin at 8 a.m. and continue until 10 p.m. Most European participants are exhausted by the demanding regime and find that [100] they benefit only marginally from the meetings.

A mini-checklist for any international meeting should begin with efforts to identify [105] the nationalities of potential participants and make provisions that cater to their specific cultural needs.

Warnings to avoid national [110] stereotypes, condescending attitudes and above all jokes, which are easily misunderstood, are among the tips given to organizers and speak- [115] ers at international meetings by Dr Ernest Dichter, a motivational psychologist. He suggests that honoured attendees should be welcomed and that, [120] when appropriate, deference should be shown to participants because of their high-ranking positions.

Speakers making presentations in English at an international meeting in [125] a country where it is not the national language, should tailor their presentation so that it will be understood by the entire audience. There are important considerations for persons respon- [130] sible for the introduction of speakers. For example, personal information or the sharing of insights about one's family life, which is common in North America, is not appropriate in Europe or [135] Asia.

TEXT 2

1 Before you read the article on the opposite page, think about the title and try to predict some of the 'pitfalls' the writer will mention. Then quickly scan the article to see how accurate your predictions were.

2 Read the article and note the key points under the following headings:
- recent trends in international meetings
- reasons for holding international meetings
- typical problems at international meetings
- avoiding the pitfalls of international meetings

DISCUSSION

What advice could you give an international conference organiser about the specific cultural needs of business people from your country and any other countries you know well? Work in small groups and outline your recommendations on paper.

SKILLS PRACTICE

Until three years ago, Eastern Architects and Designers Ltd. (EAD) was a highly profitable business with more work than it could comfortably handle. But then the property market collapsed and, like many architectural firms, EAD found itself struggling to survive.

EAD boss, Barry Jones, had always been on excellent terms with the architects who worked for him. A close-knit group, everyone at EAD got on well with everyone else. They worked hard in the office – and socialised a great deal after work. However, Barry was beginning to wonder how long the friendly atmosphere could last. Losses for two years running meant EAD could no longer afford to keep everyone on – there simply wasn't enough work to go round. He had to get rid of some of his staff to survive. The question was which of his architects should be made redundant? And how could he say to them, 'Thanks very much, but goodbye.'?

Barry thought about the problem and identified four possible approaches to reaching a fair decision:

1 **Last in – first out (LIFO):** those architects with the shortest periods of service in the company should go first.

2 **Voluntary redundancy:** a generous severance package would be offered to anyone willing to take early retirement.

3 **Selection on merit:** Barry would decide which employees were least useful to the company and make them redundant.

4 **Peer selection:** the employees would meet to decide which of them should leave.

Role-play: Meeting

1   Work in groups of between five and eleven. One of you plays the role of Barry Jones, chairing the meeting to discuss which of the four approaches – or a combination of these – should be chosen. Each of the other group members plays the role of one of the architects described in the role cards on pages 146-147.

Discuss which role each person will play and prepare carefully for the meeting by reading the role card and thinking about your situation. Barry Jones should read all the other group members' role cards.

2   Now hold a second meeting using the approach(es) selected to decide which architects should be made redundant. For groups of four to six, two should leave; for groups of seven or eight, three should go; and for groups of nine or ten, four should leave.

The Entrepreneur

INTRODUCTION

1 **Read the introduction to the questionnaire on page 122. What does it say about entrepreneurs and managers? Choose the correct answer.**

a) The role of an entrepreneur is the same as that of a manager.

b) The role of an entrepreneur is different from that of a manager.

Internationally recognised as a successful entrepreneur – Richard Branson

2 **What do you think?**

1 What is 'management ability'?

2 What are 'entrepreneurial skills'?

3 **Find out if you are cut out to be an entrepreneur by completing the questionnaire on page 122. Work out your score using the points system on page 147 and compare your results in pairs or small groups.**

4 **Discuss the following questions.**

1 What is an 'enterprise culture'? Give examples.

2 What are the main features of an enterprise culture?

Are you an entrepreneur?

THE crucial factor in a business – especially when it is just starting up – is the calibre of the person, or people, in charge.

A new business is, essentially, as good as the person who is masterminding the strategy. Too often the role of entrepreneur is confused with that of a manager. A business requires the skills of both, but it is of paramount importance that management ability is not confused with entrepreneurial skills. More to the point: a manager should not delude himself that he is an entrepreneur.

This quiz is designed to help you gain some idea of the extent of your potential.

1. Do you prefer to work on your own, with as little outside direction as possible?
a) yes ☐
b) usually ☐
c) no ☐

2. Do you feel, given well-defined criteria and adequate resources, you will produce a favourable result?
a) yes ☐
b) usually ☐
c) sometimes ☐

3. Do you find a limited working environment frustrating?
a) very ☐
b) usually ☐
c) can cope ☐

4. If something you are involved with goes wrong, do you feel personally responsible?
a) yes ☐
b) sometimes ☐
c) no ☐

5. Do you suggest changes in operations which involve you?
a) often ☐
b) sometimes ☐
c) seldom ☐

6. Do you enjoy working with other people?
a) usually ☐
b) sometimes ☐
c) seldom ☐

7. Do you enjoy assessing risks and acting on your assessments?
a) yes ☐
b) sometimes ☐
c) no ☐

8. Do you apply yourself equally to all tasks you face?
a) yes ☐
b) usually ☐
c) no ☐

9. Are you content with your achievements to date?
a) yes ☐
b) generally ☐
c) no ☐

10. Are you content with your present lifestyle?
a) yes ☐
b) generally ☐
c) no ☐

11. Do you care what your friends and business associates think of you?
a) yes ☐
b) sometimes ☐
c) no ☐

12. Do you have a clear idea of what you want to do over the next three years?
a) yes ☐
b) reasonably clear ☐
c) no ☐

13. Do you think you have control over and can influence your future?
a) yes ☐
b) sometimes ☐
c) no ☐

14. Do you put your failures behind you?
a) yes ☐
b) sometimes ☐
c) no ☐

15. Are you outspoken – sometimes to your detriment – about what you think?
a) yes ☐
b) sometimes ☐
c) no ☐

16. Do you believe you are adequately compensated for work you have done?
a) yes ☐
b) sometimes ☐
c) no ☐

17. Do poor working conditions affect your performance?
a) yes ☐
b) sometimes ☐
c) no ☐

18. Do your goals and aims have the support of your family and those close to you?
a) yes ☐
b) usually ☐
c) no ☐

19. What level of growth potential do you think the free enterprise system has?
a) unlimited ☐
b) limited ☐
c) very little ☐

20. If the situation is not conducive to your plans, do you:
a) carry on regardless? ☐
b) wait for it to improve? ☐
c) adjust your plans? ☐

© The Observer

TEXT 1

1 **Before you read, discuss the following questions. Then read and compare your ideas with those in the article.**
1 What are the characteristics of an entrepreneur?
2 Are fear, greed and dedication pre-requisites for entrepreneurial success?

Fear, greed and dedication

[1] LAST week I discussed the reasons for businesses going bust and concluded that the ultimate problem often lies in the fact that the founder of the business is [5] not cut out to start up and develop his own operation. Sometimes this is due to a lack of knowledge, skill or business experience; sometimes to personal weaknesses.

[10] So let us attempt to analyse the character traits of an entrepreneur. Although entrepreneurs are a diverse species, there are clearly some common factors. Permit me to quote from *The* [15] *British Entrepreneur* – a study prepared by accountants Ernst and Young and the Cranfield School of Management. 'Not all entrepreneurs are cast in the same mould. Indeed it would be an extremely [20] dull world if they were. Almost by definition they defy categorisation.

'Some have a strong sense of humour, some none; some thrive on publicity and adulation, others are virtual hermits; [25] some have an overwhelming need for power, others for creativity; some need the trappings of wealth, others lead very simple lives. Whatever the difference is, there is one factor which all successful [30] entrepreneurs have in common – they and their firms are always on the move.'

It must be appreciated that management skills can be learned, whereas entrepreneurial ability is a [35] matter of flair; either you have it or you don't. Business requires both skills, the flair of the entrepreneur and the solid competence of the manager.

It is dangerous to generalise but some [40] of the characteristics of the entrepreneur, in contrast to the manager, are: belief in himself and his business; belief in wealth and material gain; and belief in delegation.

[45] Entrepreneurial talent and management skills may not both be present in the one person. This may lead to the idea of partnership and, indeed, as the business flourishes and expands, the [50] creation of a management team.

The British Entrepreneur encompasses

Entrepreneurs are not easy to categorise explains **Brian Jenks** of accountants Touche Ross

the results of a survey of the views of owner-managers of the top 100 entrepreneurial firms in the UK. One of [55] the questions asked was 'what are the critical factors for success?'. The answers came under three main headings:

Marketing:
A unique product; an innovative approach; [60] a good fundamental idea; aggressive sales and marketing strategies; active selling; quality; price; heavy marketing investment.

[65] **Management:**
Dedicated senior management; hard work and commitment of staff; tight financial controls; cash flow; investment for the long term; regular views and overhaul of the management structure; [70] disciplined and cost effective management of employees; unwavering and total support from initial backers.

Personal:
Vision; hard work; concentration; [75] flexibility; persistence; ability to recognise opportunities.

The owner-managers were asked about their personal life and family background.

[80] Many came from families where the father had some form of small firm or self-employment background and the mother was a full time housewife. It was interesting to note that not one was an [85] only child and more than half came from families with more than two children.

The previous survey, in 1988, revealed that the group showed low educational attainments, 45 per cent having left [90] school at the age of 16 and very few having any post-school qualifications.

The 1989 list reveals somewhat greater academic attainments but apart from the obvious value of [95] management skills which result from taking an MBA, few of these owner-managers saw any relationship between educational achievements and their current success.

[100] There is a misconception that successful entrepreneurs fail a number of times before making the breakthrough. Not true with this sample, where only 20 per cent had started more than one [105] business.

The average age of the entrepreneurs when they started their first business was 32, while the youngest was 24. Presumably they had gained valuable [110] skills and product knowledge between school and start-up. On the other hand, the majority had started businesses which bore no commercial relationship to their previous employment.

[115] All rather confusing. Perhaps we should dwell on the wisdom of Sir James Goldsmith: 'First you must have the appetite to succeed – ambition. When you have no ambition you are dead. You [120] have to be willing to work. You have to be ready to let go of a smart, safe, socially acceptable job in pursuit of your objective. Fear, greed, dedication and luck – all play their part. The rest [125] follows.'

Brian Jenks is the partner responsible for private companies at Touche Ross.

2 As business editor on an evening newspaper, you prepared the following notes on Brian Jenks' article for use in your 'comment' section. On re-reading your notes, however, you discover that they are not accurate. Read the article and correct them.

Notes

1 it is difficult to categorise entrepreneurs

2 entrepreneurs have nothing in common with each other

3 successful entrepreneurs never stand still

4 it is possible to learn how to be a manager, but entrepreneurs need flair

5 entrepreneurs believe in themselves, like to make money, don't like delegating work

6 some of the critical factors for entrepreneurial success according to *The British Entrepreneur* include:

- a unique product
- aggressive sales/marketing
- cash flow
- effective management
- ability to recognise opportunities

7 many of the owner-managers surveyed in *The British Entrepreneur* were only children whose father owned a small firm or was self-employed and whose mother was a housewife

8 few of the entrepreneurs questioned saw a link between academic achievement and entrepreneurial success

9 most of the entrepreneurs surveyed had started several businesses before becoming successful

10 the majority of survey respondents had started businesses which were a direct extension of their previous employment

LANGUAGE PRACTICE 1

Relative clauses

Study these examples. Then complete the list in the box by writing a suitable conclusion for each item. Text 1 will help you.

. . . a unique product ***that*** will appeal to the consumer.
. . . an innovative approach ***which*** allows for creativity.
. . . senior management ***whose*** commitment to the firm is strong.

Critical factors for success include:

1 a good fundamental idea which ....

2 active selling that ....

3 backers whose ....

4 aggressive marketing strategies that ....

5 tight financial controls which ....

6 staff whose ....

7 the ability to recognise opportunities which ....

8 a management structure that ....

LISTENING 1

You are going to hear an interview with John Goff, an entrepreneur based in Surrey, England. As you listen, note down the answers he gives to the following questions.

1 Would you say entrepreneurs are born or made?
2 What is it about running your own business that appeals to you?
3 Have you always been an independent businessman?
4 What has been your most successful venture, and what made it a success?
5 Can you tell us what difficulties entrepreneurs face when setting up a business?
6 Do you have any ideas on the best way to raise capital?
7 Is a 'good idea and a dream' enough to be successful, or does it take other factors?
8 What advice can you give to would-be entrepreneurs who have an idea?
9 When an entrepreneur starts a business, what sorts of things go wrong? What have you got to be careful about once you're starting to be successful?
10 Would you advise the entrepreneur to have a partner?

TEXT 2

1 **Before you read the article on page 126, scan the subtitle, picture and picture caption for the following information.**
- Dounne Alexander-Moore's product
- the source of Dounne's recipe
- the personal quality that has helped Dounne succeed
- the professional technique has helped Dounne succeed

2 **Read the article and answer the following questions.**
1 What personal obstacles did Dounne overcome to set up her business?
2 What personal attributes does Dounne have in her favour?
3 What are Dounne's business goals?
4 Why did Dounne choose Harrods as her first target?
5 Who at Gramma's Ltd. is responsible for the following functions?
- hiring workers
- preparing the products
- administration
- getting the products to customers
- preparing the accounts
6 Why is it difficult for small companies to do business with supermarkets?
7 What are Dounne's plans for the future?
8 What warning does Dounne give to anyone thinking of going into business on their own?
9 What is the pun (double meaning) in the title?

Woman with sauce

HOT TIP: Dounne Alexander-Moore has sold her product to the nation through adroit PR

Dounne Alexander-Moore's utter determination to put her grandmother's Caribbean recipes on the supermarket shelves is starting to pay off. **Carol Dix** spoke to her

[1] HOW MANY of us, hard at work at the kitchen stove, have dreamed of turning a home-grown recipe into a millionaire-making seller? 'Gee, Ma,' says reverential [5] child/neighbour, 'you should package this and sell it in the stores.' Diane Keaton did it with designer baby food in Baby Boom. Paul Newman has made even more money out of salad dressing.

[10] But to turn the dream into a reality, without a name like Paul Newman's (or indeed Prince Charles'), can be extremely hard labour. Dounne Alexander-Moore has taken this route and has achieved [15] remarkably: her own Caribbean hot pepper sauces, based on the recipes of her Trinidadian grandmother, are now in the marketplace as Gramma's.

Dounne has managed to sell herself and [20] her product to the nation through adroit PR. Already her foot is in the door at major-league supermarkets such as Tesco's, Safeway and (as yet) one Sainsbury's. Yet, still, the going is extremely tough.

[25] Indeed, Dounne's story highlights what has become a major problem in our post-Eighties enterprise culture. Men and women, 'ordinary' men and women, have been encouraged to think big; that they can go it [30] alone, that all they need is a good idea and a dream . . .

Now in her early 40s, the indomitable Dounne found herself, a hard-working single mother with two teen daughters, living in an [35] East End council flat and on the borders of poverty, relying on income support to help out. When the idea came to her to manufacture and sell Gramma's, the first strikes against her in the Enterprise Game [40] were legion: she is black, a woman, a single parent, living in a council flat, with no capital and in need of income support. Get back to 'Go'.

But Dounne persevered and is now selling thousands of jars of her popular sauces, [45] based in a small factory unit in Hainault, Essex. She has just the personality traits required by the enterprise culture: masses of drive, motivation, initiative, and determination to succeed against all odds.

[50] 'To launch a new product on the market is always very hard, and probably doubly so being a black woman. But never once did I compromise my goals. My aim has been all along to get the product into the mainstream [55] (not just to sell in ethnic stores), educate people about the health qualities of Caribbean hot pepper sauces, sell the idea of 'quality' and of a return to natural foods, and that Gramma's is an exceptional food [60] product.

'Early on, I contacted all the TV stations and newspapers, from the nationals to the locals. And two London TV programmes covered my sauces on the very same evening. [65] I had targeted Harrods first, as a high-quality department store which would not need to order in large quantities and would not be put off by a fairly expensive product. The price of Gramma's is above that of mass-produced [70] foods, but it is right for the quality.

'My father took the jars himself into Harrods and Fortnum and Mason; for him that was a lifelong dream come true. The TV shots showed the first customers buying the [75] sauces from Harrods' shelves. Within three hours the next day, Harrods had sold 500 jars. In the first week, they sold over a thousand jars, while I was back home struggling to keep up with the supply. I was [80] still stirring the pots with a giant wooden spoon in my kitchen.'

At that point Dounne gave up her job and concentrated full time on building up the business. On her shoulders fell the full [85] marketing and business-management load – design of the packaging, the logo, the jars themselves, staffing and equipment. She relies still on her daughters for administrative and book-keeping help; her mother for the [90] food preparation and her father with distribution. Her brother-in-law is the accountant. Costs have to be kept to a minimum when, in the first two years of running a business, your main expenses are [95] equipment and advertising.

'The supermarkets demand that you must be able to spend over £1 million on advertising before they will take on a new product, a demand that in itself cuts out most [100] small companies. Yet again I have been very fortunate. Gramma's is now into 150 Tesco Superstores (next to the stock cubes, I have to let everyone know); we'll be in Safeway from June and Sainsbury's Knightsbridge [105] store. We're also in Dewhursts' butchers, will be launching soon in Ireland and there is definite interest from Asda, Morrison's in the North, and William Low in Scotland.'

Dounne's main expansion plan is to build [110] a larger factory, somewhere in the UK, and then ship her Hot Pepper Sauces across the Atlantic, where she knows the huge black market would be all too ready for her product.

[115] 'I've no intention of giving up. There's been a lot of hard work and sacrifice, but the achievement is worth it. Anyone going into their own business should be prepared for a lot of rejections and disappointment, but I've [130] learned to see them all as a plus. They teach you the next step!'

Gramma's Ltd, Unit 6, Acorn Centre, Hainault Industrial Estate, Hainault, Essex. (081-501-3530). The sauces can be purchased [135] *by mail order.*

© The Guardian

VOCABULARY

1 **Complete the following passage with words from the list.**

target	store	launch	label	charge
package	consumers	distribution	logo	outlet

Before you [1]...................................... a product, you have to decide how much to
[2].................................... and how to [3].................................... it so that it will look attractive to
customers. On the [4]...................................., you may well wish to include your company's
[5]...................................., to give the product a clear identity in the eyes of
[6].................................... . At first, you probably won't have a [7].................................... system
to get your goods to customers. You may, therefore, have to [8].................................... one
particular type of [9].................................... as Dounne Alexander-Moore did when she
approached the famous London department [10]...................................., Harrods.

2 **Working in pairs or small groups, discuss the meaning of the underlined idioms in the following sentences from Text 2.**

1 Already her <u>foot is in the door at</u> the major-league supermarkets . . . (line 21)
2 Yet, still, the <u>going is extremely tough.</u> (line 24)
3 Men and women . . . have been encouraged to <u>think big</u> . . . (line 29)
4 . . . women . . . have been encouraged to think . . . that they can <u>go it alone</u> . . . (lines 29-30)
5 When the idea came to her to manufacture and sell Gramma's, the <u>first strikes against her . . . were legion</u> . . . (lines 38-40)
6 She has . . . determination to succeed <u>against all odds</u>. (line 49)

LANGUAGE PRACTICE 2

Inversion

Inversion can be used for emphasis – and must be used when certain words/expressions come at the beginning of a sentence. Study these examples from Text 2 and the list of words/expressions in the box. Then practise inverting the sentences that follow.

*But **never once did I** compromise my goals.* (lines 50-51)
*On her shoulders **fell the full marketing and business-management load** . . .* (lines 84-85)

Under no circumstances . . .	Never . . .
Not only . . . but also . . .	Rarely . . .
Only . . .	On no account . . .
Hardly . . . when . . .	Not until . . .

1 **Finish rewriting the following sentences to make them more emphatic.**

1 You should not give up if you experience a rejection or disappointment.
   On no account ....
2 Dounne Alexander-Moore is very determined, and she has a lot of initiative.
   Not only ....
3 We had hardly launched the product, when orders started flooding in.
   Hardly..

4 A woman has rarely faced the number of problems that Dounne did in setting up her business.
Rarely ....

5 It wasn't until Harrods agreed to sell the sauces that the business really took off.
Not until ....

2 **The words in the following sentences are in the wrong order. Put them in the correct order, using inversion to make each sentence emphatic in tone.**
e.g. new products do lot money rarely a make of
Rarely do new products make a lot of money.

1 tasted have never I sauce better a

....

2 on we commercials the no television can account moment afford at

....

3 costs we only profit our can by a reducing make

....

4 the supermarkets under no put products their circumstances will our on shelves

....

5 we product not August new our on until can market put the

....

WRITING 1

1 **Dounne Alexander-Moore obtains a lot of publicity by writing press releases. These contain information about her, the company, the product range, new developments, recent events – and anything else she feels might persuade journalists to write a story about Gramma's. Imagine that the company has expanded as intended and that Dounne is now shipping her first orders across the Atlantic from her new – larger – factory in the UK. She wants to generate some media coverage in the US to tie in with her launch there and has asked you to draft a press release for circulation to appropriate American publications.**

2 **Design an advertisement (text and artwork) for Gramma's range of concentrated pepper sauces (mild; hot; super hot; extra hot). The advertisement, to be placed in a number of health food magazines, should convey the idea that the products can not only 'spice up' people's diets but also contribute to good health.**

3 **Design an advertisement (text only) – to be placed in the recruitment pages of a national newspaper – for an Assistant to Dounne Alexander-Moore. The person appointed would help mainly with the sales, promotion and distribution of the products, but would also be responsible for some routine administrative work. Think carefully about the layout of your advertisement and make sure you include the following information:**
- job title
- job description (duties and responsibilities)
- job location
- required qualifications
- required qualifications
- contact name/number

LISTENING 2

In this short interview, you will hear Dounne Alexander-Moore describing some of her early experiences trying to get her products off the ground and raise the finance she needed to develop the company. Before you listen, try to predict some of the problems she might have had. Then listen and answer the following questions.

1 What did she have to do before the supermarkets would deal with her?
2 Why did the banks refuse to lend her the capital she needed, even though her products had already been accepted by several stores?

ROLE-PLAY: MEETING

Work in groups of four as two pairs, taking it in turns to play the entrepreneurs and the small business advisers. Read your role-cards and prepare for your meetings carefully.

Entrepreneurs

Decide on an idea (product or service) for a new business that you would like to start up. Draw up an outline business proposal, inventing any information you wish, and decide how you will present it to your bank. Your bank's small business advisers have agreed to meet you and provide some preliminary feedback on your ideas, an opinion – in principle – on the feasibility of raising finance to get your business off the ground, and some advice on how to proceed. Try to present your case persuasively and expect to face some probing questions. You should be prepared to provide some basic information on the following: your planned product/service (description, name, key features, sales/profit potential); the market you are targeting (nature, size, competition); your marketing approach; financing; business structure/location; your expertise etc., but do not worry too much about specific detail at this stage.

Small business advisers

You have an appointment – an informal exploratory meeting – with two bank customers to discuss an idea they have for a new business. Your role is to provide some preliminary feedback, an opinion — in principle – on the feasibility of raising finance, and some advice on how to proceed. Ask pertinent questions about their planned product/service (description, name, key features, sales/profit potential); the market they are targeting (nature, size, competition); their marketing approach; their business structure/location etc. Try to probe their determination/capacity to succeed, but don't worry too much about specific detail at this stage. If you think the idea has merit and they have the experience/ability to make a go of it, suggest they draw up a more detailed proposal, providing more information on e.g. projected start-up costs and overheads; turnover and profit forecasts; loan requirements/anticipated repayment terms/period and anything else you feel you might need to provide the bank with adequate security for any money you might advance.

WRITING 2

1 Write a follow-up letter to the bank's small business advisers, thanking them for their time/input on your business proposal and saying you will be in touch with the information they have requested in due course.

2 On behalf of the bank, write a follow-up letter to the two entrepreneurs, confirming the outcome of your meeting.

14

Japan – Globalisation

INTRODUCTION

Discuss the following questions.

1 What do you understand by the term 'globalisation'?
2 What did Yoshikazu Kawana, Group Director of the Nissan Motor Company, mean when he said, 'We have to globalise, and to globalise we must localise.'
3 Why have Japanese manufacturers invested so heavily in Europe in recent years?
4 What are the benefits/drawbacks of a Japanese manufacturing presence in Europe?
5 Would you like to work for a Japanese company? Give your reasons.

LISTENING 1

You are going to hear an interview with Steve Kremmer, an economist with the Anglo-Japanese Economic Institute. Listen and answer the following questions.

1 When did Japanese investment overseas begin? Why?
2 Where was the first wave of investment? Why?
3 Where was the second wave of investment? Why?
4 How does Steve Kremmer describe the economic connections between:
   - Japan and the US?
   - the US and Europe?
   - Europe and Japan?
5 How has Japanese trade with Europe developed since Japan's first exports? Why?

TEXT 1

1 **According to the subtitle and photo caption, which of the following statements are true and which are false?**
1 Japanese investment in Europe brings no benefit to the host country.
2 The growing role of Japan's manufacturers in Europe is viewed positively.
3 There are now a considerable number of Japanese manufacturers based in Europe.

2 **Look at the chart and answer the following questions.**
1 Which European country had the greatest Japanese manufacturing presence in 1991?
2 How many Japanese manufacturers were there in France in 1991?
3 Which country had 109 Japanese manufacturers in 1991?

The growing role of Japanese manufacturers in Europe has attracted critical or even fearful comments. Little is heard about the achievements on both sides after 25 years of the Japanese at work in Europe.

JAPANESE INDUSTRY IN EUROPE

¹ The excitement 26 years ago of England winning its first football World Cup overshadowed the significance of the opening of a factory in Runcorn, Cheshire, by zip fastener
⁵ maker YKK. But that factory opening and the setting up of a plant in France by Pentel were to have more far-reaching effects on Europe, and the UK in particular, than any football match. Both companies were Japanese and
¹⁰ their ventures were the first trickle of a wave of Japanese manufacturing investment that has since swept Europe.

The volume has increased steadily. In 1983 there were 157 Japanese companies
¹⁵ manufacturing in Europe. By last year the number had grown to 676. They are spread among several countries (see chart) and industries.

In terms of Japan's total investment, the
²⁰ UK has attracted the lion's share – about 40% – followed by France, despite the French government's often hostile stance. Even

Iceland, not normally a beacon for inward investment, boasts a Sumitomo plant, though
²⁵ none of the executives are Japanese. The only major European country without a Japanese manufacturing presence is Norway.

Italy, which like France harbours pockets of anti-Japanese sentiment, has attracted few
³⁰ factories, but politics play little part in Japanese decisions on where to invest. Less than 10% of companies questioned for its annual survey by the Japan External Trade Organisation (JETRO) said pro-Japanese
³⁵ sentiment was a factor in their choice. Among companies that said it was important, most opted for the UK or Ireland. What matters to most companies, according to JETRO, is a good location for distribution, good infrastructure,
⁴⁰ quality of labour and availability of English-speaking staff.

Japanese manufacturers in Europe 1991			
Country	No. of companies	% of total	Annual increase %
UK	187	27.7	41.7
France	122	18.0	28.4
Germany	109	16.1	22.5
Spain	64	9.5	16.3
All Europe	676	100	27.8

⁵⁰ The greatest activity has been in the electronics and electrical appliances sector. In 1990, the latest year for which comparative figures are available, there were 178 manufacturers in that category. Chemicals
⁵⁵ manufacturers come second, followed by makers of general machinery. Other sectors, such as vehicle production, invest in fewer

Making for change: Japanese investment brings jobs and new techniques. By last year there were 676 Japanese manufacturers working in Europe.

sites but on a larger, more noticeable, scale. Yet they are not typical of Japanese
⁶⁰ manufacturing investment in Europe. Small to medium-sized businesses make up the bulk of investment. Japanese manufacturers across Europe employ an average of only 320 workers in each national company.

⁶⁵ Despite problems at home caused by the economic downturn in Japan, so far there is no hint of Japanese companies cutting back on investment abroad. But where it goes may be under review. Earlier this year Sanyo
⁷⁰ dropped plans to build a Pta1.1 billion (ECU 8.5 million) battery factory in Barcelona, saying it was investigating eastern Germany and Poland as possible alternatives. However, Japanese companies generally have been very
⁷⁵ cautious in their approach to investment in eastern Europe.

Whichever countries or industries they head for next, Japanese manufacturers already represent a significant slice of the
⁸⁰ European economy.

© International Management

3   **Read the text on page 131 and complete the following chart.**

Number of Japanese companies in
Europe in:
- 1966 [1].................................
- 1983 [2].................................
- 1991 [3].................................

Attitude to Japanese investment in:
- the UK [4].................................
- France [5].................................
- Italy [6].................................
- Ireland [7].................................

Japanese companies with a
manufacturing presence in:
- the UK [8].................................
- France [9].................................
- Iceland [10].................................

Factors influencing choice of European location for most Japanese companies:	Sectors attracting the highest levels of Japanese investment:
[11]..................................	[15]..................................
....	....
[12]..................................	[16]..................................
....	....
[13]..................................	[17]..................................
....	....
[14]..................................	[18]..................................
....	....

VOCABULARY

Match each word in the left box with a word in the right box. Text 1 will help you. Then use each expression in a sentence of your own.

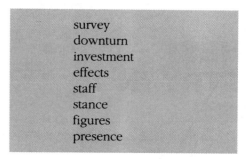

far-reaching	survey
inward	downturn
manufacturing	investment
economic	effects
hostile	staff
annual	stance
English-speaking	figures
comparative	presence

LANGUAGE PRACTICE

Tenses

Complete the following passage by putting the verbs in brackets in the correct form.

Over the years, the volume of Japanese overseas investment [1]..................................
(increase) steadily to the point where Japanese manufacturers [2]..................................
(represent) a significant slice of the European economy.

In 1983, 157 Japanese companies [3].................................. (operate) in Europe. By 1991,
the number [4].................................. (grow) to 676.

So far, the greatest activity [5].................................. (be) in the electronics and electrical
appliances sector. In 1990, there [6].................................. (be) 178 manufacturers in that
category. Other sectors which [7].................................. (attract) Japanese manufacturing
investment [8].................................. (include) chemicals and general machinery.

As far as choice of location is concerned, trends may [9].................................. (change)
if Sanyo is anything to go by: the company recently [10].................................. (announce)
it [11].................................. (drop) plans to build a factory in Barcelona and
[12].................................. (investigate) eastern Germany and Poland instead.

LISTENING 2

You are going to hear Steve Kremmer talking about Japanese inward investment again. Listen and take notes under the following headings.

- the US versus Europe
- the UK
- Europe
- culture and 'localisation'

WRITING 1

The general manager of the Japanese manufacturer you work for in the north of England has been invited to take part in a panel discussion on 'Japanese investment in overseas countries' which has been organised by the local chamber of commerce. Having heard that there will be several hostile questioners in the audience, he wants facts and figures on the following subjects at his fingertips during the debate – and has asked you to provide the information in note form. Use the charts and your notes on Listening 2 to help you.

- brief history of Japanese overseas investment from 1980-90
- extent of Japanese overseas investment by geographical area and by sector
- benefits of Japanese overseas investment for the host economy at national and local level
- the future of Japanese overseas investment

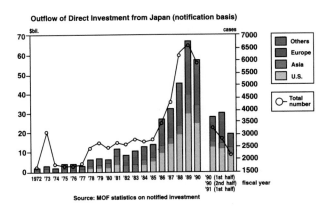

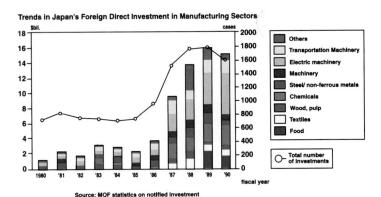

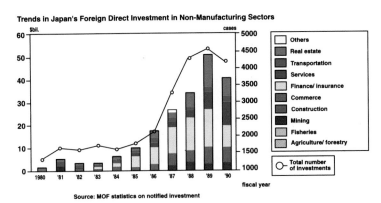

TEXT 2

1   **In this extract from his book *Mind your Manners*, John Mole compares western and Japanese approaches to business in terms of Leadership and Attitudes/Behaviour. Before you read, try to predict some of his comments.**

2   **Read the first part of the text about Leadership and decide which of the following statements accurately reflect John Mole's comments.**

1   The Japanese approach to leadership is more individualistic than the western approach.
2   Japanese bosses tend to be more decisive, charismatic and overtly ambitious than their western counterparts.
3   European employees expect defined job responsibilities and clear-cut goals.
4   Japanese employees expect regular feedback on their performance.
5   Japanese employees expect to use their initiative more than their European counterparts.
6   Success in Japanese business depends on careful observation of the boundaries of status and hierarchy.

3   **Read the rest of the text and complete the following chart. You will need to infer some of the information.**

DIFFERENCES IN ATTITUDES AND BEHAVIOUR	
Western	Japanese
1	use last name followed by 'san'
2	subtle status symbols
speak your mind	3 ....
time is money	4 ....
regular hours with time off	5 ....
humour is vital and varied	6 ....
rarely meet outside work	7 ....
meetings outside work purely social	8 ....
more to life than work	9 ....
10	karoshi

Leadership

Westerners tend to value a tough, individualistic and dominating leadership style including the ability to take independent decisions and have them successfully implemented. The higher a Japanese manager rises in a company the more pains he will take to hide his ambition and capability and not to be seen as a forceful leader. Westerners who look for a decisive and charismatic boss are likely to be disappointed.

A Japanese manager concentrates on getting his group to work together. He is expected to be accessible, to work as an integral part of the group and to share whatever information he has. Because he has spent his whole career with the company, more often than not in the same type of function, he is expected to be fully knowledgeable about his subordinates' work as well as his own.

One of the problems Japanese managers often have with western subordinates is getting them to show initiative. They complain that Europeans need to be told what to do all the time. And when they have done it they need immediate assurance that they have done it right and a pat on the back. This would be embarrassing to the boss and personally offensive to a Japanese subordinate who expects no more than a vague indication of the job to be done. Japanese do not have personal job descriptions or performance appraisal systems. Japanese job definition is for the group and it is assumed that everyone will do their best to fulfil it.

Their western subordinates on the other hand complain that they are given only vague hints of what they are supposed to do. Without defined responsibility, clear direction, and realistic goals they may find their jobs boring and without scope. When individual descriptions are instituted in Japanese companies in Europe it is usually at the European's insistence.

Europeans who discover the ground rules find that they have more scope to make their own jobs than in a circumscribed western environment. The ground rules are never do anything that is above your status, never do anything that infringes on someone else's status and never cut across hierarchical boundaries. The way to ensure you keep within the boundaries of your status is to keep your boss informed of the smallest detail. Among the sample of people I talked to it was those at the lower level of organisation who found this the most stimulating change from a European working environment where junior people are given comparatively little scope or responsibility.

Attitudes and behaviour

Etiquette

Japanese in Europe have reluctantly learned to use first names but feel more comfortable when addressed by the last name followed by *san*. Senior people may be addressed by their title plus san instead of last name. First names are reserved for family and close friends.

Titles, modes of address and language are carefully measured to indicate relative status, as are the other subtle status symbols of office life such as job titles or the positioning of desks in an open office. For example, seniors would have their backs to the windows where they could enjoy the privilege of natural light, in contrast with the fluorescent lighting pervading Japanese offices. While very sensitive to fine distinctions of rank, the western use of material goods to communicate achievement and authority are noticeably lacking. Offices are workmanlike, cars are unostentatious and so on.

More important than the actual forms of language and behaviour is pervasive politeness and a concern to avoid embarrassment to oneself or others. Displays of temper or any other uncontrolled emotions are seen as a sign of weakness.

Japanese manners are based on reciprocation, a sense of mutual indebtedness. To many westerners the excessive deference of a subordinate to a superior is less surprising than that it is returned in kind. Relationships between all levels are built on exchange, whether gifts, courtesies, help, information and so on.

Extreme politeness does not exclude openness in relationships. Europeans, especially women, may be surprised at the personal nature of conversations. This is usually because Japanese need to know people well before they can be comfortable with them. In some European countries you need not trust people to work with them as long as they do their job. In a Japanese environment there is a higher tolerance of professional and human frailty, but it is compensated with a greater demand for loyalty and trust.

Punctuality

Japanese are very punctual when politeness requires it and especially with senior people. Otherwise time is fluid. A meeting will carry on until it is finished or interrupted by the demands of a senior person outside. The working day can be very long, reflecting a demanding work ethic and a high level of commitment. Being the first to leave, even if you have no work to do, is a snub to the group and an embarrassment to your senior. As in Japan, Japanese may regularly work on Saturdays, rarely take more than a week's vacation or their full entitlement, and count sick days as holiday.

Humour

On informal occasions when they know everyone well, Japanese will be humorous and entertaining. At a formal meeting or among strangers they may be awkward and withdrawn and too nervous to loosen up. In presentations

and speeches to westerners many have learned that the audience expects jokes and informality and respond accordingly. Japanese do not usually appreciate flippancy or triviality and find self-deprecation a mystery.

Social life

The most common complaint among westerners is that most major decisions seem to be made outside office hours by their Japanese colleagues. While in day-to-day activities they are kept well informed, they are kept in the dark about the overall direction of the company. For a westerner to progress in a Japanese managed company it is essential to work late in the evening and at weekends. This can be a major impediment for women who wish to progress in a Japanese company. In the workplace itself most of the women I talked to did not find Japanese more chauvinistic than their western counterparts. The difficulty was in establishing the appropriate relationships, as well as finding the time, to join in the after-hours discussions.

It is not so easy for men either. While the expatriate Japanese is considerably more flexible and adaptable to European ways than the stereotypical image of the chauvinistic and single minded Tokyo salaryman, it is hard to break into the inner circle. As in any foreign company a first requirement is to make an effort to speak the employer's language. As well as practically useful it demonstrates a commitment to career and company to which Japanese are particularly sensitive.

It is this level of dedication to the organisation which is probably the biggest hurdle to making any more than an averagely successful career in a Japanese company. The emotional and practical commitment that Japanese expect is incomprehensible to most westerners. The term 'British disease' is a byword among Japanese for idleness and is extended to most other western countries. The Japanese disease is *Karoshi*, or death by overwork. The difference between the British and Japanese diseases is perhaps the biggest cultural hurdle for each side to overcome.

14

CASE STUDY

Shimamura Electronics, a successful medium-sized Japanese manufacturer of electrical and electronic goods for the home and office, is interested in setting up manufacturing subsidiaries in key overseas markets. To research possible locations in those markets, the company has arranged a programme of visits to regional business development groups which are interested in attracting foreign investors.

Role-play: Meeting

Work in two groups, one group playing the delegation from Shimamura, the other playing a regional business development group. Read your role-card and prepare for your meeting carefully. The meeting will take the form of a presentation followed by an informal question-and-answer/discussion session.

Regional business development group	Shimamura delegation
Choose an area you know well and prepare a presentation on it to give to the Shimamura delegation. You will need to give basic information about your area (main features, major assets, cities, towns etc.) and outline the particular advantages it offers foreign investors in terms of e.g. the number of foreign investors already in the area, the attitude of local people to foreign investment, the availability of skilled labour and component suppliers, communications, local facilities (education/training, shopping, health, recreation) etc. You are very keen to persuade Shimamura to site their manufacturing plant in your area as you know it will provide a much-needed stimulus to the local employment market – you might like to consider a package of financial incentives to tempt the company. Also, try to find out as much as you can about the company and its plans before your meeting is over.	This is a big step for your company and the choice of location might mean the difference between success and failure. Prepare for your meeting carefully by drawing up a list of questions you would like the regional business development group to answer. For example: ■ How can you be sure a Japanese company would be welcome. ■ How buoyant is the local economy? ■ How many foreign businesses are already located in the area? ■ Is there a good supply of skilled labour? ■ How many component manufacturers are located nearby? ■ What is the communications network like? Make notes as you listen to the presentation so that you can pick up on any points at the end. You may be asked by the regional development business group for some information about your company and its plans for expansion, so be prepared!

WRITING 2

1 **As a member of the regional business development group, you have been asked to design a one-page promotional leaflet outlining the advantages your area offers to foreign investors like Shimamura. The leaflet will be included in an information pack which will be sent out to all foreign firms showing an interest in the area.**

2 **On behalf of the Shimamura delegation, write a letter to the head of the regional business development group expressing your thanks for the group's presentation and indicating whether or not your company will be taking the matter further.**

15

Corporate Strategy

INTRODUCTION

Discuss the following questions.

1 What is 'corporate strategy'?
2 Why do companies need corporate strategies?
3 How should corporate strategy be decided? What factors – internal and external – need to be taken into consideration?
4 What do you understand by the following?
   1 merger and acquisition
   2 rationalisation
   3 diversification
   4 demerger

TEXT 1

1 **The article on page 138, an analysis of corporate strategies for the 1990's, appeared in *The Economist* towards the end of 1990. Read the introduction (paragraphs 1–5) and note what it says about the following dates/periods.**

   1 1960's
   2 1973-74
   3 mid-1970's
   4 1979
   5 1980's
   6 1990

Surviving the deluge

Are the corporate strategies that helped firms soar in the growth years of the 1980s the right ones to pull them through recession?

[1] After seven fat years, the word recession is once again making businessmen fear there will be one or two lean years to come. The first response of many companies will be tactical: cutting jobs, [5] excess capacity and capital spending – and forcing suppliers to do the same by pressing for lower prices. Thus are recessions made. Many American and British firms are already going through that phase, as are some of their flabbier Japanese and [10] continental-European rivals.

This kind of restructuring does not amount to a corporate strategy. It is more a way of dealing with the failure of past strategies. As recession looms, managers should be questioning the policies they [15] pursued while the good times rolled – and asking to which, if any, they should be preparing to return when the good times come back.

The first searchlight should be on the past decade's many marriages. The merger mania of the [20] 1980s was not a new phenomenon. During the 1960s growth by merger and acquisition was all the rage. In America the number of big deals tripled to 6,100 a year between 1965 and 1969. The 1973-74 oil shock helped to scupper that merger splurge: in [25] 1974 only 2,860 mergers and acquisitions took place in America, and for every two deals there was one divestiture of a failed purchase.

Undaunted, firms still sought to diversify after 1974 in order, they hoped, to offset the risk of [30] doing business in their new dear-oil environment. During the mid-1970s, says Mr Alfred Chandler, a business historian, half of all assets acquired by American firms through merger and acquisition were in industries unrelated to their core [35] businesses. It took a second oil shock, in 1979, to demonstrate the folly of that strategy.

This suggests that some of the mismarriages of the 1980s may be brutally exposed by 1990's mix of Saddamised oil prices and already-slowing [40] economies. Facing the recession test:

• **Strategic alliances** have been one of the most popular policies of the past few years. They were justified as a low-risk alternative to merger or acquisition, or as a cheaper and more culturally [45] sensitive way to enter new markets. Mr John Kay, a professor at London Business School, says that, too often, such alliances just help both partners to paper over their own weaknesses. If a recession hits one partner harder than the other, the weaker [50] partner may now find itself at the mercy of the stronger.

Other alliances may falter during the recession because their participants expected too much from them. Alliances are sometimes an expedient for [55] firms searching for a specific skill, or access to a particular market. But they cannot be relied on to provide the 'core competences' (i.e. essential skills and abilities) that companies need to gain a long-term competitive advantage.

[60] The most successful strategic alliances may prove to be those where, if bad times returned, the partners could stand back on their own feet. There is much to be said for the alliance between Britain's Pilkington, the world's biggest glass-maker, with [65] France's Saint-Gobain and Japan's Nippon Sheet Glass (NSG). All three firms have strong, but diverse, core competences. Pilkington brings its glass-making technologies to the deals; Saint-Gobain its local marketing skills in a number of [70] overseas markets; NSG its manufacturing and management techniques. If a slump in demand undermines this kind of alliance, its partners can at least walk away with their core competences intact. Who knows: they may even start competing with [75] each other, instead of co-operating.

• **Stick to your knitting.** The idea that companies should concentrate on their core competences, and eschew diversification (especially into unrelated businesses), had a good management press in the [80] past decade. That is one reason why so many mergers in the 1980s were of companies in the same industry and why so many corporate empires hastily cobbled together in the 1970s were broken up. But with the onset of slower growth, [85] unfashionable buzzwords such as synergy and diversification are creeping back. Is this a mistake?

Synergy, thinks Mr Mark Fuller, president of Monitor, a consulting firm based in Cambridge, Massachusetts, will be one of the ideas that firms [90] will be forced to re-examine as economies start to falter. By synergy he does not mean the all-purpose excuse trotted out by 1970s diversifiers, but new ways to exploit existing technologies and skills. In particular, companies will have to get more bang [95] per buck in R & D and product development.

Rather than chasing once-and-for-all breakthroughs, many companies will have to settle for moving into established markets with proven technologies. Note how Honda's motorcycle [100] engine-building skills enabled it to move into cars in the late 1960s and then into lawnmowers and generators.

Royal Dutch/Shell pioneered the idea of bringing together the skills of strategic planners [105] with those of computer whizzes, enabling it to carry out 'real-time' planning – the opposite of the bad old habit of inflexible strategic planners churning out unusable five year plans. New-product teams in the 1990s should draw together the skills of design [110] and production engineers, marketers and salesmen – even, as many Japanese firms do, suppliers and customers. Such creative synergies could make for swifter, less accident-prone product launches. Mr Fuller thinks that such developments will [115] require business structures that are far more flexible than in previous decades. Flexibility, he reckons, will separate this recession's winners and losers.

• **Financial engineering.** Along with plenty of [120] now debt-ridden corporate raiders and buyout specialists, firms like Britain's BTR and Hanson have prospered by imposing stringent financial discipline on companies in mature or declining industries. They made money by stripping away [125] the paraphernalia of corporate self aggrandisement. Hanson views the coming slowdown as a period of opportunity to pick up lots of cheap companies. It may be disappointed. In this recession many firms will be forced to impose [130] Hanson-style disciplines on themselves. Turnaround opportunities may be few and far between.

• **Globalisation** is one management fad that may survive the slump, even if it is more modestly [135] called 'geographical diversification'. Firms like SmithKline Beecham, ABB and ICI have worked hard over the 1980s to 'go global'. All now have more than three quarters of their assets outside their home country. They may find it easier to [140] weather a downturn because they have spread their risk across so many markets, and (provided they have not become smothered by a global bureaucracy) they may be better placed to seize any opportunities in an upturn because of their [145] increased knowledge.

• **Quality** has often suffered in past recessions as companies have used the downturn as an excuse to ditch those strategies that they believe add to their costs. Will they do so again? Mr Tom Peters, an [150] American management guru, believes that this recession will bankrupt any firm that skimps on quality. These days, he points out, higher quality often means making products which are simpler and have fewer parts – or providing a service which [155] offers customers more by being simpler to use. A 1990 Sony Walkman has half as many parts as its less reliable ancestor had when it was launched ten years ago; and in real terms it is now 80% cheaper to buy. Concentrating on quality can nowadays [160] help companies to cut costs in ways that give them a sustainable competitive advantage – especially in a recession.

2 The rest of the article is divided into five sections, each with a separate heading and a different focus. Read each section in turn, noting the main points in the relevant section of the following chart. When you have finished, compare your notes in small groups.

STRATEGIC ALLIANCES	
STICK TO YOUR KNITTING	
FINANCIAL ENGINEERING	
GLOBALISATION	
QUALITY	

VOCABULARY 1

Phrasal nouns

Explain the underlined words in the following sentences from Text 1. Then use each one in a sentence of your own.

1 But with the <u>onset</u> of slower growth, unfashionable buzzwords . . . are creeping back. (line 84)
2 Rather than chasing once-and-for-all <u>breakthroughs</u>, many companies will have to settle for moving into established markets with proven technologies. (line 97)
3 Hanson views the coming <u>slowdown</u> as a period of opportunity to pick up lots of cheap companies. (line 127)
4 <u>Turnaround</u> opportunities may be few and far between. (line 131)
5 Firms like SmithKline Beecham, ABB and ICI . . . may find it easier to weather a <u>downturn</u> because they have spread their risk across so many markets and . . . they may be better placed to seize any opportunities in an <u>upturn</u> because of their increased knowledge. (lines 140 and 144)

LANGUAGE PRACTICE

Prepositions

Replace the missing prepositions in the following sentences.

1 Some companies expect too much .... an alliance.
2 Firms which start by co-operating .... each other sometimes end up competing .... each other.
3 At certain times, the wisest strategy for a company may be to focus .... its main activities.
4 It is never a good idea to concentrate too much .... research and development at the expense of marketing.
5 The Coca-Cola company, which is based .... the US, depends greatly .... marketing.
6 If strict financial controls are imposed .... a company, its profitability can often be improved.
7 Multinational companies spread their financial risks .... many markets.
8 When faced .... recession, companies adopt various tactics to survive.

DISCUSSION

1 **What do these charts tell you about Marks & Spencer's:**
1 main product areas?
2 sales between 1986-1990?
3 trading results?
4 corporate strategy in this period?
5 merits as an investment?

2 **What else do you know about Marks & Spencer?**

Company: Marks & Spencer

Market value: £5.5bn
Workforce: 76,000
Interest cover: 70 Dividend cover: 2.3

Full year This time Last time %

	This time	Last time	%
Sales (£m)	5,608	5,122	+9
Pre-tax profits (£m)	604	529	+14
Earnings per share(p)	14.5	12.9	+12
Dividend per share(p)	6.4	5.6	+14

Sales (£m)

	5000		800
UK(LH scale)	4500		700
Other (RH scale)	4000		600
	3500		500
	3000		400
			300
	1986 87 88 89 90		

UK sales analysis

Clothing   Other
Food

49%
40%
11%

Marks & Spencer's flagship Oxford Street store

LISTENING 1

You are going to hear Barry Hyman, Head of Corporate Affairs at Marks & Spencer, talking about his company. Listen and take notes under the following headings.

■ the US
■ Canada
■ France
■ Spain
■ the UK

VOCABULARY 2

In groups, discuss the meaning of the underlined expressions from Listening 1.

1 We had decided even during the family days that internationalisation was necessary. . . . It would be fair to say, however, that it was <u>given an extra boost</u> . . . by our moves into America.

2 We are now beginning to <u>put our foot down on the throttle</u> in regard to European expansion.

3 (It has been a) smooth (process), yes, but some hiccups along the way and <u>learning curves</u> to be taken note of and absorbed.

4 I think <u>with hindsight</u> we made some careless decisions.

5 One of the things we've learned . . . is that the route for us . . . is <u>organic growth</u> rather than acquisition.

6 Brooks . . . gave us a national perspective across America under the guise . . . of a highly-respected <u>high street name</u>.

WRITING

You work for a firm of financial consultants. Use your notes on Listening 1 and the information in the charts on page 140 to write a brief profile of Marks & Spencer for circulation to prospective investors.

TEXT 2

1   **Before you read, look at the title and discuss the following questions.**

1 What do the letters ICI stand for?

2 What do you know about ICI?

3 In the light of Text 1's reference to ICI (page 138, line 136), what do you think 'comes to a fork on the road' means?

ICI comes to a fork on the road to its future

by David Bowen

[1] At 3.30 pm on Wednesday, Tony Rodgers left ICI's Millbank headquarters in London and headed in his Daimler for Heathrow Airport. Mr Rodgers, a Colonel Sanders lookalike who [5] runs the group's Far East activities, did not know whether he was going to depart, however, because the main board was still deciding whether to go ahead with its Grand Plan.

[10]   He rang from the airport, was told it had been approved, and flew to Singapore. Soon ICI's Asian managers were converging for a meeting with him. Around the world, the pattern was repeated. David Barnes, head of [15] US operations, left Millbank to fly to Wilmington, Delaware, where senior American managers were heading; Sir Denys Henderson, ICI's chairman, and Ronnie Hampel, the chief operating officer, were [20] driven to the group's conference centre just outside London to meet the European bosses.

At the same time, word went out that 120,000 letters could be released to employees.

The plan was to split ICI in two: to follow [25] the fashion for demerger by creating two companies that should do better on their own than together. One, ICI Bioscience, would have pharmaceuticals, agrochemicals, seeds and speciality chemicals – the supposedly go-[30]go parts of the group. The rest – mainly paints, industrial chemicals and explosives – would remain in a company called ICI.

For ICI, as for most big companies, decentralisation had been a theme of the [35] 1980s. Following the 1980-81 recession, when it went into loss for the first time in its history, Sir John Harvey-Jones, the then chairman, decided that ICI should be totally reshaped. He considered turning the headquarters into [40] a holding company that would allow subsidiaries almost complete autonomy. He decided this would throw away too many cross-benefits, but from then on the group stressed that decentralisation was the [45] watchword.

As the ideas crystallised, groups were set up to see just how ICI would be split.

It will take many years – probably until the next recession – before we know whether the [50] division has been a success. What will decide the future is the quality of the management and whether ICI can survive on its own when times get rough. Both Sir Denys and Mr Hampel retire in 1995. It will be interesting to [55] see whether in the years after that the memories of Tweedle Dum and Tweedle Dee are revered, or reviled.

© The Independent On Sunday

2   **Read paragraphs 1 and 2 of Text 2 and complete the following chart.**

Name	Position/responsibilities	Destination	Reason
Tony Rodgers	running group activities in the Far East	Heathrow/Singapore	meet Asian managers
David Barnes	1	2	3 ....
4	chairman	5	6 ....
7	8		

3   **Now read paragraph 3 and summarise ICI's 'Grand Plan' briefly in your own words. Then finish labelling the following diagrams.**

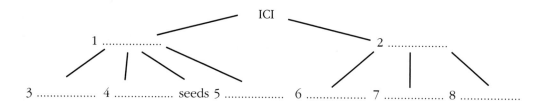

4   **Read the rest of the article and answer the following questions.**
1   When was decentralisation first considered as an option?
2   Why did Sir John Harvey-Jones reject the idea of turning ICI's headquarters into a holding company?
3   When will ICI know whether its Grand Plan has been successful?
4   What will the Grand Plan's success depend on?

LISTENING 2

In the second part of the interview, Barry Hyman summarises Marks & Spencer's strengths, weaknesses, opportunities and threats. Listen and take notes on the key points. Then complete the following chart.

The "Jewel in the Crown" – Boulevard Haussmann in Paris

MARKS & SPENCER	
STRENGTHS	**WEAKNESSES**
OPPORTUNITIES	**THREATS**

ROLE-PLAY: MEETING

Work in small groups of up to six people. Imagine you are senior managers at Marks & Spencer and hold a meeting to discuss the future direction of the company. You have been asked to consider corporate strategy for the next five years and to submit your ideas and recommendations to the board.

Choose one of the following positions (1-6) and prepare for your meeting carefully. Use your role-card as a starting point and outline some more detailed ideas on paper so that you can present your case persuasively. You may invent any information you wish.

1 You are chairing the meeting. Your task is to keep the discussion relevant and constructive, and to ensure that you reach an agreement on the future direction of the company.

2 You believe that M & S is doing well and should not be thinking of any major expansion at all. Instead, the company should be trying to increase turnover in existing stores (for example, by widening the product range further) and to reduce costs where possible.

3 You want M & S to be more adventurous. The company should be taking over some European food companies which are having financial problems, for example. Also, M & S could set up alliances with some of the bigger European food and clothing stores. You are in favour of withdrawing from North America and focusing strategy on Europe.

4 You want M & S to start selling lower-priced food and fashion lines to compete directly with the big supermarkets and other department stores. You would particularly like to see the company develop its range of high-fashion clothing aimed at younger buyers and expand its wine selection, which is considered rather limited by some people.

5 In your opinion, M & S should expand internationally by developing more of its own stores. You want to see the company develop its image in Europe just as it did in Britain. You think it should begin by selecting two or three markets (for example, France, Spain and Italy) and concentrate on these.

6 You are pleased that the company's recent diversification into financial services has been a success and you would like to see *more* diversification. Why can't M & S exploit the strength of its brand name on other products and services?

Complementary Materials

Unit 5, p53

Presentation Outline for Product Presentation

1 The Product
design
material, colour, etc.
use(s)

2 The Market
possible markets
forecast for market size
assessment of possible competition

3 Marketing Strategy
pricing
name/slogan
presentation/packaging
supply

4 Promotion
where/how to promote
sales promotion

5 Conclusion
You may, if you wish, provide any other information, e.g. financial data, production targets, etc., pointing out that at this stage these can only be estimates.

Unit 7, p71

Role-card for Chief Buyer, Trendsetters Inc.

New York

Trendsetters Inc. is a major American clothing retail chain, based in New York. As Chief Buyer, you have not previously done business with Island Silks, a medium-sized clothing manufacturer based in Hong Kong, but you were very impressed with the silk scarves in their new 'Miriam Designer Collection' on show at last month's Hong Kong Clothing Fair. You have been quoted a unit price of $US50, including the cost of insurance and shipping, and are keen to place an order for 50,000 scarves from the collection.

It is now November 1 and you need the goods quickly as you are approaching your peak selling period - the six weeks before Christmas. The scarves should sell well if they hit the shelves at the right time and mid-November would be ideal. Your customers like bright colours and intricate patterns, and expect to be able to choose from a wide range of designs.

Your objective is to negotiate a satisfactory deal, making as few concessions as possible - the retail clothing market in the US is highly competitive. Use the following points system as a guide to your priorities. You should try to score as many points as possible, and you will need to decide your objectives, negotiating limits and strategy accordingly.

Decisions	Points
Delivery Date	
Nov. 15	3
Nov. 30	2
Dec. 7	1
Different Patterns	
20	3
15	2
10	1
Colours	
12	4
10	3
6	1
Terms of Payment	
By irrevocable letter of credit:	
90 days presentation	5
60 days presentation	3
30 days presentation	2
at sight	1
Discount	
4%	5
3%	3
2%	2
1%	1
0	0

Unit 8, p83
Role-card for Peter Kahn

Peter Kahn

You are keen to take up this offer as you know it would be an excellent career move and provide you with the kind of challenge your current job lacks, but you are determined to negotiate a *very good* package. Going to Zurich is not an easy option for you – you will be leaving behind a secure position and a lovely home for a very unknown quantity; Paula is unhappy because she will have to appoint a manager to look after the business she loves to run herself; you'll have to let your house, with all the problems and risks that involves; and you'll have to pay for your children to travel to Zurich in the holidays. With all that in mind, you have worked out the following negotiating position.

Salary	£160,000 (your current salary is £100,000, but your boss offered to raise it by 20% when he heard you were thinking of leaving.
Bonuses	A 'golden hello' (i.e. a payment for making the move to Hi-Style) of three months' salary plus a guaranteed six monthly bonus of at least 10% of your annual salary
Accommodation	Free accommodation (preferably a large rented house in a smart area of Zurich) plus telephone costs and a subscription to the local golf club
Car	Negotiable – but a model appropriate for the position
Hours of work	A guaranteed five-day week
Length of contract	Five years – in the event of the contract being terminated before the end, you must receive financial compensation
Employment for Paula	A managerial or executive position with Hi-Style (nothing too 'low level')
Other	Stock options? Education allowance for your children? Paternity leave? etc.

Unit 12, p120
Role-cards for EAD meeting

Pat (aged 45)
You have been with the firm 20 years, and have won many awards for outstanding design. You spend most of your spare time flying aeroplanes – an expensive hobby. You have been married three times and have four young children to support. You are particularly friendly with Mario/Maria.

Mario/Maria (aged 42)
You are talented, especially in the area of marketing, but very emotional. Last year you had a nervous breakdown, but are slowly recovering, due to the support you are receiving from senior colleagues at work. You want the firm to diversify into new areas, such as the design of hypermarkets and apartment buildings – this is where the big money is to be made. You think the traditional LIFO system is the fairest way to solve the present problem.

Don/Donna (aged 26)
You joined the firm three years ago. You have just bought a large new house since you're getting married soon. You are a brilliant young architect and have just submitted plans for a major building project on the River Thames. You will know soon whether your plans have been accepted by the local council. You quite like the peer selection approach to the redundancy problem in the firm.

Carl/Carla (aged 30)
You are an Italian-trained architect. Besides speaking five languages, you have superb design skills. Because of this, you are frequently in demand by clients. You are smart, good-looking and charismatic. You add a certain glamour to EAD's rather conservative image. Because you are in love with one of the other architects, you are determined to stay with the firm.

Paolo/Paola (aged 27)

You joined EAD a year ago. You were delighted to get the job as you had been unemployed previously for over 18 months. You are dynamic and exceptionally creative. You believe that your future prospects are excellent because EAD needs young people with new ideas. You are excellent company and give wonderful parties, which everyone attends.

Hiroshi (aged 32)

You are Japanese and very business-minded. You have excellent contacts with Japanese companies wishing to set up companies in England, but EAD does not seem interested in exploiting them. You like the job, but do not enjoy living in London. You must stay there, though, because your wife – an English woman – has an excellent job as manager of a fashion house. You believe firmly that consultation is very important in decision-making.

Felix/Felicity (aged 55)

Unmarried, you are well-connected socially. You went to the right school and know all the right people. You are fairly talented and very popular. You are a sociable, extrovert person, liked and trusted by the financial experts in the City. You spend most of your time having lunches with well-known business people. You love working for EAD and do not intend to retire. You believe there is no substitute for experience in your profession.

Simon/Simone (aged 35)

You are the 'life and soul' of the firm – full of energy and ideas. However, you have a weakness. You are a big spender and always heavily in debt. You live life 'in the fast lane', as they say. If you are made redundant, you will face financial ruin. You like Felix/Felicity, whom you consider to be the best architect in the firm. In the present situation, you believe selection by merit is best for the company.

Matilda/Matt (aged 55)

You joined the firm five years ago, but have long and varied experience as an architect. You believe that, more than anyone else, you have kept the firm afloat in these difficult times – that's why Barry depends on you so much. You have a personal problem. You have an elderly mother who is in very poor health. Because of her, you might be willing to take early retirement if you were offered enough money to keep you and your mother in comfort until she dies.

Byron/Byrony (aged 38)

You are American-born and very efficient. You organise everyone – including Barry Jones! You feel that EAD would not be losing money if it were better managed. You want the firm to be more international, and to look for business in Europe. You believe that EAD should reward first class architects (like yourself) and that the company is 'carrying' too many low achievers.

Unit 13, p122

Scoring for "Are you an entrepreneur?"

1 a) 3, b) 2, c) 1. 2 a) 3, b) 2, c) 1. 3 a) 3, b) 2, c) 1. 4 a) 3, b) 2, c) 1. 5 a) 3, b) 2, c) 1. 6 a) 1, b) 2, c) 3. 7 a) 3, b) 2, c) 1. 8 a) 1, b) 2, c) 3. 9 a) 1, b) 2, c) 3. 10 a) 1, b) 2, c) 3. 11 a) 3, b) 2, c) 1. 12 a) 3, b) 2, c) 1. 13 a) 3, b) 2, c) 1. 14 a) 1, b) 2, c) 3. 15 a) 3, b) 2, c) 1. 16 a) 1, b) 2, c) 3. 17 a) 1, b) 2, c) 3. 18 a) 3, b) 2, c) 1. 19 a) 3, b) 2, c) 1. 20 a) 2, b) 1, c) 3.

Rating Yourself:

Over 55: You probably know exactly what you intend to do – if you have not already started on it. And the chances are that you did not need the confirmation of this quiz to reassure you about your entrepreneurial drive. But since you appear to have the motivation and attitudes to succeed, make sure you seek out expert advice before you go any further.

50 to 55: You are on your way. A full profile of your personality would probably place you firmly in the 'likely to succeed' category.

45 to 50: The ability, the motivation and the attitudes to win through are probably there. But there is also the possibility of a lack of commitment in some areas. Perhaps family responsibilities give rise to caution: perhaps you are not committed to the accumulation of wealth. More likely, you are already in a job and, not being an intending entrepreneur, lack the clarity of goals.

40 to 45: Definite need for close reappraisal if you are intending to launch yourself forth as an entrepreneur. Perhaps your skills are more management orientated? Or perhaps a co-operative or partnership would be more suitable?

Below 40: A decided scepticism, even lack of belief in the system is indicated here. You may be highly skilled, but are perhaps unwilling – or unable – to do battle as a business entrepreneur.

Resource Materials

PROMOTIONAL LEAFLET

A leaflet is a single sheet of printed paper sometimes folded to form several pages.
It either advertises a product/service or gives information on how to use it.
No particular layout is required but the leaflet must be eye-catching, easy to read, and
have a contact address and date. Key information, e.g. the offer of a special discount or
bargain rates, should be highlighted.

Up To 35% Off

SUPERVALUE

HOGG ROBINSON TRAVEL

AVIS HOLIDAY CARS

SuperValue Winter Promotion

from the car rental company
that's voted the best

We've shaved up to 35% off our Summer rates in the
most popular European Winter destinations*

So now you can get the best deal from the best car
rental company — that's really **SuperValue**

PLUS

Win a free week's Group A car rental for your next
Summer holiday!

We're giving away 10 free week's car rental to our
customers, in Europe — for SuperValue rentals in
Europe between
1st November '91
- 31st March '92
Winners will be
announced in
March '92.

Opel Corsa

Avis features Opel and Vauxhall cars

So you can enjoy the benefit of the lowest Avis holiday
rates, plus the reassurance of unbeatable service,
reliability and the best choice of up to date cars around

To make a reservation contact your Travel Agent

*Example refers to saving on previous rates for 5 day's rental in
Germany; saving will vary for other destinations.

SuperValue Winter Promotion

Our special Winter SuperValue rates are shown
below. Rates include: Unlimited Mileage, Collision
Damage Waiver, VAT and all Local Taxes. Theft
Protection and Personal Accident Insurance are
optional.

Advance reservation is required.

Destination	Car Group	Daily rates (£)	
		2-6 days	7-13 days
CYPRUS	A Suzuki 800	16.00	14.00
	B Suzuki 1,000	17.00	15.00
	C Austin Metro	18.00	16.00
GREECE	A Subaru M.70DL	25.00	21.42
	B Nissan Cherry 1.0	27.00	23.14
	C Nissan Sunny 1.3	32.00	27.42
MALTA – 1.11.91 -10.12.91)	A Ford Fiesta 1.1	11.00	10.00
7.1.92 -31.3.92)	B Isuzu Gemini 1.3	12.00	11.00
	C Ford Escort 1.3	15.00	13.00
MALTA – 11.12.91 - 6.1.92)	A Ford Fiesta 1.1	14.00	12.00
	B Isuzu Gemini 1.3	15.00	13.00
	C Ford Escort 1.3	16.00	14.00
PORTUGAL	A Opel Corsa 1.0	11.00	10.00
	B Fiat Uno 45	12.00	11.00
	C Opel Corsa 1.2	14.00	12.00
SPAIN - MALAGA)	A Fiat Uno 1.0	14.00	12.00
ALICANTE)	B Fiat Uno 60 1.1	16.00	14.00
BALEARICS)	C Renault 19	19.00	17.00
SPAIN - OTHER AREAS	A Fiat Uno 45 1.0	17.00	15.00
	B Fiat Uno 60 1.1	19.00	17.00
	C Renault 19	24.00	21.00
		3-6 days	7-13 days
FRANCE - CANNES)	A Opel Corsa 1.0	29.00	25.00
MONACO)	B Opel Kadett 1.3	31.00	27.00
NICE)	C Opel Vectra 1.6	35.00	30.00
FRANCE - OTHER AREAS	A Opel Corsa 1.0	30.00	26.00
	B Opel Kadett 1.3	40.00	35.00
	C Opel Vectra 1.6	52.00	45.00
GERMANY	A Opel Corsa	24.00	21.00
	B VW Polo	26.00	23.00
	C Opel Kadett	31.00	27.00

Vauxhall Astra SRi

N.B. Rates valid 1.11.91 — 31.3.92 unless otherwise indicated. Previous
brochure rates apply for all other destinations.

Standard Terms and Conditions of rental apply.

AVIS ON ISTEL: X # (ABTA NUMBER) AV #

TRAVEL AGENT

AVIS We Try Harder for your peace of mind.

BLACKIE INTERNATIONAL PLC.

25 High Street, The Broadway, London SE16
Fax: (071) 321 1000 Tel: (071) 321 1888

*Your company's
name and address*

November 27, 1993

*The date.
This may also be
written 27/11/93*

*ur correspondent's
me (or title) and
dress*

Avril Stapleton
52 Knighton Drive
Leicester
Midlands

The greeting

Dear Ms Stapleton

I am replying to your letter of November 18. I am pleased to hear of your interest in our new atlas and delighted that it has been so well received by your more senior students.

Our company does have representatives in your area and they frequently give presentations of our new publications to colleges and schools. One of our sales staff would certainly be willing to visit you and your students to talk about the atlas and answer any questions you may have. If you are interested, could you please call me on (071) 321 1888, ext. 205. I will then put you in contact with the co-ordinator of our field visits.

I enclose our most recent brochure since you may wish to have information about some of our other publications. We have, for example, produced an excellent encyclopaedia (see page 56) which is now widely used in schools and has been greatly praised by teachers and pupils.

Once again, thank you for the positive comments you made about our atlas. We always enjoy receiving letters like yours!

*gning off:
you begin Dear Sir
d Yours faithfully.
you begin Dear Ms
apleton or Dear
ril, end Yours
ncerely*

Yours sincerely

S. French

Stewart French
Administrative Assistant

enc.

PROMOTIONAL FLYER

The purpose of a promotional flyer is to encourage or persuade your prospective customer that she needs what you are trying to sell and that (s)he should buy the product or services you are offering.

You take something attractive and make it seem necessary, or you take something necessary and make it seem attractive! Your letter should make an appeal to some buying motive, e.g. it will help someone to save money, get promoted, look more attractive, feel healthier, etc.

A good promotional flyer should have four elements. It should:

- **ATTRACT**
- **AROUSE INTEREST**
- **CREATE DESIRE**
- **INDUCE ACTION**

ATTRACT
Your opening paragraph must be interesting, so that the reader notices what you have to say and is encouraged to read further, rather than throw your flyer into the waste-bin.

AROUSE INTEREST
As mentioned above, you do this by appealing to some buying motive.

CREATE DESIRE
There are many ways of doing this. You may support your claims by facts, e.g. by giving the results of tests or official statistics. Another way might be to offer a free gift, or to send the goods 'on approval'. You could also offer to return goods without obligation if the customer is not satisfied.

INDUCE ACTION
In the final paragraph, you try to persuade the customer to take action. For example, you may invite him/her to visit your factory or showroom, in which case you will probably include a contact telephone number. Or you may provide a tear-off coupon if you wish the customer to place an order or ask for further information.

HI-STYLES STORES

30 Main Street, York, England. Fax 025 640 3200 Tel 025 641 3000

December 10, 19 . .

Ingrid Nielsen
Latchford Manor
Green Lane
Middletown
Staffordshire

Dear Ingrid Nielsen,

ATTRACT — What would you say to a gift that would be a most judicious choice for Christmas? A gift that would make your relations, friends or family happy? And even more so, a gift that could be the pretext for a wonderful dinner party?

YOU can enjoy these advantages by buying our **'DELUXE HAMPER',** a traditional willow hamper, with a double-hinged lid and leather straps, padded with velvet. It is a gourmet's delight. It is separated into three **AROUSE INTEREST** — compartments which include charcuterie products like 'Foie Gras', directly imported from French farms, together with two elegant bottles of red 'Château Margaux' claret and liqueur truffles, mulled fruits, continental biscuits and a deliciously crisp champagne.

This superb **HAMPER** is offered in two different sizes and its cost **CREATE DESIRE** — ranges from £100 for the small one (see description above) and £130 for the largest size, to which is added a smooth, well-rounded brandy and port.

We offer a trade discount of 10% and a further special discount of 5%, **INDUCE ACTION** — making 15% in all, on orders received on or before December 10. Because of rising costs, we cannot extend these terms beyond that date, so why not take advantage of them now and send us an immediate order?

We are offering you goods of the very highest quality and would welcome the opportunity to serve you.

Your sincerely,

Bernadette Peters

Bernadette Peters
Promotions Manager

MEMORANDUM

A memorandum is a written *internal* communication designed to inform employees about policies, procedures and other matters relating to the organisation.

Each paragraph should contain only one idea, and paragraphs may be numbered.

ANITA FASHIONS

MEMORANDUM

Sender's name and/or position the company

FROM   Marketing Director

TO   Sales staff

SUBJECT   Spring collections

DATE: 8/6/19 . .

Addressee's name(s) and/or position(s) in the company

This indicates briefly what the memo is about

Date the memo written

This is an update on our plans for the Spring collections. Our marketing mix will depend heavily on in-store promotions backed up by aggressive TV advertising.

Women's leatherwear and accessories promotion

We have to finally decide what the theme will be for this promotion. Suggestions from your end would be welcomed!

However, we have agreed on these elements of the promotion:

Use lists to be concise

- Window displays in a major London store
- Full-colour flyer to be sent to all our distributors
- Regional fashion shows in selected cities
- Full page advertisements in quality magazines.

With each purchase of a leather jacket, a free gift of a leather purse, wallet or key ring will be offered.

The approximate value of these gifts is £25.

P.K.

The sender may initial a memo, but (s)he never puts a signature

Initialling a memo shows that the text is complete and that you take responsibility for it

RESOURCE MATERIALS

MINUTES

There are several ways of recording what was discussed and decided at a meeting. The minutes below are known as 'resolution minutes'. They show the decisions that were taken at a meeting, but they do not give any indication of the discussion which led to the decisions.

MINUTES OF THE MANAGEMENT MEETING

Held at head office on Wednesday, July 16, 19.. at 10 a.m.

Present: R Pullin (chair), P Sheldrake, J Latour, H Reiss, M Goldoni, C Lee, W Thomas (secretary).

Apologies for absence were received from P Spiropoulos.

Minutes of the last meeting
The minutes of the last meeting, previously circulated, were taken as read and signed as a true record.

Matters arising
There were no matters arising.

Advertising and promotion
In spite of increased advertising and promotional expenditure, the company's performance had been disappointing. In view of this, it was resolved that the present contract with PHK agency be terminated. With effect from January 19 . ., the London advertising agency, Sykes Pemberton, would be appointed to handle the account.

Company logo
It was resolved that a specialist company would be commissioned to design a new logo. M Goldoni agreed to provide a list of suitable firms.

New brochure
It was resolved that P Sheldrake would provide a detailed costing for the production of a new brochure using in-house personnel and facilities. This would be compared with estimates provided by 'outside' firms.

Date of the next meeting
The date of the next management meeting was scheduled for Wednesday July 30, 19 . .

R Pullin
General Manager

July 22, 19 . .

REPORTS

Reports may be formal or informal, and may be sent within the organisation or to outside organisations. They are used in every area of administration and therefore have many different purposes. The function of regular routine reports is simply to provide information, e.g. monthly sales returns, safety inspections, etc. Such reports are produced as a matter of course by whoever is responsible for them, and they generally have a standardised form. Other reports contain the results of investigations. They will put forward ideas and possibly make recommendations.

Format

There is no set layout for reports. Whatever the layout chosen, however, reports should always be presented *schematically*. They should be divided into *sections* and *subsections* which are numbered systematically under headings and subheadings. A longer report will require a more formal and detailed scheme and layout, so that the reader can find his/her way through the material.

Using sections and a numbering system in a report enables people to refer quickly and easily to specific parts in it. Generous use of space and signalling will make a report more readable. Therefore, try to:

a) Leave a margin each side of the page.
b) Leave a line between each section.
c) Use a consistent scheme of headings, subheadings, numbering and indentations.

The following format is common in many reports:

1 Title
This should indicate concisely the subject of the report.

2 Introduction
This section is sometimes called the 'terms of reference'. It states what you are reporting on, who commissioned the report and by when it should be submitted.

3 Body
This presents the main contents of the report.

It could be giving information, setting out findings, putting forward ideas and arguments, etc.

4 Conclusion and Recommendations*
The conclusion says what *you* think about the facts, how *you* interpret them. You will probably do some of the following:

– summarise the discussion in the body of the report.
– summarise findings.
– make recommendations.
– state what action should be taken as a result of your recommendations and by whom.
* Note: Recommendations should only be included if you have been asked to do so. They should, if possible, be *practical* suggestions as to what should be done.

The report should signed with your name and title, and should be dated. The signature and date are put either on the title page of a report or at the end of it.

Format for formal reports

The following format is common for the longer, more formal, report:

1 Title page

2 Terms of reference
   (see *Introduction* above)

3 Procedures
   How you obtained your information, e.g by interviews, questionnaires, observation, desk research, etc.

4 Findings
   The facts you discovered from your investigation.

5 Conclusions and Recommendations
   These are sometimes separate sections.

Writing effective reports

In order to write effective reports, it is essential that:

* You have a clear understanding of the *purpose* of the report. This will influence how you will organise your material.

* You present information in such a way that the reader can understand it quickly. Readability is achieved by:
  – using titles, headings, subheadings, spacing, a numbering scheme, indentation and visual presentation, where appropriate. Statistics, for example, are often better presented in charts, diagrams or tables.

* You select carefully the material to be included in the body of the report. Any material which the reader needs but which would make the report too lengthy and dense should be included in an appendix.

TO: All Staff

FROM: Personnel Director

Date: Jan 5, 19 . .

REPORT ON THE PROPOSED FLEXITIME SYSTEM

1 Our study of the proposed system has now been completed. Under the system, staff would choose their preferred working hours from 6.00 to 22.00 Monday to Saturday. They would, however, be expected to work their normal period of eight hours, with a 45–minute break for lunch. The scheme has been worked out after extensive consultations at all levels in the company and has now been approved by our Board of Directors.

2 The advantages of the new scheme are as follows:

- We shall have greater flexibility in dealing with our customers, especially those in overseas countries whose time zones are different from those in England.

- Staff will be able to avoid the rush hour when they come to work. As a result, their transport costs may be reduced, and they should be less tired at the beginning of the day. This should lead to improved efficiency and morale.

- Staggered hours will mean that the canteen staff will be able to provide a better service. Queues will be less frequent, and tables less crowded.

- Employees will be able to work on Saturday, therefore they may take a day off midweek when, for example, shopping is easier and more convenient.

- Flexible hours should lead to better utilisation of machinery and to a more spacious environment. The latter should have a beneficial effect on employee performance.

3 Although the scheme will bring increased costs – heating and lighting are obvious examples – there are great benefits from introducing flexitime. Besides bringing increased productivity and producing a happier workforce, flexitime allows staff to have greater control over their working lives.

4 After analysing the information provided by questionnaires and receiving feedback from all department heads, we obtained a costing estimate from Finance which showed the scheme was feasible. We knew that it would be popular, and it was for that reason that we have recommended it should be introduced from July 1, 19 . .

Tapescripts for Listening Activities

Unit 1, p12

KF = Kate Farara   RP = Roger Partington

KF Advertising really can work in a number of ways. I mean, if you go through any magazine at the weekend – pick up a Sunday mag., you can pull out a whole selection of pieces of advertising, which are all designed to work in slightly different ways. The most, er, immediate way that advertising can work is to look for an immediate response from the consumer, so that would be the kind of advertiser that has a coupon in the bottom, and is maybe for a . . . send off for a dress, or send off for a tape or something like that.

The second way in which advertising can work is to impart information, and this is particularly true of very expensive products which you're not going to rush out and buy immediately having seen the ad., nor are you going to fill in the coupon and send off for a £15,000 car.

The third way I think in which advertising can work is to relate to your own needs, your wants and your desires. They're things that you feel like you might have, but you don't already have. And advertising in this situation is generally selling you a new product or telling you new news about an old product. Unfortunately we can't keep telling people new news about brands because most of them have been around for quite a long time. So one of the most important roles that advertising has to do is to remind. And this is very important for products which you purchase day-in day-out and you don't really think about: breakfast cereals, confectionery, washing-powder. Chocolate is perhaps a good example where creating brands is particularly important. When you go into the newsagent's on your way home from school and you're feeling peckish, there are probably 20 or 30 products that would fulfil your need.

RP We spend a huge amount of money on advertising. The reason why we do that is because I need to make sure that Rowntree's brands are differentiated from those of our competitors. The basic products are probably not very different one from another. Advertising helps to generate an image, er, around a brand. It helps to generate a, if you like in the case of Smarties, a playground credibility we call it; it's cool to be seen walking around with a tube of Smarties. But if you're aged 15 you wouldn't want to be seen dead carrying them! 50 years ago we didn't have, er, television. In those days the only way that you could communicate, er, the benefits of your product versus your competitors' product was probably through a billboard on the side of a house or something like that.

Advertising is an important part of being able to communicate what the difference is between one type of product and another, but it's not the only part. Er, advertising is one element of what we call the marketing mix. Within the marketing mix you have issues such as the packaging, pricing, distribution and manufacturing. We spend a lot of money on product development, and so our researchers are very important.

Market research of course is very important to us; we need to know what it is that we're doing. So we actually go out to, into the, er, big wide world outside there, and we ask you what you think about this particular product. So what we try and do is, we work out in our own minds, well, who do we think this particular product or brand concept would be, would most appeal to, and test their opinions. Now that gives us a quantitative check. At the end of the day we are what we call a marketing-led company, and that means that we take consumer opinion, er, above all else in the way in which we, er, design our products and our brands.

KF When a manufacturer decides he wants to, er, advertise, erm, a brand we will sit down, and obviously if it's a new brand, then, er, there is a very specific role for the advertiser to perform, which is to launch that brand, to do the news bit, to tell people about it, to create a personality for it. And what we will do is, we will sit down with the manufacturer, and we will agree which is the best way in which advertising can work most effectively to achieve his marketing objectives.

It's very important to keep a constant check on how your target audience is changing because, if you take a brand like Smarties, the target audience has stayed the same since we first started advertising the brand on television in the 50s. But the nature of kids' lives has changed enormously, and the advertising has to reflect the changes in kids' lives and the things that are influences on them.

Unit 2, p21

NB = Neil Beeson   DC = David Cotton   SR = Sue Robbins

NB Puma is renowned for its soccer shoes, and that's where the company's built its base. We also do tennis shoes.

DC Oh really, the first product was soccer?

NB Yes, Puma has been a soccer company right from the beginning, that's its main foundation, and it sells endorsements to go with that, right from Pele, Eusebio, Cruyff, Kempes, Maradonna, Gascoigne and Matthäus; at the world cups all the best soccer players have always worn Puma boots.

SR So does Puma the company produce sports shoes then, or does it produce fashion shoes?

NB It produces sports shoes. Sports shoes come first, and if they become fashionable it is a bonus. It is a major bonus really because unfortunately, er, these days, er, I would say up to 80% of sports shoes are bought for fashion use. Never actually reach a tennis court, a football pitch, a squash court or anything like that. When it's being used for sporting purposes, er, target audience is far wider than the fashion implications. The fashion implications are basically 16-24-year-olds.

SR So you've two different markets there. You've got those buying for sports purposes and those buying for fashion. Tell us a bit about the people who buy them for fashion.

NB Well the age; they're young, they're 16-24-year-olds, they're currently very heavily influenced by peer groups, by peer pressure, by advertising, by imagery and all that, that's associated with the glamour of sport, sport has got a certain amount of glamour, so that does appeal.

SR What kind of life-cycle do the products have?

NB Well unfortunately the UK's got one of the shortest life-cycles in the sports market world. We currently run on approximately at the minute, especially if it's associated, if it becomes a fashionable product, three months. We try to make products work for as long as twelve months to eighteen months; that is a good product if it can last

157

that long; but I mean if it becomes fashionable, if a colour of a certain shoe becomes very fashionable it expands at a tremendous rate and then it's not wanted any more.

DC I'd like to come back to your main product, the football boot. What have been some of the major innovations in designing football boots?

NB Erm, I would say something like having removable studs. There's been all sorts of material innovations in terms of reducing weight, making them more flexible, making them more comfortable . . .

DC So you've constantly been innovating?

NB Yes, I mean this is the segment of the sports category that we have been the most innovative in that, that is why we're still known for that, and that's why we're still ahead of the competition. We've been talking to Linford [Linford Christie, Olympic 100m Gold Medallist] on the development of our latest technology which, I don't know if you're aware of, is the PUMA disc system.

DC Can you tell us about that?

NB Well basically what the system does, it replaces laces in the standard form. Er, it is a single wire that is connected to a planetary gearing system that, erm, you turn a disc on the top of the shoe clockwise and it tightens the whole of the lace rote, and you can also turn it anti-clockwise to loosen it slightly if you feel that you've overtightened it, or it becomes too tight when you're playing sport, and there also is a quick release on it; by pressing the centre of the disc and pulling the tongue forward you can be out of it in seconds. That's what the company's focusing its marketing on at the minute. That's what we're spear-heading the company's strategy behind.

DC It will give you an edge over the competitors?

NB Yes, because what it is, it's a fit system; basically there's been a lot of technologies around in mid-soles, in the part between your foot and the ground, but those technologies don't work correctly unless your foot is firmly placed above the mid-sole, and it's not slipping about, it's not moving about. So what the system does, it acts like a second skin and it holds your foot in the correct position above the mid-sole.

SR Are you in a very competitive industry?

NB It is incredibly competitive now, yes, because it is such a big world-wide market. There's a lot of companies want a share of that market . . .

SR So innovations like the disc system are vital, really, to the survival of the product?

NB They are, yes, yes, definitely.

DC Can I just ask you a little bit about market share. Can you tell us anything about the market share of the big companies?

NB If we talk purely UK terms, the market leader currently is Reebok, who have approaching 13% I think of the market. Erm, then there's a close battle behind that, I'm not quite sure who's in the lead at the minute, you've got Adidas, Nike and Hi-tech somewhere in there, but that's purely because they sell, um, volume; they sell entry-level products which are cheap products and they sell massive volume of them; and then it is ourselves – Puma.

DC Do you advertise here, or does Puma, head-office?

NB Yes, we, Puma AG which is Puma Germany advertises on a pan-European basis; through the likes of MTV. We're on MTV for five months – we started in January and it'll take us forward to July – with an advert.

DC So they do a European advert, do they? A similar one in every country?

NB They do, yes, which we then use on the national TV, ITV, Channel 4 and BSkyB. What the disc system advert was designed to do in actual fact was basically be a brand advert. It is an awareness advert. Puma's been off the advertising market for a long time now and our name has dropped tremendously, so basically what this was, it was a brand exercise, er, that we could get behind, through disc, and it was an awareness campaign, which did target 16-24-year-olds heavily.

For the spend that we had in the UK, which was approximately 1.5 million, in the TV campaign the results that we had from the advert, in the latest marketing magazine actually, we've scored number 15 on the recall of being associated with the advert and the brand.

p23

JW = John Williams

DC Can you describe the product?

JW Yes. Reebok, erm, manufacture a wide range of high-performance athletic footwear, er, training shoes, in other words, and complementary clothing or apparel.

DC Can you, erm, give us a sort of consumer profile, I mean what sort of people are they aiming at?

JW We are aiming at anybody who has an interest in sport, er, it doesn't mean that you've got to be a high class or top quality athlete, it's anybody who wants to perform sport at whatever level they want to perform. Our marketing philosophy is that we manufacture shoes and clothing to enhance sporting ability at whatever level, so with Reebok you can achieve your own personal best; so it's, it's across the board, from, it's men and women and of course children and teenagers.

SR And what main marketing techniques do you use?

JW The main marketing techniques we use are of course advertising, television advertising, er, and then we use the whole range of below-the-line support which is an intensive public relations, brand awareness campaign, and of course point-of-sale material in all outlets that link into particular ranges of shoes.

SR What about sponsorship?

JW Yes, we do do sponsorship. Each country, er, will have a range of . . . that comes from the international area, erm, and we also have a range of UK-based sponsored athletes. We do a lot of different sort of youth sponsorships, erm, targeting specifically at young sports people, we have 'Reebok Fives' which is a junior five-a-side football tournament which takes place throughout the country; we should have at least 25,000 youngsters taking place in that this year. That's for soccer. We've just introduced 3-on-3 basketball, which is a similar young basketball competition; Junior Grand Prix which is specifically for tennis. Erm, at the more professional end we have the Reebok national aerobic champions, which is for fitness, and aerobics, both men and women. We obviously sponsor various road races at different levels and different locations for the running. We have running clubs, erm, we have sponsored running clubs and various running events throughout the country.

DC Do you have any exciting new products? Anything that's leading edge technology?

JW Yes. We launch new shoes obviously twice a year, linked into spring and summer, and autumn and winter. But this year we are unveiling very state-of-the-art technology for the running market, which will filter down to other sporting disciplines, and that's known as the Insta Pump, Reebok Insta Pump. The Insta Pump is utilising our pump technology which basically takes into account that no two people's feet are the same size, and you need superb cushioning and superb fit of an athletic shoe, to be able to perform at a superbly high level. So what the pump technology is, is it's an inflatable air chamber which you pump up in various key areas of the feet, which needs, sorry, the areas of the feet that would need specific cushioning. So it's either the insole, the outsole, the forefoot or whatever, and you inflate that to make it like a glove so it fits like a glove. The Insta Pump basically, erm, is a shoe that is comprised of purely pump, and the pump is on the outside of the foot and it's inflated by using a CO_2 gas cannister, and so it is incredibly light, there are no laces, it's the nearest thing to running barefoot but with the added benefit of the traction of spikes.

Unit 3, p27

FJ = Francine Jason

DC Can you just tell us what marketing ethics are, or what you understand them to be?

FJ Right, well marketing ethics is a bit of a controversial area. It's basically all about these moral principles. It's a decision that has to be taken about an issue, or a potentially explosive issue, erm, regarding whether it is morally right or morally wrong.

Erm, it's very much taken at a strategic level, erm, about a particular issue. Erm, obviously who is going to judge whether it is morally right or wrong is a debatable question. I mean, what is morally right to one person is morally wrong to another. Erm, using the example in fact of the Benetton advertisement, erm, where they're showing . . . the first advertisement was this new born baby in all its blood and glory, and everything, erm, and the idea is that 'united by birth' and the latest one 'united by death' and they're showing this father, you know, leaning over his son dying of AIDS and everything. Now some people say, you know, that is ethically wrong. How can you cash in on somebody's misery and this, you know terrible thing about AIDS. The other side, the other camp is saying, well ethically we believe it's right because we should be, you know, exposing this AIDS issue. And there's nothing wrong with it at all. So, it's very difficult to say what is right and what is wrong – that's why it's such a controversial area.

DC In a company who would decide? I mean in a large company. Who would set the tone as it were, do you think?

FJ Well, I think in any large company . . . they have to have some kind of uniform guiding, some kind of code and policies that have to permeate throughout the organisation, even inasmuch as how the employers treat their staff, they have to do it in an ethical way, and once they set this code, this code should then be translated into everything else including marketing, and . . . as I said before, marketing ethics really relates to a particular, erm, problem, so the person or the group of people who would be concerned with it would be at a strategic level, management level. What should we do in this case? But the organisation should run along certain ethical lines . . .

p31

FJ = Francine Jason

DC Is it reasonable for a business person to accept, I don't know, a box of chocolates or a [FJ The bribes of business, yes.] bottle of whisky? At what level does a present become a bribe?

FJ It's an interesting area, I mean does this all come into corporate hospitality, you know, if you entertain your clients, and take them to Ascot and send them lovely gifts, should they give you all their business? It's like with . . . going back to the medical profession, do the doctors only prescribe those pills which are the trademark of the chap who's giving him a lovely free holiday? or a weekend away?

DC Is a free holiday a bribe? To a doctor?

FJ Is a free holiday a bribe? Well, again we don't know what goes on, but I'm sure there are certain bribes that do go on, and it puts the sales rep. in a favourable light, and you feel obliged in a way. Erm, again, you still have your own free will, and you are under no pressure, you know, you can still say if this is a wrong product. If you have a choice between two identical products, OK, perhaps a box of chocolates might, you know, persuade you one way or another. Erm, it is yet again questionable. If, you know . . . one party might say it is morally wrong to accept bribes, and the other one might say well, you know, what difference?

DC So it's a personal choice.

FJ It's a personal thing, but really it should be in the consumers' interests. Marketing is all about, you know, er, trying to give the consumer the best, whilst pursuing this profit motive, and as long as the consumer does get the best product at the best price, and where there is . . . you know, they have a free choice, there's competition in the area, erm, they have the right to say 'I want this one or I want that one'.

Unit 4, p36

AW = Alan Wroxley

DC Alan, I know that you've done many presentations in your job as a sales manager. Can you tell me why do business people have to make presentations?

AW Well, really there'll be three reasons, three main reasons why people make presentations, and they can be divided quite separately, although they're all linked together.

The first one will be a new product, when you're trying to launch a new product to the sales force, into the UK, maybe to a group of sales managers from different companies. That would be a totally different approach to say, when you're launching a sales campaign, which might be used to promote that new product. And then the third area would be an incentive to actually get the sales campaign underway. So they're all linked but in themselves they'd all be different promotions. Sometimes they'd be made on the same day, but most of the time they'd be made separately.

DC I see, are the techniques required for those types of presentations, are they very different?

AW They differ slightly. Erm, the presentation for a new product, we would actually try and get your product there amongst the delegates, and you'd probably try to limit it to a small number of delegates. With a sales campaign it's not so important that you have the product there. The main message to get across is the benefits that the new product will bring and, if you like, the, er, incentives that go with it.

DC So you have to be pretty enthusiastic, for that type of thing.

AW Yes. The key to all of them is to be enthusiastic because what you've got to leave your delegates going away with is as much enthusiasm for the product as you've got. And if they've got that enthusiasm, they'll go out into the market, they'll promote your new product, they'll get involved in the sales campaign, and indeed they'll want to take part in an incentive, which is the third reason I was going to give you. They'll want to get involved in the incentive that will actually ensure that the sales campaign is a success, and that incentive might be a trip abroad, it might be to win a television or something like that. But, if you can infuse them with that enthusiasm they'll take that out and they'll do your job for you which is what you want them to do. That's, that's, I suppose the ultimate aim of a sales presentation is for them to go out and do your job.

DC I see. Erm, you've done a lot of presentations. Do you get nervous before them?

AW You do. I think the larger the presentation, or the presentation to more people, the more nervous you get. Also, er, the more you know about a product the least nervous you'll get. So, I think the idea is to have, er, good preparation for any presentation, it does take the nerves out of it.

DC What ways do you use of getting your information across, Alan, in the presentation?

AW Well, there are various ways to use, and again it would depend on the type of presentation you're doing. If you're doing a small, rather intimate presentation, you might limit yourself to handouts, having equipment available for people to look at and use personally. If it's the larger presentation, or slightly larger presentation, you'll use an overhead projector. And then for the very big presentation when you're hiring a hotel, and you've got a lot of delegates coming from a long way away then often you'll use a professional media company, and you'll have a very slick presentation with music, with lights, erm, with slides and indeed often with video to get your message across. So those are the, if you like, the main tools of the job.

I always find it useful to have handouts because when people come they might not write down the relevant points that you want them to write down, a lot of them won't make notes. Whatever presentation you're doing, whatever it is, you've always got to give something to go away with on what you've been presenting, or else it's forgotten.

DC Well that's useful information. What would you say are the elements of a good presentation? What are the secrets of success?

AW I think the main secret is enthusiasm. If you've got enthusiasm for your product then the people who are listening to you will have enthusiasm. Keep it pertinent, always keep it pertinent. You can wander off, so it's important that you do your research, as I mentioned earlier, that you know what you're talking about, and keep it, keep to the objective you've set yourself.

p40

AW = Alan Wroxley

Good afternoon everybody. I'd like to thank you all first of all for giving up your time to come here today and listen to me. I hope that by the end of the day you'll think that your time has been well spent.

You're not of course going to remember everything that you're going to hear of course but I hope you will leave with a knowledge of what the equipment can do for you and for your customers, and I suppose most importantly how you can make money by selling it.

Some of you I know will want to take notes, and please do so. However, all of you will be given a handout at the end of the day which will give you some details about the information I'm going to give to you, and also it'll give you some graphics that you can use in your sales presentations to your customers.

I'm going to talk today about a new product, a new range of fax machines, and I'm not going to tell you only about the product but how by selling it, we can all make profit by doing just that. And that I suppose is the most important effect. How we can make profit.

The new range of faxes I'm going to familiarise you with are the fax 430, the 450 and of course our brand new 1200 PX. Now the main purpose of the talk, of my talk, is to outline the major benefits of using these models and I shall discuss these benefits in terms of Ease of Use and Cost Savings – probably the most important to your customers. So remember I shall discuss the major selling points of the machines under those headings.

Before doing so, I would like you to look at some very interesting statistics which I hope you'll find very encouraging. I'd also like to tell you about some trends in the fax market. Then I'll move on to my main topic. Is that all right? Is everybody happy with that?

Let's look at some figures, I'll put them up on the screen now. The first you can see are that there are 15-20 million fax machines being used in the world. In the US alone there are five and a half million faxes in use alone. Now what does that mean to the UK? For most of the time when we're selling, what we're interested in is the size of the UK market. What do those world statistics mean to us?

Well, what it means is that every machine we sell in the UK can communicate with those machines out there, so if there are 20 million in use, that means all of the machines that we're selling can speak to those machines out there.

Now there are 800,000 in use in the UK, and that's an equivalent for one in three organisations having a fax machine. Now there are 800,000 machines in the UK and as you can see they can communicate with five and a half million machines in the US and 20 million worldwide. That's food for thought, isn't it? Just looking at those two figures. What does that mean to us?

One in three organisations in the UK have a fax machine. Well of course what it means is that two out of three organisations don't have a fax. So I would suggest to you that in fact the home market has hardly been touched.

Let me give you an example which I think really brings out graphically what I mean. I walked into a chain store in Manchester the other day and I needed a leaflet that the chap didn't have. I wanted some information on a product he was trying to sell me, so I said to him, why don't you ask your office to fax that information to you. He didn't have a fax machine. Now that particular chain store has 500 branches, and he informed me that none of them have a fax machine. Now the head office has two or three machines, but think of that potential, a potential of 500 machines from just that one organisation. Forget going along the rest of the high street and finding out how many other branches of other chain stores that have any fax machines they can use.

Right. Well, I've given you some statistics and discussed what I think they mean in terms of potential sales for all of us. And I've pointed out that say in ten to fifteen years time, almost every office in the country will have a fax machine, and when I say office, I don't just mean every company, every office within that company will have a fax machine just as only the principal in the old days would have a computer or even a calculator, now everybody has a calculator or a computer. Just so in the future, everybody will have a fax machine that is available for their own use.

Now let me turn to some other trends in the market. You will be aware of some of them, I'm sure. But it might be useful if I remind you of some of them.

Now if you would please look at the screen again, you'll see that I've listed them under the headings of 'memory models,', 'high speed transmission', 'plain paper', 'ease of use' and finally, 'cost savings'.

Right. Well, I'll start with memory models. I'm sure you've all noticed that more and more machines today have those memories. Very important for when you're getting an incoming fax, you run out of paper, you can still receive that message. No messages are lost, one of the most important benefits of having a memory. The other, of course, I'm sure you and your customers, I suppose, have all waited in a queue to use the fax machine. With a memory, of course, you can programme your fax to go later when the fax is not quite so busy. So two benefits for the memory machines.

OK. We've looked at some of the figures and we've examined the major market trends in the industry. I'm going now to discuss with you the major benefits of our new models.

Put it quite simply, all of the new features on them are designed to make the machines easier to use and to reduce the cost of using them. So the major advantages are Ease of Use and Cost Saving. These are the benefits I shall come back to again and again as I talk to you about the features on the models which I'm sure you'll then emphasise when talking about them to your customers and end users. These two areas, these two benefit areas, give our models the edge over the competitors' products.

Now in the handout which I'll give you at the end of the talk I've listed under the heading 'Ease of Use' all of the features that contribute to this – and there are quite a few by the way – and these are the features which make the machines so user-friendly and which give the user all of the facilities and the quality of reproduction that users expect when they buy a new fax machine. I'll comment now on each of the features one by one, but don't hesitate to ask me any questions because it's much better we cover the points now rather than having to come back to them later when perhaps we've passed that topic and it's not quite so relevant.

So, by turning to the first feature which you can all see if you look at the screen now. It's 'Simple to set up' and let's think, that applies to every single product we sell. If you can't set the thing up, you can't use it properly. You don't get the benefits that are in those machines.

All of the models that you'll see that we show you today are very easy to set up. Why is this so? Quite simply, because there are step-by-step programme instructions in the very large liquid crystal display and a very simple Alpha key system for entering in that data.

I've explained to you why the new fax models are so easy to use and we've looked at each of these new features in details. Now let's now talk about 'cost savings'. And when I say cost savings, I don't just mean cost savings when you buy the machine, I mean cost savings when you use them. A powerful argument with our customers, and a major selling point of any fax machine – as you all well know.

I'll start by talking about 'fast transmission speeds'. Probably the most important, the most obvious, – the less time you spend on line, the less it will cost you in your telephone bill. The most obvious reason to save money.

Now would you please look at these new figures showing the improved transmission times for all of our new models. Quite impressive, aren't they? You'll notice immediately that the transmission speed of the 1200 PX is ten seconds faster than our previous models.

I hope that I've given you all now a clear idea of the benefits of using the new models which are, of course, 'Ease of Use' and 'Cost Saving'. Thanks to them, you should have no trouble at all in convincing our customers that we've got the best fax models on the market. Models which are user-friendly, fast and cheap to operate, and which provide really high-class, high-quality reproduction.

Well thank you very much everybody for coming. I do appreciate it, and for giving so much attention. Thank you for showing so much interest in our products. That's all now. Let's get out into the market place and show everybody what we can do with them.

Thanks everybody. Have a safe journey home. And let's do it now.

Unit 5, p51

VE = Victoria Ewin

DC Can we just start by asking you about any successful products or ranges of products . . .

VE Well obviously our most successful product is the silk scarf which everybody knows Hermès for. It makes up about 25% of our business, which is phenomenal. Other things that have been great successes, and still are for us, but obviously in a much smaller market, are our handbags, the leather Kelly bag, which was made famous by Grace Kelly; erm, the ties, which have become extremely fashionable over the last five years, having been sort of normal business really until then, picked up as soon as we started doing small animal prints on our ties and things like that they became the rage, and Prince Charles wears them, and, right the way down the line.

DC What is special about the scarf to you think? I mean why is it so popular?

VE We choose a very special silk which is made into a much thicker twill than most of the other scarves that you find, so it makes it a heavier feeling scarf. Erm, we also have developed a method of printing our scarves in a much more sophisticated way than anyone else. We can do up to 34 colours in our scarves, all very, very effectively printed . . . and I think that people have just fallen in love with that colour and amazing designs that we have. We've done over a thousand scarf designs now.

SR Who designs them?

VE It's a huge body of people. Anyone could design a Hermès scarf. We're very open to young ideas, and young talent – and things like that.

SR And who are the customers who buy the scarf – and also the other products?

VE Completely different. I mean everybody from, sort of, the most obvious and traditional sort of Sloane Ranger type lady that one would see walking down Sloane Street, to very young, very fashionable people who wear them as belts to jeans or sort of round their Jean-Paul Gaultier suit and things like that; people who've saved up for years to buy a scarf who may come from the Outer Hebrides and come travelling down to London and sometimes spend two hours choosing a scarf.

DC Do you segment your market at all, or is it really that wide a range, or are you aiming roughly at higher income groups?

VE I think that we like to imagine that anybody can come to us at some stage during their life and have a part of Hermès. Things start with our fragrances – which is the first step in the dream. We're not selling, I don't think we ever feel that we're selling luxury, I know that my chairman is very averse to the word luxury, erm, it's a wonderful generic term that's used over here, but we like to think we're selling an amazingly beautiful piece of whatever it may be. And so that therefore we don't want to say you know, we're putting it at this price so no one else can have it and we only want to be seen on the most chic ladies in Paris and London. Erm, we would like to feel that anyone could aspire to having something from Hermès.

SR So your image is really of a beautiful or a classic piece of . . .

VE Very much so, I mean craftsmanship is everything to us, more so than price or name. There are very few things that we make that actually have Hermès emblazoned over them. Everything that we make is made by Hermès, we don't give out anything to anybody else, all our perfumes are made by Hermès. And if it's another company that makes it then we usually own at least part of that company.

DC Have you ever considered diversifying, or licensing your name?

VE Certainly not. It's one of the things that we feel very strongly about, that it would just ruin our whole Hermès thing. As I said we're very tight-knit and the family still own Hermès. . . . Jean-Louis Dumas Hermès is still our Chairman, he's the fifth generation of the Hermès family, and I think he feels that to licence his name would be admitting to that terrible sort of snobbery of branding rather than of quality and of tradition and craftsmanship. . . .

SR What are the plans for the future then; if you're already international, and if you don't have plans to bring the brand downmarket? What is the way ahead for the Company?

VE I think it's, just, we're constantly expanding our product lines. We just this year launched a new range of cutlery . . . beautiful silver cutlery, and a new range of porcelain, in fact our whole, what we call, 'Art de la table', which is the tableware side, is getting bigger and bigger, and that's something we've expanded wholesale as well so we'll sell in for example to Harrods, to Thomas Good, to Mappin & Webb and those sort of people with those products. With our perfume as well . . . Perfume is very important to us. Calèche was our first perfume in the 60's, and we've just launched a new Calèche which is called Soie de Parfum Calèche, and that again is a way of expanding our market. We believe that the Hermès customer will not feel that by bringing in porcelain or cutlery that we're kind of becoming a sort of mad marketer of goods. We feel that everything should complement everything we already sell.

VE We've been going for 155 years, making saddles and harnesses which we still make.

DC Is that what you started with?

VE Yes.

SR And you still make them?

VE Yes! We still make them, . . .

DC So the earlier product ranges were leather goods, and then presumably the scarf and the silk.

VE Well what happened was we started off as wholesale harness makers, to the carriage makers of the Champs Elysées, and when we got more and more well-known we decided to start selling things properly to the retail market, started making saddles and things like that, and then the car came along and we realised we were going to be in a bit of trouble if we didn't do something so we started applying the same technique we were using to make our saddles and harnesses which is this double, knotted stitch, so that if one stitch breaks the whole lot don't go, which they do with machine stitching, we started applying it to luggage and wallets, and eventually to leather jackets and coats and things like that and we became a huge success. In fact our scarves didn't start until the 1950's, no, actually that's not true, no the scarves started in '37 the ties started in the 50's, as a kind of add on – they were sort of the fashion accessory that everyone wanted, and we used to buy them in from other companies and we realised that we could make them better.

Unit 6, p58

SB = Stella Beaumont

DC Is it possible to make an advertisement which crosses borders?

SB Yes it's perfectly possible to do so, providing a number of different criteria apply. Firstly, it will only work providing that the brand, that's the product that we're trying to sell, works in the same way in the different countries under consideration; that it's got the same image, that the same values are attached to it, and that as a result of that it's bought by the same type of person.

An obvious example of a brand of that kind would be, say, Coca Cola which is obviously the one that springs to most people's minds when they're thinking about transnational branding. Now providing all that happens, and that the media consumption habits of the people who you're trying to influence are the same in different countries, then it is perfectly possible to do so.

The other factor that will determine whether it's a success or not is whether the organisation itself is geared up towards selling, distributing and marketing in a pan-European manner, because otherwise the whole thing will break down completely. If you're talking about a multi-national organisation, which is still structured in a vertical way, with the manufacturing, marketing, distribution happening at country level, you can't then make an advertisement which crosses borders. You have to have that central, logistical organisation in place first, before your transnational advertisement will work properly.

DC I see. Right.

SR So are more companies moving in that direction? Are companies beginning to restructure as . . .

SB Yes. It's starting to happen. I mean, it's not happening as fast as people thought it was going to happen, erm . . . certainly a lot of British companies, my perception is in the run-up to 1992, aren't quite there yet. But I think we're going to see over the next decade that that will be the way companies are looking to organise from now on.

DC Can you give us any examples of campaigns that you think have been very successful or unsuccessful?

SB Erm . . . I was at a conference in the autumn at which we had a very interesting presentation from the vice president, marketing, for American Express, and he gave an exceptionally interesting presentation, because he showed an advertisement which I'm sure we'll all have seen, without probably realising that it actually was a pan-European advertisement; and that, I think, is critical to its success. The one I'm thinking about was an advertisement featuring a woman fashion photographer who was on the way to shoot the designer collections in either Milan or, or Paris, and she had her camera equipment . . . went on the wrong flight so she had to go into a local camera dealer's and buy a new set of equipment. Now the interesting thing about this advertisement was that although the backdrop to the set was exactly the same, the footage of the collections themselves, the camera seller, the friend in the café, what was interesting was that in each different country the fashion photographer herself was played by a different actress. Because we in England have a completely different perception of what a fashion photographer should look like; what she should wear and what sort of luggage she's carrying, to the way that they would in France, or to Italy or to Spain. So I thought it was an exceptionally good advertisement, because none of us would have thought, 'Oh, this is a pan-European advertisement'.

SR So the key there is making each market feel as if that advertisement was designed for them?

SB I think that's absolutely critical. A danger that you can fall into with pan-European advertising is that it's too bland, that it hasn't got enough character, that it doesn't appeal enough to the local audience; and anyone who thinks that everyone in Europe is exactly the same, even if they would fall into the same income groups, or did the same occupations, would of course be crazy.

DC The example you cited was very interesting. What they did in fact simply was tailor that advertisement to the taste . . .

SB Very wise. So they got both. They did get those economies of scale on the shoot, as you were saying. They only have one tetchy prima donna of a creative director to deal with, and one set of expensive location shots, and the rest could all be done relatively cheaply in the studio.

Unit 7, p65

SQ = Siobhan Quinn

DC What is your actual title?

SQ My actual title is Manager, Bulk Sales, Texaco Fuel and Marine Marketing Department, Europe. So you're probably sorry you asked that!

DC Well let's get into negotiation. I mean are negotiators born or made would you say?

SQ I would say a very rare few are born, most of us are actually made, and I'd say just about anybody can learn to be a negotiator, because negotiation is really taking skills that exist within yourself, and honing them to the appropriate situation, so although some people, you could say that the market trader or somebody selling bagels in the East End is a born trader or negotiator, I would say most negotiators are, are made, whether from necessity or desire.

SR What are some of those skills then that you need to be good at negotiating a contract?

SQ You don't want a business deal where you have left the other person so crushed that they are not ever going to come back to do business with you again. You actually want to reach that middle ground where you've achieved something, they've achieved something, and if you can't reach that middle ground then the chances are you shouldn't be looking at a deal at that particular time anyway.

SR So it's important to go for a win-win situation.

SQ Yes it is, yeah.

SR Do you trade, or do you negotiate with a lot of people whose first language isn't English then?

SQ Yes, I would say I do. Probably 50 – 60% of the business we do are with non-native English speakers.

SR Right. And does that affect your strategy during a negotiation or not?

SQ I wouldn't say whether or not English was their native language necessarily affects the strategy, because most of the people that we deal with do speak English rather fluently. What would affect your strategy is a knowledge of, possibly their cultural bias; which you could say also exists within native English speakers. You might approach an American slightly different from you would approach an English or a Scots person you were negotiating with – so it's, it's an awareness of a little more than the language that you're dealing with that would influence how you would approach the negotiation.

SR So do you, do you usually try to familiarise yourself with the background of the people you're dealing with?

SQ Oh absolutely, that's your . . . biggest asset in a negotiation. There is no one winning formula for a negotiation, it is very much a case of not only knowing your own business, but it's an understanding of the personality of the other party involved; and in the course of a day you might take three or four different approaches to negotiations depending on the personality of the other party.

DC What sort of approaches would these be though, I mean would you play it very tough with an American or . . . ?

SQ In terms of the people I deal with, and I'm just running through my mind right now, some of the utility buyers that we work with, . . .

DC Can you give us a profile of some of these people in broad terms?

SQ Right OK. There's erm, there's one person I deal with who's Irish, well-educated, he actually has a background from a major oil company himself, very gregarious, talkative, knowledgeable about the industry but also quite erratic in the way he deals with things. If you catch him in a certain mood on a certain day he will make up his mind just instantly, and say 'right, I feel good about this – that's that.' On another day, or another week even, it could take you, take you hours and hours of chatting through and you'd get 'Mmm, I don't know, I'm not sure about this, I don't feel good about this.' He's a very intuitive buyer. Whereas somebody else we deal with is very much plays by the book, by the numbers, so it's no use going to buyer number 1 saying, 'this is what historical figures will tell you and this is definitely the time to buy, and this is a fair price', you have to say, 'Ooh, you can feel the market's moving this way, you know now's a good time to buy because if you wait a week it's going to be $10 higher'. Whereas the second buyer you would very much approach with a straightforward – 'well the PLAS', which is an oil-related index, 'PLAS is telling you that you have a price of X and this is a fair price that we're giving you and therefore you should buy' – and he would buy it on that, whereas trying to put an intuitive approach into this person's mind wouldn't get you anywhere. So it's knowing the person you're dealing with.

DC What areas of a negotiation cause most trouble, would you say?

SQ The areas of a negotiation that would cause most trouble really are when you have somebody on the opposing side that doesn't recognise that they're in a position of negotiating, i.e. you get no feedback whatsoever, so you are speaking and negotiation . . . it's a bit of a dance really: two steps forward, the other party two steps forward and just edging around maybe even like a boxer is, edging around each other until you actually make contact. But when you have somebody that refuses to give anything back, well then there's not too much you can do about that. Because you . . . you have one of two options – you either give up before you start or you lay all your cards on the table instantly and say that is my position, there's no room in this, I can't budge, and either take it or leave it. That's the only way you can deal with a person in those circumstances. But most business, there should be enough factors at hand that there should be a give and take in the terms of how you negotiate.

DC What advice would you give to someone who wanted to be a sales negotiator?

SQ The advice I would give is, erm . . . know your own business as much as you possibly can; know their business as much you possibly can, and know them. If you know where you're starting from, if you understand your business then you're not going to make a mistake on your side. The more you know their business the better chance you have of actually pitching your own sales strategy appropriately. And the more you know of the person you're dealing with, the better chance you have of success.

To be successful in negotiating you actually need to listen to the other party and hear . . . it's not always said in the words they're saying, but hear the hesitations, hear . . . if you're face to face, you can actually read the body language. Since most of our business is not face to face you don't have the body language, so it's even more important that you can pick up over the telephone the clues as to what is actually going through that person's head, whether you are way off mark with the approach you are taking or whether you're actually just two cents apart from each other, so I would say listening is a very important skill.

p68

Dialogue 1

JM = Jerry Mullins   CH = Charles Ramsay

JM I've come to see you about the course I applied for. I couldn't believe it when I got your memo. What's the problem exactly?

CR I thought I made it clear, we can't let you go. There's just no money for that sort of thing, anyway not for the moment.

JM Oh, how come?

CR It's the cutbacks, our budget's been reduced, so we can't do all the things we'd like to do. I'm sorry, I know you're disappointed, but then so are a lot of other people.

JM Well it's not good enough. You can't tell me that a company this size can't find the money to pay for the course. It only lasts three days, and it's not that expensive. What's three hundred pounds these days, for goodness' sake.

CR It's a lot of money, I can tell you and . . .

JM Oh come on now. In any case, they promised me back home, I could go on any course I wanted during my attachment here. Now you're trying to worm out of it with all this talk of cutbacks . . .

CR Hold on now. Let me explain how things are here. When money's tight like it is now, middle managers get priority. If there's anything left over, it's the turn of people like you. OK?

JM No, rubbish! It's not the way to do things at all. Totally unfair. I can't miss a chance like this. I've really got to go.

CR Sorry.

JM Look, how about . . . erm . . . if I were to offer to pay something towards the course . . .

CR Eh?

JM Yeah, I'd be willing to put some money towards it . . . say, erm, well maybe a hundred pounds. How about that?

CR I'm sorry, we couldn't consider it. We just don't do things like that.

JM All right then, I'll pay a hundred and fifty. But I can't afford more than that. Surely that's reasonable. What more do you want?

CR Listen, Mr Mullins. You've got to understand – there's no way you can go on the course, right? It's company policy – I can't change it. And you've just got to accept it. If you work in a company like ours, you've got to toe the line sometimes.

JM Mmm . . . so that's it, is it?

CR Afraid so.

JM I was hoping you'd be a bit more flexible. Didn't expect to be refused point blank. I can't believe it.

CR We'd better leave it there, I think. Things may be different in a few months time. There could be more money around for . . .

JM It won't help me. I'll be back home by then.

Dialogue 2

HG = Hans Guertler   HD = Helen Dawson

HG OK, Helen, come in to my office.

HD Thank you very much Hans. I must say that was most interesting. That's quite good equipment, isn't it?

HG Yes, they're certainly good machines.

HD Mmm.

HG And they are worth a lot of money.

HD Well I'm not sure about this yet but, erm, we are in the market for second-hand equipment, so let's talk.

HG Right, well, for all the equipment as you've seen it, we would like to bill you a hundred thousand pounds.

HD Oh my goodness! I'm not sure that, er, we're going to be able to get anywhere near that, Hans.

HG Well, you know they are top quality machines and they're in excellent condition.

HD Yeah, that may be so, but we're going to have to, er, look at this a little differently. I had in mind something nearer seventy thousand pounds.

HG No way Helen, sorry.

HD Well I'm afraid we're not going to be able to do business then.

HG No no, just a moment. Er well, what about . . . let me see . . . well I could manage eighty thousand.

HD Eighty, you say?

HG Yes, but you would have to pay a deposit, of thirty thousand up front and the balance within six months.

HD Thirty thousand, and the rest over six months.

HG That's right. How does that sound to you?

HD Well, I think we might be able to do that.

HG Fine then. That's agreed.

HD Good, but I think we ought perhaps to cover one or two other points before we get too far.

HG By all means, what are they?

HD Well, first of all, could we talk about servicing and spares?

HG Sure. As you know the spares are OK – they're off the shelf. And the servicing, if there is a breakdown, we'll fix it.

HD Uh huh. And what about warranty? You know we'd really like a one-year warranty.

HG Oh well, that's a bit difficult, Helen. You know company policy is three months. And I'm sorry I can't go along with you on that. We have to stick to three months.

HD Really?

HG Yes. I'm afraid so.

HD Oh, all right, well let's leave that point then, erm, what else haven't we talked about, what about delivery?

HG Well, we could get everything to you probably within two months.

HD No, no, no. That's no good. I'm afraid, no good at all. We shall probably want this equipment by the end of the month. Is there any way you can do that?

HG Oh, that's a bit difficult, but let me think. Well we could manage it, I suppose if we laid on some special road transport . . .

HD Yeah, well, that's probably the only solution. Look, I wonder, when could you get back to me and confirm that?

HG Well, I'll confirm the details next week, but your request is fair enough. You'll have the equipment by the end of the month – and I think we've got a deal! Let's just summarise it, shall we?

HD OK, well, first of all, there's the price – £30,000 deposit, a further £50,000 over six months. And then what we've said about servicing and spares – you'll provide both.

HG Right.

HD And er . . .

HG The delivery, special road transport by the end of the month – details to be confirmed.

HD Yeah. And don't forget the three months warranty.

HG OK.

HD Fine. OK, that sounds good.

HG Good, Helen.

HD We've got a deal, Hans.

HG OK, let's go for a drink.

p69

CM = Carson Martin   PE = Pieter van Eck

CM Let's agree first on how to organise today's meeting, shall we?

PE Uh-huh.

CM OK, well, how about starting with the contract itself? Then we could move on to the product range, sales targets and discounts. How does that sound for the morning session?

PE That sounds fine. There's plenty to talk about there, for sure. Do you want me to start things off?

CM Why not? Go ahead.

PE OK, well, as you know, we've signed up quite a few overseas agents recently. What we're looking for really is exclusivity – we think an exclusive agent can offer us more – more commitment, more motivation and better service. We'd like to build up the relationship gradually, based on trust, and common interest . . .

CM I've got to stop you right there, Pieter. Sorry, but we just can't agree to that. An exclusive agreement is out of the question. Absolutely impossible.

PE Oh, how's that then?

CM It's just that we're agents for a lot of big manufacturers, European, North American, a couple from the Far East, and we're locked into agreements with them. There's no way we can break them. In any case, we wouldn't want to – we've always handled competitors' products, it's the way we run our business.

PE I see.

CM Look, exclusivity isn't everything, you know. We'll look after your firm well if you give us the chance – there'll be no lack of commitment on our part. I guarantee it.

PE Hm, I suppose we might be able to make an exception if you, erm . . .

CM Yes?

PE . . . if you offered us a realistic sales target for the first year.

CM I see. Well, I suppose it depends what you mean when you say 'realistic'. What do you have in mind exactly?

(Fade)

CM I want to be clear about this – could you run through that again for me?

PE Yes, of course. What I'm saying is that we're prepared to offer you a non-exclusive contract, providing you stock our whole range of products and an agreed quantity of spare parts for each item.

CM Right.

PE What I'd like to know now is are you prepared to commit yourself to a figure for sales growth, say, over the next three years?

CM No, I don't really think so.

PE What, not even a rough figure?

CM I'd rather not. It's going to depend on a lot of variables – any figure I give you won't be very accurate.

PE OK, I won't try to pin you down on that. Let's move on to discounts. I'd like to suggest 2% on orders up to $200,000, 5% on orders from $200,000–$500,000, and 10% for anything over that. It gives you a strong incentive to exceed your target. How do you feel about that?

CM Well, a bit disappointed, really. I was hoping for at least 5% up to $200,000. It 's the going rate over here – or weren't you aware of that?

PE I'm sorry, I can't improve my offer on discounts. We've worked them out very carefully.

CM I see. Well, I don't know . . .

PE How about this? If you accept the discount rates, I could help you with your mark-ups. I was going to set some limits, but if I were to say you can set your own mark-ups and we won't interfere . . .

CM Hm, yes, that'd be useful. It'd give us plenty of flexibility with our pricing.

PE Exactly. What do you say?

CM Right, OK, I agree to that.

PE Great, that's a deal then. Let's summarise, shall we?

Unit 8, p75

FW = Francis Wilkin

DC Do you consider yourself to be a headhunter?

FW Definitely, yes! Some of my colleagues have hang-ups about being called a headhunter because they think it has certain negative overtones. I don't share those feelings. I think it's a quite clearly understood term, and to me it means somebody who actively goes out looking for people for particular jobs. We're in the business of finding people for jobs rather than jobs for people, if you understand the distinction. And so as a headhunter I'm looking for specific types of individual for specific positions. They may not be looking for a job. My job is to engage their interest and persuade them that there might be some alternatives. And that's what a headhunter is, and I'm quite happy to call myself that.

DC Fine. Do you specialise, does your firm specialise in any area?

FW Yes and no. Our firm started on Wall Street in New York in the late 60s. It was therefore very strongly a financial services and banking organisation. Today, slightly less than 50% of our business comes from financial services, and the rest comes from a wide range of industries, so as a firm, we've become generalists. We started as specialists, and have become generalists. For me personally, yes I do specialise now, probably more than I used to. I specialise in areas such as computer systems; the use of computer systems and indeed the manufacture and sale of computer systems. I also have a City background so I do work in banks and financial institutions, particularly in the technology and systems area.

DC How would you define the main job of a headhunter?

FW When people talk about headhunters or executive search, they generally mean people like ourselves who find people for jobs. We have a brief, from a client, to fill a particular position. By far the majority of so-called recruitment agencies however work the other way round. They are actively bringing in people who are looking for jobs, and they are trying to place them – by phoning up potential clients and trying to sell them.

DC So what sort of people would you look for? I mean, what sort of positions.

FW Generally, I think you can loosely define it as either senior management, main board directors, divisional directors, heads of functions such as sales or marketing, finance or systems. Erm, sometimes if it's a large organisation, we may also be looking for the number two or number three. Erm, but there does tend to be a salary cut-off point where our fees are such that it doesn't become worthwhile using us, if you're going to pay less . . . If you're paying less than, say, £60,000 a year in salary, probably a firm like ours is not the best way of recruiting.

DC Well, how do you go about getting someone. I mean, do you invite them to the Ritz?

FW Sometimes. Yes, sometimes we invite them to the Ritz! The problem with the Ritz is it's full of headhunters! Talking to candidates, and so sometimes we pick more discreet places. Erm, we identify potential candidates in a number of different ways. There are obviously those that we simply know, by having been in the industry a long time. There are those who are in our computer system, i.e. they're known to somebody else in the firm. And we have a computer system with about 15,000 names on, so there's a fair chance there'll be somebody in there. But the real craft of a headhunter is knowing how to find out who's around, and that means talking to what we call 'sources'. That means phoning people up, people you know, sometimes even people you don't know, and engaging them in conversation on the telephone and trying to persuade them to give you the names of people who would match the particular specification. And that really is part of the art; a lot of telephone work, being able to win the confidence and trust of total strangers on the telephone in thirty seconds flat, and then have them spill the beans, is really where the art of headhunting comes in. So once . . . using all those different avenues, our aim is to identify individuals who have been recommended to us by at least two, or maybe more people. Because then you know they have a good reputation, and that's the sort of person we're after.

p81

FW = Francis Wilkin

DC How are recruiting agencies, and people like yourself, how are you paid, if that isn't an indelicate question?

FW No, not at all. Erm . . . The fees that we charge are based on a proportion of the person's earnings. Quite straightforward. We charge a fixed percentage of the first year's earnings; cash earnings. That generally means salary and perhaps bonus if there is one. We don't include car and pension and those sorts of things. That's pretty much the industry standard. Some maybe a bit less. Some maybe go for . . . fees that are not based on a proportion, but rather on the complexity of the assignment. On the whole though, what I've described is the standard way. In terms of how am I personally paid. I work on a salary, and I also have a bonus, and the bonus is based on my own performance, and on the performance of the business. I think again that's fairly typical as well.

DC In your view, is it an ethical activity?

FW That's a good question. I mean the answer must be yes, from my point of view, but why? How do I justify that? Erm . . . I think I would justify it on the basis that we are not 'stealing' individuals. We are merely presenting them with opportunities. The final decision must be theirs. And the final decision for somebody to move jobs has to be a function of two things: We say there has to be a 'push' and a 'pull'. There has to be a push from their existing organisation, and there has to be a pull to the new organisation. We spend a lot of our time making it clear to them what the pull is, i.e. bigger job, more money, better location or whatever. We can do nothing at all about the push, that's up to them. If they are perfectly happy and successful where they are they will not move. I can guarantee that, however good the job is that we're dangling in front of them. And that is sometimes the case, and part of the skill of the job is identifying when that is the

case and when you're wasting your time trying, because the person simply won't go. The people we successfully move are those who, . . . perhaps they hadn't sat down and thought about it, and actively decided to do anything about it, but there was something not right with the job they're in. It could be they've just simply been there too long, or they're blocked politically or there's a career progression by a boss above them. It could be they're underpaid. It could be any of those things, although rarely people move just for money.

DC Do you make them an offer, I mean, how does that work out when you're actually talking with . . .

FW The initial discussions we never mention money at all, we try not to mention money till very late in the stage. It's . . . the view that headhunters phone up and say 'I've got a great job for £100,000' is a naive and unrealistic one. It doesn't happen, at least not with good headhunters. We want to avoid people who are simply interested in moving for money. Money comes in right at the very end. We may have a preliminary discussion where the candidate will say 'Look I'm currently earning £70,000, is it going to be worth my while.' And you need to say either 'yes' or 'no'. But the discussion over compensation comes at the end, we act as go-betweens between the client and the candidate, to try and make sure that neither is disappointed, and to try and avoid embarrassing situations where one makes an offer which is considered derisory by the other, or makes a claim that is considered extravagant. Erm, so we're . . . a critical part of the search process is what we call the closing; and that is, you know, having decided that this is the person they want, and the person having decided this is the job they want, we need to make sure then that the money and all the conditions are right, and that is the most difficult part.

DC So you don't want them to waste their time going to a company, and then being disappointed.

FW That's right. It's not in our interests for people to join a company and leave quickly afterwards, partly because our clients will get their money back if they . . . if the person leaves too quickly and it can be shown to be our fault. But that's a point where deals fall apart for the most ridiculous reasons. We had somebody who simply refused to take the job because his company car would not have leather seats! People behave in the same sort of irrational way when they're changing jobs as they do when they're moving house. You know the sort of crazy things people do when they move house, people do crazy things when they move jobs. Small things can tip the balance. An extra five miles commute, or some silly benefit can tip the whole thing out . . .

DC Are there any interesting stories about headhunters? Or are they all very confidential?

FW Oh no no. they're not very confidential at all. There are stories from my own experience of . . . for instance, the time I was making an approach to a particular individual who I was determined to get hold of, because he'd been strongly recommended. I called his office number – he answered the phone himself, it later turned out his secretary was away from her desk so he picked it up himself, he was in the middle of a pep talk to his managers. He was trying to persuade his immediate managers not to leave the company because morale was poor, he picked me up on the telephone on the speaker phone, not on the actual handset, so he had this voice fill his office saying 'My name is Francis Wilkin, I'm a headhunter, and I'm calling to talk about a job.' He was very embarrassed. But he did call back, and he did eventually end up moving.

Unit 9, p90

AB = Angela Baron

DC What do you see as the different cultures which affect how a company is run?

AB Well, first of all, I could turn that question around for you and talk about the way in which a company is run which creates different cultures, because when you start to look at the culture of an organisation, that culture is created by a number of things. It's created by people who work in the organisation, it's created by the kind of management systems which exist in an organisation, and quite often it's created by the style of the leader of that organisation.

DC Hm hmm.

AB So for example, an organisation which exhibits a very bureaucratic culture would have quite strict systems of control. There would be a lot of management systems in place to control people, to tell people when they're doing something wrong; there would be a lot of company directives, a lot of company rules. You probably would find that the senior managers would be fairly autocratic, erm, probably respected by, erm, their subordinates in the company, and generally the company would be run along very strict and rigid lines.

Now in a company which exhibits what I would call a facilitating culture, which is the culture whereby employees or subordinates are empowered to do their jobs, responsibility is devolved, people are encouraged to express themselves, to work in different ways, to get things done in their own way, rather than the way in which the boss says, you would tend to associate that kind of, erm, organisation with much looser control systems, or very few control systems. Erm, the senior managers would probably tend to be much more relaxed, far less autocratic, erm, possibly also fairly charismatic characters who have the confidence to devolve responsibility to their subordinates, respected for themselves rather than for the positions of authority that they hold within that company.

SR So, if those two different types of companies were interviewing, looking to employ new people, how would they ensure that the type of people they employed were the type of people that fitted in with those two very different styles?

AB Well, there's a number of ways in which companies can do that. First of all, they have to identify that there's a type of person who's going to work better in their organisation. Now that may or may not be true because what I've described are two very extreme styles, obviously there are lots of shades of grey in between those two extremes. Erm, so if a company feels that they are looking for a certain type of person, a person who's capable of taking on responsibility, who can be self directed and self motivated, they should include that in their job specification or person specification when they . . . before they recruit anybody, an organisation should draw up a job or person specification which states all the qualities that they are looking for – skills and personal qualities.

DC Can I move on to my second question. Do you get cases where someone's personal culture doesn't match the company culture? Does that happen at all?

AB Oh definitely, I think that happens a lot. When anyone starts a new job, they have to learn the ways in which things are done in the new organisation that they've entered. So it's a traumatic process for anybody, even if the new organisation is very similar to the last organisation that you worked for. But there's certainly a number of well-documented instances where managers from fairly bureaucratic companies have gone to work in the more facilitating laissez-faire culture companies, and this has come as a great shock to them because they've been used to being, erm, quite strongly directed from above, told what to do, how to do it, and now they're expected to simply be given a task, and they have to get on with it, and they have to devise their own ways to do it. There's no accepted way of doing things. They're expected to come up with ideas, and they're not given any direction, and that can be very traumatic, in certain cases it can be extremely stressful for people, and in very extreme cases, people never learn how to cope with that way of working. Some people need direction, and they cannot cope with a facilitating culture.

DC So they're like a square peg in a round hole.

AB Absolutely. Now in most cases, people will adapt over a period of time. People will adapt to the new way of working either by, erm, peer pressure conforming to the way their peers within the new organisation are working or because the employer has recognised there's a problem, or maybe has given them some additional training to enable them to cope with the new system of working. But in some cases you will find people will simply leave because they simply can't cope with that way of working. And of course, erm, the other way

round. People who go from a fairly relaxed laissez-faire style of management to a more bureaucratic style of management often can't cope with that. But the evidence suggests that those kind of people recognise that's a bureaucratic style of management and therefore do not apply for those types of jobs.

SR Another point I wanted to ask you about was other buzz words, erm, that I've heard along these lines about learning cultures, for example, and performance cultures. Can you tell me a little bit about those two?

AB Well, it's creating the kind of company culture in which it's OK to perform. I mean, we've been talking very generally about overall cultures. When you get down to the more practicalities of company culture, erm, it's things like creating a high productivity culture whereby the norm among the workforce is to be highly productive.

Now, erm, very basically, that's eradicating things like absenteeism. There've been a number of cases or organisations which have had horrific absenteeism problems, and that's mainly because its been the accepted norm with the company, within the employees that, 'Oh if I have a bit of a sniff this morning, I take a day off because everyone else does.' Or 'I haven't got any holiday left and I really want to go fishing, so I'll have a sick day because everyone else does.' So, it's, it's overcoming those kinds of attitudes. That's very much what culture is. It's changing the attitudes of your employees. And obviously the most powerful motivating tool that a company can have is to encourage their employees to relate their own personal goals of working to the organisational goals, so that by achieving your personal goals, you're going some way to achieving your organisational goals. Now, in order to do that, erm, the best way that a company can do that is to identify themselves as an employer who cares about developing their employees, so encouraging things like personal development and personal growth, erm, and, erm, expanding jobs so that they are actually interesting jobs that people are getting something out of work other than just a living wage, so that they're actually getting something personally out of work.

SR Actually having various needs met as well . . .

AB That's right.

SR . . . Which help to meet the needs of the company at the same time.

AB That's right.

Unit 10, p97

JL = John Lawrence

DC And what are you trying to change, John, exactly?

JL We're trying to change all the ways we manage people, so that they fit together. So that there is integration between how you recruit people, how you manage, how you train them, how you develop them, how you reward them. And that people get a consistent set of messages from the way the managers behave. If you manage people to say 'what I value is innovation' and then you pay people purely according to their length of service, they get inconsistent messages. It's aligning the messages from each of those areas so they're saying the same thing. That we care about the people, that they're an important part of the business, and their future as well as the shareholders' return depend on the success . . .

SR So how are you going about this?

JL The style with which we have gone about it is very much to involve the employees as customers. So in the first instance we went to the whole workforce through the line managers, to say we believe we now need to think more strongly about how we invest in people. What would you like to see us do? What are the areas you believe should be priorities? What are the areas that you don't like about the way you're managed at the moment? And although there could be an endless agenda of all the different ways you manage people, the areas that the employees highlighted were: how we structure jobs in the first place, both in terms of variety, the number of layers we have, the degrees of freedom that people have not only to think about something but to do it as well.

DC Mm hmm.

JL How we then manage the performance of people in giving them a clear idea of what's expected of them, and feedback about how well they're doing. And then how we reward them. Such that their reward is related to the contribution they make to the business.

SR So you actually let the employees, erm, more or less dictate which areas the project would deal with from the word go?

JL We defined the overall aims of the project, recognised that that was too much change to try and manage all at once, and asked the employees for their preference about which areas they'd like to see us address first. It would be wrong of me to say there was a common view of all the employees about which of the areas that needed addressing. So at the end of the day it was a judgement about well, this is where the main body of people feel we need to look. A decision was then made to look at how we design the organisation, how we manage performance and how we reward people. But that sucked in issues from other areas like training, like trade union relationships, like other parts of terms and conditions. But the prime aim was to say, 'You are a customer, what would you like to see us do?'

SR So having selected those three main areas, how did you go about, erm, changing what happened in them?

JL The change in the first instance was brought about by . . . several different mechanisms. One was a project team, which was a combined project team of line managers, professionals from personnel, and trade union nominees, to look at what are the issues, how do they relate together, and what should we do. Also, consultations with the employees, of saying this is what we're thinking about, how does it grab you? And also a general education process as to why are we doing this, what does it mean? What are the issues?

SR Can you say why you chose the consultative approach or a consultative process as the one that would bring about change?

JL Fundamentally because of a belief that it would work better. I can't prove that it did . . .

SR Why did you think . . .

JL Why did I think . . . Because I've tried it both ways. I've done it the other way, of seeking to negotiate change which affects employees, through the full time negotiating machinery of trade unions, and that is a difficult process. This was a different approach of saying, well let's go and actually ask the customer, i.e. the employee, what they'd like to see.

SR So where are you now in the programme, how far have you got?

JL We have reached a point where we've, after what eighteen months, two years, we've got a shape of organisation which we're much happier with, in terms of the number of supervisors we have compared to the teams we're supervising.

DC You've got fewer layers of management.

JL We've got few layers of management. We have launched for all employees, at least on an annual basis, a discussion between that person and their manager about what are they trying to do, where are they going, how well are they doing it, and what training they need.

p98

JL = John Lawrence

SR And what happens now?

JL What happens now is that we finish off the design and implementation of a new pay structure. But that we accept that we can always further improve upon that. Also in the two years that the programme has been running in consultation with the employees, everybody has learned more, so therefore our initial view has now been modified as we've learned more about it, and therefore we've identified quite a lot of areas where we want to go next, both in terms of training, in terms of development and in terms of working practices.

SR So those three areas that you have already been working with, are you now at a stage where the people who, erm, the people themselves involved can run that themselves from now on?

JL It's not totally at the stage where you can take your hands off it, and it will run for evermore, and the culture change is completed. There's still a lot of work to be done to fill in the detail and reinforce that change by behaviour.

DC What do you think's the greatest benefit of the programme? I mean, if you could look at the positive . . .

JL The greatest benefit is what was the original target. It's a more profitable and secure business.

SR Imagine right at the beginning when you were planning this programme, if the initial feedback had been, we don't want any changes in those three areas, what could you have done then?

JL We wouldn't have gone out and asked a question where we didn't think there was an issue. We had a business which had, at that time, seven different pay structures, and we were managing a lot of friction between different groups claiming that . . .

SR And everybody realised there was a problem . . .

JL Everybody knew there was a problem, the easy part is saying, there's something that needs doing here, the hard part is what do we do, how do you do it, and how do you get it to stick.

SR The 'what' is less difficult, is it? It's the 'how' that . . .

JL It's the 'how' because your view on any change that affects you is not only what happened, but how did it happen, was I involved in it? Or did it happen against my wishes? Did I even know it was happening?

SR Well even if it's something you really want, if you're not happy with how it happened, you're not going to . . .

JL Right, and therefore, that's why at the core of this, the 'how', through a process of consultation, of involving people every step along the way, was important.

DC As you say, you were changing the whole corporate culture of the organisation.

JL Yes, and we still are. The issue of culture change is one that is not something you start and finish. You start it and it continues, and as you go through the process . . .

SR What kind of culture would you say that Ilford had now?

JL It's not stable yet. Because as I say . . . two years sounds a long time, changing how people live and breathe and work, it's not a long time at all. We are changing to a culture where people feel they are part of the business rather than purely affected by it. And that means that the whole way in which we manage people, and how they relate to the business is going to change. We've concentrated on how we define roles to increase flexibility, to remove demarcations, how we reward people, such that they feel that it's their contribution they get rewarded for . . .

SR Rather than the hours that they put in.

JL Rather than the hours or any other factor which they believe managers have used in the past to decide how much to pay people, and they are clearer about what their own personal contribution is to the business, how it fits with others and how well they're doing. There are vast untapped areas still to move into. In terms . . .

DC Training, you mean.

JL Training we do. But more in terms of development . . . what's beyond the current role that I'm performing, and how can I change the shape of that role to the benefit of both me and the company. And development is a more difficult area. What we are clear about is we're into the area of people development, not solely management development. We don't regard development as an exclusive club only for managers. So it's people development whoever you are in the business. How can we develop so that you can make a better contribution to it.

DC Well it sounds to me as though you're developing a very interesting culture there and one that employees would enjoy, you know working in, as it were.

JL I believe that they will, I believe they'll find it more secure. And I hope that they find it interesting and rewarding as well. What will matter at the end of the day is whatever we end up with, they have been involved in that process of change, and had an option to say 'yes, on balance that looks better than what we did yesterday.'

Unit 11, p109

PW = Peter Wallum

DC Can I first ask you about what type of work your company is engaged in?

PW Well Strategic People is an integrated human resource consultancy – what we used to call personnel consultancy – and by integrated I mean that we're involved in a number of areas and we all work in these different areas, and try to cross-fertilise between the different aspects of our business.

DC Do you have to advise organisations in aspects of team-building?

PW Yes, we've found that we get asked to do this a lot – as do other consultancies, er, in recent years.

DC Erm, what are some of the problems that managers have in building teams?

PW Well, there are lots of aspects to building teams. Managers still have problems, believe it or not, in today's high unemployment context, in recruiting externally able people. So that's one problem of building a team.

Within big companies, erm, the problem often is that the manager doesn't have total control over who joins his team. It may be the central personnel function or his boss will actually allocate people to a team and the teams keep changing. But of course once you've got your team together, you're only just starting to build your team, and it's that area of training and development in team building that most of our work is involved in these days.

DC I'd like to come to that in a minute. Can I first ask you if you can give any examples of, erm, the problems they have?

PW Well there's the classic problems of course of people having different management style, and the style clashing, er . . . Other problems might be that within a team everybody, erm, is wanting to run things when in fact only one person ultimately can be in charge. In fact, teams that have everybody with the same characteristics are often less effective than teams that have a real mix of abilities and approaches.

DC Erm, are there any ways of training managers to develop effective teams?

PW Yes, there are. Erm, there are a lot of general methods and some specific to Strategic People. One general method, for example, is to get the managers together to talk about how they work as a team and to use models like the Belbin's model that I know you've been using to give insights into how people behave in the management team group. Another approach is to give people personal feedback about their management style and how they're seen by their colleagues. Er, another approach is to actually observe the processes going on in management. But at Strategic People, we, we try to approach all our work from, er, the angle of culture and management.

DC Oh yes?

PW And we have a unique approach to team building based on a management simulation called 'Dilemma'. Now 'Dilemma' is a board game that we developed five or six years ago working with a bank, in fact, that was concerned about developing ethics within the business, er, and what 'Dilemma' does is present members of the management team with business dilemmas, and they have to decide which of a number of answers to specified dilemmas they would adopt, and then defend that viewpoint with the rest of the management team. Now it's a game, and it's fun, we call it serious fun. And people play this game for an hour, an hour and a half in groups, er, well in management teams, but it does really test managers' mettle, and gets them talking about the things that really matter – the culture of the business, the values of the business . . . (telephone rings) . . .

DC Very interesting. What sort of people should be in an ideal team, would you say?

PW Well, I know a lot of management theorists bang on about ideal teams. Er, having been working in the team-building area for six, seven years now, I'm convinced that you never do get the ideal management team and the fact is, you have to work with, with what you've got, and, er, not aim for perfection.

DC Can I now turn to the sort of cultural side? What sort of problems emerge when a team is formed of people of mixed nationalities?

PW Well, this is very, very interesting. Er, and it will vary between the types of company that one's dealing with. Some international companies, er, have such a strong culture, and I suppose IBM would be a publicly recognised example, that the company culture is so strong that the people who join the firm buy into that culture at an early stage. And actually the IBM culture in some senses is stronger than the local national culture, so when one plays 'Dilemma', with those sort of firms, when one talks to management within those sort of firms all over the world, er, you find people are very similar. And I, for example, have consulted with, er, a US investment bank, and visited all their worldwide branches, and every branch one walked into, the décor was the same, the people seemed to be the same, no matter what their nationality. A very strong corporate culture, but of course there are very strong local national cultures, and the firms that haven't got that history and, and the strong culture, obviously you observe tremendous differences between the approaches of different nationalities. I had an example last week, a manager who'd worked in South East Asia, was telling me that he'd worked for a, for a British boss with, erm, locals as his, his peer group, and he had a problem in the sense that the local managers were terribly terribly polite, and never criticised, never gave any feedback on, on poor performance whereas his approach was the very straightforward British approach of, of, saying, er, what you think about things. And he found that cultural gap quite difficult to deal with.

DC Mmm. Er, can I now throw in a question at the end? Is there room in a team for the complete maverick, the person who doesn't follow company rules all the time, and is a difficult, possible even disruptive element. I mean, is it possible to have that kind of person in a team?

PW Well, I think so. In fact, I've, I've always welcomed having people like that in, in teams that I've been a member of. Unfortunately, they're too rare because they tend not to reach the, the management level, either by self-choice or, or they're not appointed. But a maverick in a, in a team of people who very much follow the company line can be extremely useful both in pointing out, er, you know, the emperor has no clothes, and this kind of thing, and also stimulating discussion. Erm, people have to understand, er, where that person is coming from and, and allow them to express their ideas and views, but of course, not necessarily, er, undertake to act on all their mad ideas, but I think it's a good idea to have a mix of people and one person like that in a team's very helpful.

p111

Dialogue 1

P = Philip   J = Jack

P I tell you, Jack, we've got to do something about Dennis. I know he's our best salesman and all that, but he's upsetting everyone in the office. If he doesn't get what he wants, he behaves like a spoilt child. He's so rude to people when they don't do exactly as he asks.

J OK, Philip, I'm not going to accept that sort of behaviour from him or anyone else – but don't you think he's like that because he wants to look after our clients really well? To make sure the systems are installed on time and working perfectly for them?

P Perhaps. But the problem is he never thinks of anyone else. He promises the earth to his clients and then expects everyone to rush around and make it happen. It's not right, we simply can't work to his completion dates. We're having to take technicians off other projects – important ones – just to meet his deadlines. It's really not fair on the other members of staff. No wonder people dislike him.

J They don't like him, huh? Maybe they're jealous. Maybe that's the real reason why he's unpopular. I don't want to upset him unnecessarily. As you know, Dennis is far and away the best salesman we have. He brings in a lot of money and a lot of prestigious clients. We can't do without him.

P Well, he's certainly very popular with the clients. They all insist on having Dennis to sort out their problems. He knows how to treat them, I'll say that for him. But no one's indispensable and he's making life very difficult.

J Dennis is a key man for us – there's no doubt about that. But that doesn't mean he can do whatever he likes. I'll have a word with him, Philip. I know he'll listen to me.

Dialogue 2

D = Dennis   J = Jack

D I don't see why you should be blaming me, Jack. We're in a competitive business – you know that. I can't get contracts from you if I don't look after my clients properly. They expect the best treatment, and if they don't get it from us, they'll go somewhere else.

J I know that. You don't need to tell me how important service is in our business, all right? Look, all I'm asking you to do, Dennis, is to check with Philip's department before you commit us to a completion date, OK?

D But Jack, I can't be spending every minute of the day on the phone to Philip. My job's selling systems and software.

J Yes, and you do it very well . . .

D Precisely. I make a lot of money for this firm. Sometimes I wonder if it's worth all the effort. Maybe I should look around a bit, see if one of our competitors might appreciate me more.

J Don't be ridiculous, Dennis. You know as well as I do we bend over backwards to support you here. You've nothing to complain about at all.

D I still say we don't have enough technicians. Why don't you hire a few more?

J They don't come cheap these days, that's one reason. Anyway, I'm not going to add to our wage bill at the moment – I'm sorry.

D Huh! Well as long as no one interferes with my work, I won't complain, I suppose. All I ask is to be left alone to get on with the job.

Dialogue 3

H = Heather   R = Robert   J = Jack

H You can't accept that sort of behaviour, Jack. You've got to discipline him. He just took off without saying a word to anyone. And then left everyone in sales to pick up the pieces.

R I must say, I'm fed up with him too. One of our salesmen – Peter Jones – phoned me just now. He said he'd resign unless something was done about Dennis. He seemed to think he wouldn't be the only one to go either. Everyone in the department's unhappy. They say we favour Dennis too much.

J What's the problem with Dennis, Robert, would you say? Is he unstable? Is that it? Or just too arrogant, too full of himself?

R It's not as simple as that. He's a bit of a split personality, really. Polite, charming, helpful, persuasive with clients. And in the office, rude and uncooperative. A prima donna type. There's no doubt about it, he's causing a lot of trouble. Upsetting the whole organisation.

H I agree, Jack. He's not a team member, he does it his way all the time – not our way.

J Hm. So the big question is: do we have room here for Dennis? Can we keep a brilliant salesman who won't follow the rules? Of course, if he left, he'd probably take a lot of customers with him – you realise that, I'm sure. Something has to be done though . . .

Unit 12, p115

RM = Roger Myddleton   P = Presenter

P First of all Roger Myddleton outlines the range and frequency of meetings at Grand Metropolitan. Are they held very often?

RM Yes we do hold a lot of them. When you ask a question like that, I tend to think of larger meetings first. Formal occasions, with ten or fifteen people round a table, and a chairman, and an agenda, and then someone taking minutes as a record of the meeting. That's one kind of meeting, but of course far more common than that are the much smaller less formal meetings when just two or three people get together to discuss something, and carry a particular business matter forward.

(Fade)

RM Well, we do have quite a lot of large formal meetings in a worldwide business like ours, that's inevitable. But in sheer number, I would say that probably ten or fifteen or twenty times as many meetings are of a much more intimate kind than, than that.

P Are they very time-consuming?

RM They do tend to be, and I, I think that is often the fault of the person who has called the meeting. I think much can be done to make meetings shorter if people have a clearer objective in mind as to why it was called in the first place.

P Is decision-making the main objective?

RM Well, making decisions of course is, is what you traditionally think of as doing at meetings, particularly the formal board meeting kind, kind of situation that I described before, but actually in reality, an awful lot of meetings don't make decisions, they just carry a matter forward. You just edge towards a decision, because you need a lot of input, from a lot of angles, from a lot of people. And you can't do that on one occasion in a formal way, you do it informally through meetings and in that way, matters do get decided, although not perhaps as formally as people would expect.

(Fade)

RM Well I think you have to have in your mind a pretty clear objective of what you want out of it. Do you just want input from someone, you're telling them something, and you want to know whether they like it, dislike it, have something to add – that's one reason for having the meeting. But you ought never to go into a meeting, in my view, without feeling, erm, that you know and that the person who's having the meeting, or the people that are having the meeting with you know what is expected of them. And how they should be leaving the room. But let's face it, if you don't leave the room with the world slightly different, I mean very very slightly, then why are you having the meeting in the first place? Nothing has changed.

P What are his experiences of chairing meetings, and what advice would he give?

RM Er, yes, I, I chair all sorts of meetings. But chairing sounds very formal. As I say, an awful lot of meetings are with small groups of people, and although I'm in control of the meeting, I wouldn't call it chairing in any formal way.

(Fade)

RM Well, I think so far as chairing a meeting is concerned, as I've already said, that if you have a good idea of what you're trying to achieve, then you're half way there. I think also you have to be very sensitive to the way people are reacting to what's going on in the meeting. You have to watch them carefully. You can easily see whether people have turned off, and are bored and snoozing or, or inattentive, doodling, what have you. And perhaps one person is monopolising the meeting. They're doing all the talking. Erm, that's not a good way of conducting a meeting. You ought to try to draw out contributions from everyone because some people are much shyer than others about speaking, particularly if it's a large meeting. A large formal meeting is precisely the occasion that some people will never say anything. I don't say you have to try and share it totally equally, that would be artificial, but you do have to be sensitive to someone who seems to want to say something but doesn't actually have quite the nerve to do so, and allow them to. Also as a chairman, I think it's very helpful if you can clarify what other people are saying, you can summarise it. And so everyone is clearer at the end of the meeting what people's views may have been, than they, they were when they came into the meeting. And that summary function is very important, and very helpful if you're taking decisions. And of course it's particularly important if you're dealing with people for whom English is not their native tongue.

P Does it often happen that meetings involve people whose native language is not English?

RM Oh yeah, it does certainly, we're a multinational company, so obviously we have dealings with Europe and around the world. So certainly, quite a lot of the time, I'm dealing with people for whom Italian or French or whatever, is their natural tongue, and I'm afraid being English my linguistic ability is about, er, well, is not too good! But yes, I do find repeating back to people what they have said, in my words, slowly and clearly, is a very helpful way to see that I've understood properly what they're saying, and that they've understood that I've understood it. And communication is what meetings are about, if you don't have that feedback, then you're not getting the full benefit of meeting face to face.

P What advice would he give on participating in meetings?

RM Well, I think again, you've got to, erm, be clear what the object of the meeting is, and how you can contribute to it. Too many people I think go to meetings, without any very clear idea of what they're expected to do. They're there, are they being told something, are they being expected to participate in a decision, and I think holding large meetings is often a mistake for that reason. That there isn't enough focus by the participants on what their individual contribution is. If there are only three of us round a table, it's very noticeable if someone doesn't speak. But if there are twenty, you can keep quiet the whole time. And have you really gained much from being there. So I think the first thing is to think what you want to contribute; secondly when you do speak, try and do so in a pithy clear way, and don't ramble, keep to the point – that's another thing that the chairman, of course, can help with, bringing people gently, politely, back to the point. The last point I'd make about both participating and chairing meetings is that an awful lot of them are greatly improved by an element of humour. And I think the ability to defuse a tense situation, or just to put people at their ease, not by being a raconteur and, and telling funny jokes, but just by making a witty remark, an aside, thus putting people, erm, at their ease and relaxing the atmosphere. Very very helpful in making a good meeting.

P Finally, how important are the minutes of a meeting?

RM Again, it depends very much the sort of, what sort of meeting it is. If it's a formal board meeting, erm, then minutes are statutory and a proper requirement. They should be brief, clear, erm, they needn't be terribly formal, but they should essentially record the decisions that have been reached, and however much of the discussion, erm, that the chairman wants to record. Basically, going on too much about recording discussions seems to me, and I'm a secretary, as well as legal director, to be unnecessary. Normally, you don't need to be reminded of all that, you just want the action points, but I think doing that, doing it crisply, doing it quickly, because having the minutes two or three weeks after the meeting, is no use at all, having them within a day or two is very valuable.

Dialogue

F = Frank   D = Derek   J = Jennifer

F Let's get started then. Erm, what we've got to do is, er, discuss how Derek's interview with Charlie should go. Jennifer can offer advice on how to go about this sort of thing, she's very experienced in this area, and I'm interested in knowing more about it, so I'd like to minute the meeting, if you don't mind, so we can use our discussion to draw up a procedure, erm, for doing this in the future.

D I've been thinking about it over the weekend and there's several areas I think we should cover. I need to know when I should tell him, er, where the interview should take place, and how to go about it and handle his reaction, OK? I mean, is there a time scale for this? Have you thought exactly as to when this might best be done?

J Well, I think it's usually useful to break this kind of news midweek, rather than doing it on a Friday afternoon.

F Certainly, I absolutely agree.

D The other thing obviously which he'll be concerned about once he's bitten the bullet, swallowed the bad news as it were, is what is the time, when is this going to come into effect.

F Yes.

D Do you want me to try to deal with this, or is that going to be left to a later follow-up?

J I think that's something you and Frank could decide on a little later. There should be a package that we offer him, and quite a few details to sort out.

F Yes certainly. Erm, I think we ought to move on now, so the next question really is, erm, you know, how are we going to do it, and where? What do you think, Jennifer?

J Yes, this is where Derek can really help more than any of us, knowing him as you do. How you're going to do it would depend, to a certain extent, on what you know of him.

D Well, thinking about it, I mean, we have, you know, not a regular basis, gone off and had a game of squash after work. And I'm not, I mean I haven't really thought this through, but erm, I mean I think it might be better to do it outside the office in a sense.

J I'm afraid I don't agree with you. It needs to be you in your managerial role, not you in your role as a personal friend, in order to make it clear to him that it's not you who's making him redundant. It's the company, and it's his role that's going. I certainly think it should be done, er, somewhere in the office, and preferably in his office rather than in yours. Then he can be left in his office after you've finished talking to him.

F I don't know, Jennifer. I'm not sure I . . .

D It's a little bit cold and clinical, that approach. I mean, I think the point you're making, that perhaps it would make the role issue a lot clearer both to myself and to him. But I . . . don't know, I mean it's the emotional aspect of this, I don't feel I can deal with it terribly well.

F Well how about a lunch, Derek, in a quiet pub or restaurant?

D So the in-between thing, it's a working lunch. It's work, but it's not in the office. It could be a compromise, yes.

J Well, could I just come in here please? I tend to think it might be better if you did it in the office. That you could do it . . . it's going to have to be fairly brief, rather than beating about the bush. Because you've got to remember, Derek, how you're going to feel about this. You're going to . . .

D Yes.

F I mean, Jennifer, you've had a lot of experience of this. How do people react when they . . .

J People tend to be rather shocked, they tend to be angry, but rather briefly, and they do tend to . . .

D In other words, they're not able to formulate an immediate and rational response. It is an emotional . . .

F Uh huh.

D The effect it has on them.

F In which case, a lunch might not be a good idea. I don't know.

D Well, I see what you're saying. It's just . . .

J Sometimes, although you may not believe this, people go away not really being sure whether or not they've been made redundant because the person breaking the news finds it so hard to . . .

D To put it bluntly. (laughs)

F You think you're being promoted yes. (laughs)

J You may think a variety of things. (laughs)

D In communication, I mean there is a certain degree of directness required here, I think I appreciate that. You know, it's bad news, but it's better to be short and brief and clear about it, rather than beating around the bush.

F Yes, it's worth, er, bearing this in mind.

D Well, I mean, taking Jennifer's expert advice on this, I mean, I suppose I am convinced in a sense that I might just follow it up in the evening with a phone call or something at home.

F Yeah.

J I think that would be a very nice thing to do. Yeah. So recapping then. Erm . . . Derek will break the news . . .

F Have we discussed how he breaks it, I mean, are you just going to come out with it . . .?

D Well, I will contextualise it to a certain extent. You know, saying, 'well as you're aware, you know, the business has not been doing as well, as good as it was last year, and particularly certain areas have fallen away, and unfortunately the areas that are most affected seem to be the areas that you've been dealing with, and so the company has reached, you know, the sort of decision which it's had to make with deep regret, but . . . ' I think really that's the kind of . . .

F Give him the background.

D Yes, I mean, but briefly. You're saying that I should get get to the point and say, 'You know, Charlie, it has been decided, that, basically, you are being made redundant, and the normal terms and conditions of our contract will apply, and that's it.'

J So be brief and specific. And move straight on to talk about the package you're offering him.

F OK, so . . . Let's recap. I think we've agreed, Derek, that you will, you will actually be telling Charles . . .

D Yes.

F And that you'll do it, er, inside the company, and you'll do it probably in your office. Right?

D No, in his office.

F Sorry, I do apologise. Yes, in his office. And you'll give him the background, and the reasons why we have to do this.

D Mmm.

F And you'll make it fairly short, and to the point. And you'll phone him in the evening.

D Yes, and I'll leave that a little depending on the reaction I get from the initial one, but that's . . . some kind of follow-up that evening, whether it be going out after work or whether it be a phone call after I've got back.

F OK.

Unit 13, p125

JG = John Goff

DC Erm John, can I ask you my first question which is, would you say entrepreneurs are born or made?

JG Well I think that question possibly oversimplifies the, the issue because whilst I don't believe that courses of business studies necessarily will make any sort of entrepreneur, I don't think anybody is born an entrepreneur. I think luck also can play quite a large part.

DC What is it about running your own business which appeals to you?

JG Well I think first and foremost the independence to be able to make one's own decisions and guide one's own lifestyle.

DC Have you always, er, been an independent businessman?

JG No, in earlier days, shortly after leaving university, I worked for a large company, in fact BP, and had several years of, er, working in a fairly bureaucratic environment.

DC Erm, what has been your most successful venture and what made it a success?

JG Well I think in recent years it's been the formation of our partnership, PC Challenge. Business accountants specialising in getting the most out of personal computers for small and medium-sized businesses. I think what's made it a success really is the relationship between myself and my partner, and the fact that on most issues, we think along similar lines. Also, the fact that I think both of us are extremely interested in the work, particularly in software publishing, small task-related programmes, to do nitty-gritty jobs in business, rather than the very large software that's on the market, which on the whole can be described as tool boxes, which do nothing when you get it home from the shop.

DC And have you here found a niche market, as it were?

JG Yes, I think so, erm, but we've found that we have to do this on the back of a large publisher, rather than try and market it ourselves. And it's a question of the numbers game with small margins.

DC Yes, I asked you what is your most successful venture. How would you define the word 'successful' in this respect?

JG Well I think there is a problem because some of the things I've done, particularly in the property business, have made quite a lot of money, although I wouldn't have said that there's a great deal of job satisfaction necessarily in that type of thing. I think it's extremely difficult to have a successful business, which is extremely enjoyable, and the two don't necessarily go together.

DC And in your present venture with the computer software, what, er, do you find particularly enjoyable about that?

JG Well I suppose to some extent I must have an aptitude for certain aspects of personal computer use, and I'm slightly addicted to the whole environment.

DC Thank you. Can you tell us please what difficulties entrepreneurs face when setting up a business?

JG Well, first and foremost, I think it's making sure that the product or service which they're going to market is, er, viable, and that there is sufficient market demand for it. Everything else must follow from this key issue. Secondly, in the present environment, the huge problem of raising capital, particularly with very little to back up one's application, e.g. assets. And thirdly, I think it is finding reliable and well trained staff, er, in the early stages to help the business to grow.

DC Yes, erm, do you have any ideas on what is the best way to raise capital? Is one way better than another, have you found?

JG Well, I think as far as possible, having heard the experience of certain friends of mine, mortgaging one's house is probably the last option. And, erm, if one can raise it in some joint venture capacity, i.e. giving up some of one's equity, to get capital on board, I think this is a preferable option. I mean there are organisations who, erm, will help in this respect, but I think we're not talking necessarily of the mainstream high street banks, one's looking at more the commercial banks.

DC Can you tell me this, is a 'good idea and a dream' enough to be successful, or does it take other factors?

JG Oh I think it certainly takes other factors although the, the dream is essential, and the perseverance that follows from it, to see it through in difficulties. But I think there are skills which can be taught, and in business there are a whole list possibly of useful skills, erm, such as accounting, the use of computers, handling communicating with staff, some of these areas can be taught. But I don't think one can produce the entrepreneur through the educational system.

DC What advice can you give to would-be entrepreneurs who have an idea?

JG Sound out the market thoroughly to see if your product or service has a good chance of success. Don't launch into a lot of capital investment until you've tested the product thoroughly in some way, and you may need some help from an outside company or, or organisation to do this. I think too many people fail because they convince themselves about a product which does not succeed because there isn't the necessary demand for it.

DC When the entrepreneur, erm, starts the business, and perhaps he's doing quite well, in your experience, what sort of things go wrong? I mean what have you got to be careful about once you're starting to be successful?

JG Well, over-commitments, over-rapid growth can cause problems. Cash flow problems. Not budgeting sufficiently for the capital needs of a programme in the coming initial years of the business. More businesses go broke, not because they are unprofitable, but because basically they run out of cash, and hadn't, er, achieved the necessary commitment from their bank or, or partners in advance.

DC So would you advise, erm, an entrepreneur to have a partner? Is this a safeguard, would you say?

JG Well partners have dangers, and I've had plenty of partners in different enterprises. Er, it's easy to get into bed with a partner; not so easy to get out!

DC (laughter) Thank you very much, John.

p129

DA = Dounne Alexander-Moore

DC Could I ask you a question that I think interests us very much, and that is, did you have any problems getting your products onto the supermarket shelves?

DA Right well. By the time I got to the supermarkets, right . . . when I was in my flat . . . I developed a product over two and a half years, working from home, and basically wrote to various people as I started getting better at it to find out whether or not they would be interested. Now a supermarket or a store which will, erm, order in large quantities will not deal with you from a private dwelling, so you've got to find a small unit or a small factory.

SR And that's how you moved from the kitchen into your unit?

DA Yes, but my problem there, before we go into the supermarkets, my problem there was that no bank . . . I had already . . . I was in like in 20 individual department stores, and small fine food delicatessens and health stores. I already had so much press coverage over the years, but no bank will take me seriously nor lend me money because I had no collateral or capital. So it took two years trudging round every bank, being told how brilliant my business plans were, how excellent my promotional skills were, but no one will lend you the money to get out, to develop. Eventually, I met a wonderful bank manager, erm, who was also ambitious and said, 'well look if . . . I wanna help you, if I help you, would you help me?' I said 'fine', and he says 'Would you ensure that all your press coverage says . . . helped by such and such a bank at such and such a branch.' I says, 'By all means'. Once I was here I approached the supermarkets again, arranged meetings and so forth, . . .

On my first meeting TESCO said 'Yes, we would love to stock your product'; in fact, he was very very nice. He literally laid out a red carpet. You're lucky if you get a 15-minute interview, normally it lasts five, ten minutes. I was in there for about two hours!

Unit 14, p130

SK = Steve Kremmer

P First of all Steve Kremmer outlines historical trends in Japanese investment in general terms.

SK Well er . . . the first thing I should say is that Japanese investment overseas started about twenty years ago. Erm, Japanese companies which had become fairly cash, cash-rich from their exporting activities realised that in order to expand markets overseas they needed really to have, erm, investment sites, manufacturing sites within the markets. Now, the American economy has always been very important towards the Japanese, or for the Japanese, and so the first investment from Japan started really, or the first serious investments started in, in the States, and they started making all kinds of er, all kinds of consumer goods, and, er, eventually cars and so forth, because they were investing within the market where those things were going to be built. Erm, a second sort of wave of investment if you like, er, was concentrated in East Asia and places like Korea, Thailand, erm, Taiwan, as well, places where labour is very cheap but the quality of, erm, the skills available is very high and education and resources are very good as well.

P And the move into Europe?

SK Well the movement into Europe has really been a result of the fact, if you can imagine the world economy as being a three . . . let's say three pillars to the world economy. You've got Japan, the States and Europe which between them account for, er, the majority of, erm, world economic production, and count for a large share of total wealth and total manufacturing ability in the world economy, those are three core areas. Erm, now the connections, economic connections between Japan and the States, as I said before, have been, erm, very strong. The Japanese have sold quite a lot of materials, quite a lot of finished products to the States, and they've relied themselves on the States for, erm, initially technology, ideas and certain key bits of equipment, and kinds of things they can't themselves make like aerospace products, aeroplanes, aero-engines, that kind of thing. So those connections have always been very strong. Between the States and Europe the connection has also been strong, erm, throughout history for the last two or three hundred years. But that leaves the connection between Europe and Japan, in modern terms, relatively . . . weak compared to the other two relationships, the two bilateral relationships.

After a number of years of exporting directly to the European market, and finding that it was accessible, and European people did like Japanese goods, initially motorbikes and cheap electronics, then after that televisions, video cassette recorders, compact discs, a whole range of consumer electronics; and a whole range of industrial goods as well which we don't see so much but are still there, and are very important. Erm, it became apparent that really to expand and to capitalise entirely on the European market they'd need, again, to set up manufacturing operations over here. That was one reason. Another reason was that, erm, there were some restrictions placed on investments, or placed on exports by the European Commission. Now, one way of getting around those imports is to build cars inside the country.

p133

P Next Steve Kremmer compares Japanese investment in the United States with that in Europe and explains why Japanese companies are particularly interested in investing in the UK.

SK I'm not sure how many companies there are, but, erm, the level of investment in the United States is something like four times as much in manufacturing as it is in Europe, and something like twice as much as it is overall. So . . . the financial sector is quite important here, and there's been a lot of Japanese financial investment in Europe, in fact there's much more financial investment than there is manufacturing investment. Erm, so what it means is, because the, because the European economy is actually larger than the American economy, the potential for more Japanese investment is absolutely enormous. There have been three big Japanese car investments, car manufacturing investments in the UK, in fact in the whole of Europe, and all three of them have gone into the UK.

(Fade)

SK Communications between the Japanese and the line workers, or the local workers in the factory is very important, so obviously if they're familiar with English, it makes their life, it makes their job much easier. That's one thing. The government in Britain, and that's government both Conservative and Labour, and local government and national government have been historically very much in favour of foreign investment. It's always been promoted in Britain.

P Is the cost of labour a relevant factor?

SK Certainly. It's always, it's always a balance between the cost of labour and the quality of labour. Erm, now British labour is cheaper than labour in Germany, erm, substantially. It's also cheaper, depending on the labour, than it is in France, I think, erm, but obviously it's more expensive than Spain, as a European site. Now Spain is taking more investment recently, and Portugal. And all of the south European countries, or the ones that are relatively poorer than Britain. But it's a balance between the levels of skills available and the cost of labour. And in Britain during the 1980s, erm, it was a very good balance between those things for the Japanese. Now the problem that they're finding at the moment is that, er, there aren't really enough engineers in Britain to . . . engineers and skilled and highly trained people to fulfil the requirements of new investment. That's starting to have an impact on new investment coming into Europe. So in the last year or so we've seen an increase, a dramatic increase in Japanese investment in Germany and France, erm, where they can find more engineers.

P Are Japanese companies introducing their own management styles and working practices into Europe?

SK Well basically no. Because the thing is that the British culture and the Japanese cultures are quite different. I mean there are some similarities, but, er, they are very different, and work practices anywhere depend very much on the cultural background of the people who are working. Erm, communications, social organisations, business organisations, even language determine or have an influence on how a business will operate, er, and so it's quite difficult or virtually impossible to bring in Japanese ideas and place them in anywhere in Europe or America, without taking some account of how the local culture actually works. So what this means is that, er, by and large, Japanese companies have brought in the best practice, or the best ideas, the best philosophies they can from Japan, but they've combined them with the best philosophies, and the best ideas, and the best practices that are available in the UK, or in France or in Germany, or wherever they're investing. And so you'll find that if you go to somewhere like Nissan, which is making cars in the north east of England, they're quite proud, and the British workers and the British managers there are quite proud to say that, er, the company's a British company.

Erm, Nissan has brought in a number of revolutionary ideas, but they've been, erm, implemented by British managers and they've been worked by British workers if you like, using, using a lot of ideas, a lot of background from, er, or lessons from British industry.

P The usual practice is then to use nationals as senior managers?

SK Certain, yeah. And that was from the word 'go' with Nissan, because they realised that they couldn't, it's really impossible to move into the country and build up an effective, erm, company or build up an effective manufacturing, er, facility without any detailed and sensitive understanding of how that country works. And so you've really got to, and this is not just for the Japanese, it's for any, hopefully, any country, has to take a lot of account of local, of local conditions. Which is why generally in other multinational companies, erm, Unilever for example, they'll have Indian managers in India and they'll have Japanese managers in Japan. It's standard, it's standard practice throughout the world generally to try and become as localised as possible, because the more localised you are, the more effective you will be in accessing the markets that you're targeting.

P So localisation and globalisation . . .

SK They're working together, that's right. But the other point I should make here is it does take time to globalise, and to localise. So with the Japanese because they're quite a . . . because they're quite a recent phenomenon, as far as investing in Europe is concerned, erm, they aren't as localised as their American counterparts in Europe.

Unit 15, p140

BH = Barry Hyman

SR In terms of the corporate strategy, do you plan to internationalise further?

BH Oh yes. Internationalisation's very much an important part of the strategy as a whole. I think we had decided even during the family days that internationalisation was necessary. Indeed we first went abroad to America and Europe, what . . . early 70s. So that happened long before the family finally relinquished control. It would be fair to say however that it was given an extra boost, certainly during the Rainer era, by our moves into America: acquisitions of Brooks brothers and Kings supermarkets in the United States, and under Sir Richard Greenbury we are now beginning to put our foot down on the throttle in regard to the European expansion.

DC Has it been a smooth process, internationalisation?

BH Smooth yes, but some hiccups along the way and learning curves which have had to be taken note of and absorbed.

DC Can you tell us a little bit about them?

BH Yes, the problem area has been predominantly Canada. We went into America, bought two very good businesses but at a time when recession was about to hit. Consequently we've had to ride that storm, and are still riding it, as is everybody else. Europe has perhaps been rather easier. We took it very slowly there, some would say too slowly, I think we'd probably agree. But the advantage was that we learned as we went, and we made our mistakes in a small way rather than a large way. So that by the time we decided Europe was right for us we had in place our jewel in the crown – our Boulevard Haussmann Parish store, which is very profitable and very successful, has just been extended yet again. And that gave us the encouragement to go forward with France, and with other countries. The major development now of course is Spain.

DC Can you, can you tell me why, obviously you were very successful in Paris, but in Canada you, you, erm, had problems. Is there any . . .?

BH Yes, I think the problems were those of distance and lack of population to be honest. We went into Canada 20 years ago and I think with hindsight we made some careless decisions about what we acquired, and one of the things we've learned from that is that the route for us, by and large, is organic growth rather than acquisition, unless it's a very targeted acquisition, like, the acquisition of the chain we wanted in the States, Brooks, which gave us a national perspective across America, under the guise, if you like, of a highly respected high street name there.

DC Is expansion basically through internationalisation or is diversification an important element as well?

BH The international dimension of expansion is very much an important one clearly, and will continue to be. I'd like to think, the company would like to think, that we may have up to ten or fifteen stores in Spain for instance in five or six years time, against two now. In this country though development continues. We've been putting on something like half a million square feet of selling space in the UK every year for the last six or seven years, and we will continue with something like that.

p143

BH = Barry Hyman

DC What are the strengths and weaknesses . . . well let's take the strengths, the strengths of the company, the sort of SWOT analysis, you know, strengths, weaknesses, opportunities, threats, but particularly the strengths, would you say of Marks and Spencers . . . ?

BH I think the strengths are its ability to buy its merchandise very accurately and very quickly, and that is what this is all about. If we stopped selling goods we might as well all of us go home!

We have a dedicated and committed supplier base, built up over decades, some of the suppliers with us since the founding of the company. If you add on to that, and when I say 'that' I mean their willingness to give us the right merchandise, because it's in their interests as well as ours obviously, the technical developments which have taken place in the last few years. Our capacity with electronic point of sale and astute suppliers, to change colour, change fabric, change style much more quickly than ten years ago is an integral part of the success of the business at the moment.

That's the major strength. I think another strength is the innate flexibility of the people who work in the business. Erm, you have to turn it to a strength, sometimes it can be a weakness – that we change people around too often, but essentially the strength is that you can have somebody who has learned the management skills of the business buying fish this year and buying jumpers next year, and applying the same sort of management skills of buying to whichever industry he's in.

If there is a weakness it is, or was perhaps an inclination to change people around too often. I think it's a weakness we've overcome and we're now recognising that, er, strength of knowledge counts for something, so while you want to develop people, a) give them an opportunity of a number of career chances and b) make sure that you've got flexible people, the first prerequisite is to make sure that people spend a sensible amount of time in an area to their benefit and to that of the business.

DC Opportunities?

BH Opportunities are boundless. When I joined the business in 1959 the best I could hope for as a Londoner was to go south to Falmouth and north to Aberdeen . . . but if I work for the company now I can go to America, I can go to Europe, I can go to the Far East. The world is now literally at my feet, and young people coming in now have the most fantastic opportunities to travel and develop their skills, and are encouraged to do so.

DC So the internationalisation is the big opportunity?

BH Yes. Great development, yes.

DC Erm, what are the major threats, would you say, to the business? Are they any?

BH It sounds arrogant, doesn't it, to say that we have no competition, and I don't mean it in that way. Of course there is competition. Every other retailer is a competitor, erm, I don't see any of them at the moment as major threats, and the reason I say it is this. In the 80s when the high street was developing rapidly and a variety of other bright traders were coming along, and a variety of retailers who I won't name at the moment, we were told that Marks and Spencer's day was over. We were looking tired and jaded, and they were going to modernise their stores and put in systems and merchandise which would see us off! With hindsight, many of them are not there any more. If their companies are, they're trading at a loss. We are still trading at a profit . . . It's a race in which we're very happy to be the tortoise rather than the hare. So no immediate threats, but we're not complacent. We are aware of other retailers and other techniques and we keep an eye on them all the time.